An NVA squad circled behind us in an attempt to finish off our casualties and attack the main part of our company from the high ground we occupied.

In assault formation, the NVA steadily moved up from their draw, firing from the hip at our group. These NVA were bigger and stronger looking than any Vietnamese I had seen before. They wore green uniforms and helmets, and had bushes tied to their backs.

With scarcely a word of command from myself, our group began a countercharge. Sinke staggered and began firing right away. . . . The Marine from the Deep South who had the arm wound ran out in front of us all, firing and yelling madly. Sinke, my radio operator, myself, and the two injured men formed a skirmish line and moved down the hill, firing and screaming loudly.

In my case, the noise was meant to make our motley force seem larger and more ferocious than it really was. It worked. . . .

Books published by The Ballantine Publishing Group are available at quantity discounts on bulk purchases for premium, educational, fund-raising, and special sales use. For details, please call 1-800-733-3000.

NOT GOING HOME ALONE

A Marine's Story

James J. Kirschke

BALLANTINE BOOKS • NEW YORK

A Ballantine Book
Published by The Ballantine Publishing Group
Copyright © 2001 by James J. Kirschke

www.ballantinebooks.com

ISBN 0-345-44093-5

Manufactured in the United States of America

First Edition: August 2001

10 9 8 7 6 5 4 3 2 1

To my men of the 81 Platoon, 3d Battalion, 5th Marines, and of 3d Platoon, Company H, 2d Battalion, 5th Marines—*Semper Fidelis*

CONTENTS

INTRODUCTION

This book is a personal narrative. In January 1967, I was severely wounded while leading my rifle platoon through a mined area southwest of Da Nang. *Not Going Home Alone* deals primarily with my tour of duty in Vietnam, the months leading up to it, and the weeks in which I struggled to stay alive after I was wounded.

This book is a personal narrative, but it may have a more than personal meaning. My experiences may not be entirely typical, yet I believe they are not altogether untypical. If this is so, then in setting down the significant things I saw, heard, thought, and did during this period, there may be some value. In writing my narrative I have been conscious of adding, if only by a little, to the sum of our knowledge about this period in the past. If Montaigne was right when he said that "each man bears within himself every attribute of humanity," then perhaps others may profit by reading of my experiences.

The Allied effort in Vietnam was unsuccessful, but this was not due to an absence of courage or a lack of effort on the part of the men with whom I served. In writing this book, my wish is to assure that the good deeds and heroic actions I witnessed will not be allowed to vanish like a sound without an echo. A study of numerous captured North Vietnamese documents, POW interrogation reports, books, and pamphlets published in Hanoi during the war, and interviews with innumerable Ralliers (Communist defectors) convinces me that we will not hear anything like the full truth about the war from the Vietnamese Communists, and it is seldom offered to us by anyone else; on this account I have done my best to utter it as I have understood it.

Perhaps in some of the opinions I have expressed I may be said to be prejudiced. If so, then this is an accusation I can accept. My prejudices have provided much of the driving force in my life; to neglect to express them, in a narrative which aims above all to record my thoughts and experiences, would seem to be a grave omission.

In writing this book I have drawn primarily upon my personal correspondence and notebooks that I kept from the period. Whenever possible I have checked the accuracy of my recollections by consulting other sources. Chief among these are the archives on the war at the History and Museums Division of Headquarters, United States Marine Corps. From this repository I have obtained copies of the unit diaries and situation reports for the two battalions with which I served in Vietnam and numerous other, once classified, documents of the war. I have also obtained taped interviews with many of the Marines who served closest to me overseas and who survived the war, as well as transcripts of interviews with most of the senior Marine generals who were in-country during my tour of duty. In addition, I have made use of many captured Vietnamese Communist documents.

I have written *Not Going Home Alone* by myself, but it would have been written less well were it not for the assistance of many others. Chief among these are the members of my immediate family. To Juanita, *querida de mi corazon*, I am the most grateful. She has discussed the book with me, aided me with her strong and enduring love through the difficult times when I was writing it, and sustained me with her unshakable confidence in its worth.

For some three decades already Joe and Linda have brought me joy and inspiration every day. My continued sincerest wish for both is that they have a peaceful life with honor. May the only war they ever know be found in books.

My mother, the late Margaret McGill, and my aunts, Betty and Nancy Kirschke, saved my correspondence from the period. Were it not for their having done so, my narrative would lack much of the completeness it now has. Betty, too, is now long deceased, but she and Nancy were the ideal aunts for a boy and then young man without siblings who grew up without a father, and whose mother was perforce rarely around.

For the scholarly cooperation afforded by the History and Museums Division of Headquarters, United States Marine Corps, I am very grateful. From this division I would like to thank especially the now deceased Henry I. Shaw and Benis M. Frank, and the director, Jack Shulimson. To Dr. Shulimson I am particularly thankful for his having provided me with the working draft of his then unpublished monograph, *U.S. Marines in Vietnam, 1966: An Expanding War*, and for a great deal of additional thoughtful assistance.

In Washington, D.C., Douglas Pike kindly welcomed me into his home, provided me with access to his full collection of documents on the war, and shared with me his ready knowledge of Vietnamese history and politics. I have further profited from advice and discussion with John F. Lulves, Jr., executive vice president of the Intercollegiate Studies Institute. For other kinds of assistance I should like to thank Maj. John P. Farrell, USMC (Retired) and Thelma Martin, Navy Reference Branch, National Personnel Records Office.

As in my previous writing projects, I have received the steadily warm, intelligent, and courteous assistance of the staffs of the Falvey Memorial Library, Villanova University, and the Bryn Mawr College Libraries. Mrs. Barbara Mathers has typed the first draft of this book. My assistant the past two years, Sean Flannery, has done outstanding work in assisting me with preparation of the final draft. Our departmental chair, Charles Cherry, and our departmental secretaries have proven steadily supportive. The help of Mrs. Susan Burns, in particular, is beyond praise. I am also greatly indebted to the following: Wendy Schmalz, of Harold Ober Associates, Inc., Jerry Doherty, Bob Brown, Jim Graves, Owen Lock, Gary Brozek, O. K. Batte, Steve Saffel, Al Sproule, Christopher Evans, and Nancy Delia. Ms. Patricia

Crouch and Hans S. Haupt read the page proofs with admirable diligence.

I would also, however, like to express my gratitude to the many others—relatives, friends, neighbors, university colleagues and students, former teachers, casual acquaintances, and often total strangers—who have helped me through the personal crisis I have experienced, and whose daily acts of kindness have helped to make my life the great joy it generally is.

Finally, I would like to thank the men to whom this book is dedicated. When I left them overseas, I was not able to bring myself to say good-bye. But that may be just as well, since I have always made an awkward bow.

AUTHOR'S NOTE

In the narrative, names of certain individuals have been changed. All Vietnamese words have been spelled phonetically.

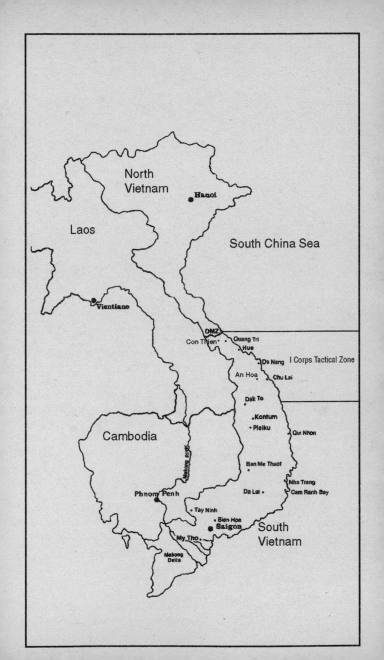

NOT GOING
HOME ALONE

ONE

Leave-Taking

The day I left for the coast I felt the strongest premonitions of loss. When I awoke, the sun was reflecting off the brick walls of the neighbors' houses behind us, but I had a hollow feeling inside that signified more than mere hunger. I dressed quickly, grabbed a double armful of uniforms, and scrambled downstairs to begin loading my car. I stopped on the way out to say good morning to Granny, my mother, and aunts. Betty and Nancy helped me load the car while Mom checked around to see if I had forgotten anything in packing. The bustling about helped subdue the hollow feeling a bit. I went upstairs once more, checked my room again, took a last, long look at it, then got washed up, packed my shaving kit and workout gear, and came back downstairs to have what would be my last breakfast at home for nearly two years.

Granny was waiting for me as usual in the kitchen. Her arms were folded. In the same tone as always, she asked, "What will you have, Jimmy?" I paused a second, to reassure her I was "making up my mind," then announced my usual large order. While I ate, Granny sat watching and attending to me in her special ways. I told her again that I would be heading for California, where I would be safe, and that I would write to her as often as I could. Since my letters home always bore either a California or a Fleet Post Office, California, address, she did not learn I was in Vietnam until the day Captain Lavin came to call.

After breakfast I kissed everyone good-bye and told them not to worry. I'd be home before they knew it. My pale blue Chevy II was loaded and filled with gas. I was ready to drive west, to take command of an infantry platoon, I hoped, to train them, and to take them into combat in Vietnam.

I had grown up in the closely knit neighborhood of South Philadelphia where much of *Rocky* and *Rocky II* were filmed. Growing up in this area alone constituted a great and lively education, valuable to me the rest of my life. As I pulled out from in front of our Wolf Street home, I turned around to wave good-bye to everyone, and then the hollow feeling came again—stronger this time—a feeling more palpable than that induced by a blow, one that stayed with me until I left the South Philadelphia neighborhood of my youth and got onto the Schuylkill Expressway, heading northwest toward Valley Forge.

TWO

Training

The first thing one notices about Pendleton is its size. I had become accustomed to large bases, since neither Quantico nor Lejeune was small. Pendleton, however, covered an area roughly two hundred square miles, some twenty miles long by ten miles across. In addition to a mainside the size of a small town, the base had numerous training areas, and five camps, each of which housed several thousand Marines. On my first day aboard (Marine speech for "on-base"), I wound my car around the wide-swerving roads to the temporary officers' quarters a few miles into the hills. As on most days I was in southern California, the afternoon sun was bright and the sky clear, an atmosphere that induced in me a continual feeling of restless exhilaration. As I drove I observed the steeply rising hills with their autumn foliage, as if covered with sleek brown rugs. The TOQ at the time comprised a series of worn-out-appearing wood barracks that looked almost as much like a ghost town as did some of those towns I drove through on my way across country. My first evening aboard I squared away my uniform, polishing shoes and brass until they glowed even in the dimly lit, dusty room where I stayed. The next day I arose as usual at first light, did PT outside the barracks, had a brisk road workout, snatched a hasty breakfast, put on my uniform, and drove to headquarters to report for duty.

The 1st Marine Division headquarters at the time was a large, austere, wood-frame building. I was greeted inside by an enlisted man who escorted me across the room to the desk of a slim, late-twentyish, dark-haired and crewcut warrant officer.

He rose, smiled, and said, "Good morning, Lieutenant. B. F. Beggs," as he extended his hand to shake. "Gunner" Beggs leafed through my officer qualification record (OQR) and noticed I had had a rifle platoon in the 2d Division, and had before that been assistant 81s—mortar—platoon commander there. He pointed to the spot in my folder and said, "See you've been with the 81s in 3/6." I nodded yes. Quick as a thrush he flipped through the table of organization file on his desk and placed his finger on the place where it said BLT 3/5 (Special Landing Force). "They need an 81s platoon commander in 3/5. Interested?" My smile was answer enough. "Outstanding," he said as he penciled my name with a question mark into the block on his TO chart that read, "81s, Battalion Landing Team 3/5." He gave me directions to Camp Margarita and advised me to report to the 3/5 headquarters there, to a Lieutenant Prince, the battalion adjutant. We stood up to shake hands before I walked out. My heart was thumping in anticipation. Before I was out of hearing distance, Beggs was on the phone to tell Prince that I was on the way.

Camp San Margarita was one of about five similarly constructed camps at Pendleton. Set a few miles into the hills, several miles from the main road that ran through the base, Margarita was then headquarters for the 5th Marine Regiment. At the time the Vietnam War started, the 5th Marines was the most highly decorated regiment in the Corps. It remains so today.

Margarita consisted primarily of several dozen Quonset huts with unpainted cinder-block walls and aluminum roofs. Each hut had two large squad bays, one on each side of a large "head," or bathroom area, and a small bachelor NCO quarters. Also at the camp were several warehouses, PT fields, parade decks, handball courts, administrative buildings, a chapel, a small library, a large mess hall, an NCO club, and a "slop-chute" or enlisted men's club. Behind the camp a rough, narrow road led to a steeply rising series of high shoulders of ground that the troops referred to as "goat-shit." The plateau was so high it was generally only traversed by several herds of goats.

As I entered the 3/5 headquarters a first lieutenant built like Gunner Beggs* and wearing airborne jump wings emerged from his office to shake my hand: "Lieutenant Kirschke? My name's Paul Prince. I'm the S/1. Welcome aboard!" He invited me into his office, drew us each a cup of coffee, and sat down to look through my file, pausing now and then to smile. After a few minutes he looked up and asked about my trip, my family situation, housing setup, and whether I would like to command the 81s. He seemed pleased by my response to the last question and told me he would recommend me for the position to the colonel.

Paul told me a few things about himself, the Pendleton area, Colonel Bronars, the battalion, and its general mission. Then he asked leading questions about my background, the answers to many of which he probably already knew from having looked through my OQR. I told him I was from Philadelphia, where I had gone to college, that I had been commissioned through the Platoon Leader Course program in June 1964, and that I had gone to the 2d Division after Basic School. I mentioned our Caribbean cruise, and he asked me a bit about my experience in the Dominican Republic. I think we also talked briefly about rock climbing school. Someone mentioned the NATO cruise I had made, and we spoke briefly about Europe.

In a few minutes the colonel buzzed to say he was free to see me. Paul took my officer's qualification record into the CO's office and came back shortly to say the colonel would like to see me. Like Lieutenant Prince, Col. Edward J. Bronars had graduated from the Naval Academy, where he had been a superior athlete. At the time I joined the battalion, Bronars was about thirty-eight years old and a newly promoted lieutenant colonel. He was one of the first Marines to serve as an adviser with the Vietnamese at the outset of our involvement in that country in the early 1960s, and had served there with distinction. When I first met him, Ed Bronars, now recently deceased, had penetrating

---

* Gunner is a traditional term used by Marines to indicate a warrant officer.

blue eyes, gray hair turning white at the temples, a fullback's shoulders, and large powerful-looking hands. He also had a gentle, deliberate manner of speaking that we junior officers came to refer to as "the ho-hum style."

He expressed right away his desire to have a solid 81 platoon in 3/5 and said I could have command of the 81s if I wanted. I responded enthusiastically, and he said he would do whatever he could to help me build the kind of platoon we needed.

A famous general once said one can judge the effectiveness of a military leader by the feeling one has upon leaving a conference with him. From my experience in the Corps, I would say that observation is generally correct. By the time I left the 3/5 command post (CP) that day, I knew Colonel Bronars belonged to the stallion-class of men. He showed those traits in everything he did, and nothing I saw of him afterward altered my first impression of him.

As I stepped out to the bright sunshine that day, I was determined to mold the best 81 platoon in the Marine Corps. I set out right away to plan to do so.

Most of the rest of that first week aboard I was occupied by getting "processed" into the battalion. To my recollection the only really significant occurrence, subsequent to meeting the colonel that week, was one that proved timely and important.

On my way out of the division disbursing office I came face-to-face with Staff Sgt. J. E. Murray, who had been my platoon sergeant in M Company, 3d Battalion, 6th Marines and had served with me closely for nine months in the 2d Division. He and I had developed what both of us considered an outstanding professional relationship. Murray was the kind of solid and reliable staff NCO the Marine Corps breeds in abundance. A heavy-set, slightly evil-looking man of about thirty-two, with his bearish aspect and tough thoughtfulness concerning the troops, it was impossible for me not to like him.

Sergeant Murray was on his way overseas within the next week or two to serve as a replacement in one of the battalions already deployed in Vietnam. I hope he returned safely, but I would not be surprised to learn that he did not.

After we had brought each other hastily up to date on what we had done since we had last met in September, we shook hands and I began to take my leave, but Murray paused and came back. Bending slightly toward me with a furrowed brow, he said in low, earnest tones: "Watch out for those troops, Lieutenant. Remember to take good care of those troops." The words went directly to me. Until I had seen Murray, all my friends and well-wishers, both at home on leave and while I was on station in the Corps, had told me to watch out for myself, to be careful—"Don't get your crazy ass killed" as one officer colleague put it. Until then I had given little thought to the more important subject of how I could best serve the men who would be under my command. Murray's words, therefore, came at just the right time; since they had come from a staff NCO whom I admired and respected, I heeded them as best I could.

As the days passed I grew increasingly absorbed in working with my platoon. One of my first jobs was to select personnel. Almost as soon as I reported aboard we began receiving a steady stream of new Marines into the battalion. Of these men, I was pretty much able to choose the ones I wanted for my platoon.

At the battalion aid station I also established an instantly good rapport with Dr. James Thornton, one of the two battalion surgeons who would sail with us. Jim came from Pittsburgh but now lives not far away from us in the Philadelphia suburbs, where he is a gastroenterologist. He responded to my request for "a tough corpsman who can really hump" with a smile and the words: "We've got just the man for you." He turned to a second-class seaman* nearby and said, "Send Joey Jardina to 81s, will you?"

The TO strength for an 81 platoon at the time was approximately ninety men and two officers. Before we had gotten far into our training cycle, however, we received over 150 men. From that group we were able to select the ones we would take into combat with us.

Of the men assigned to our platoon in training, we of course looked through the service record books for items

---

* Marine medical personnel are corpsmen furnished by the Navy.

such as high GCTs (roughly equivalent to the standard IQ), meritorious promotions, high performance marks from previous duty stations, letters of recommendation, and strong educational backgrounds (few, however, possessed much beyond high school; many had less). I also always welcomed into platoons I commanded in both California and Vietnam men who had either military or civilian records of disciplinary offenses.

The latter is not a practice I would necessarily recommend to every officer; but I seemed successful in doing so, and none of those Marines ever performed in less than outstanding ways under our command. By precept and example I let each of them know that they were welcome in our platoon, and that each man in our unit would be treated fairly (which meant "fairly sternly"). Without exception, each of the men with criminal records, usually 10 to 15 percent of the active strength of the platoons I commanded in the field, responded with pride in belonging to an outfit that frankly aimed to be the best.

I believe there are two fundamental reasons why those men performed so well: first, men who have had disciplinary problems often seem to have an extra charge of aggression that, if properly channeled, can be put to effective use; second, it has been my experience, both in the Corps and outside it, that men with records often are individuals in whom no adult has ever believed and who feel they have been "written off" as incorrigibles. When such individuals find themselves in a cohesive unit that not only accepts them but positively welcomes them aboard, they often develop into loyal and dedicated people.

When we were in garrison I usually checked into the company office around mid-morning to see if there were messages for me or my men and to get to know the members of our company staff. The CO of Headquarters and Service (H&S) Company, of which the 81s platoon was part, was Capt. Hans S. Haupt, a wiry, chain-smoking, intelligent officer with actor Glenn Ford looks and perhaps twelve years of commissioned service. Our company gunnery sergeant, "Gunny" Chapman, in appearance was the conventional stage figure of a Marine gunnery sergeant. Weighing around 260 pounds and standing well over six feet, he had a brush haircut that was beginning to turn gray, close-set eyes, and a loud, powerful voice. He was about as intelligent as Hans, and the two made a formidably effective pair.

About the time we had pretty much decided on the people we were going to take overseas with us, I prepared a brief speech to my platoon. From my experience on the East Coast, I knew that H&S company members were often considered by the men in the rifle companies to be un-Marine. There were several probable reasons, chief of which was the service and staff aspects of the H&S company, which often made for a lack of unit cohesion. Moreover, I had often heard H&S company referred to as "Hide and Slide," because many rifle company members had the impression that all the H&S people ever did was goof off.

I knew there would be no shirking in any platoon I commanded, and I saw the need early in our training cycle to dispel any thoughts that we might have a unit that would be anything but hardworking. On a bright day in early December, therefore, I had the platoon sergeant assemble our men in formation outside the platoon headquarters. Here I delivered an introduction.

I find it easy to recollect the essence of that speech. I told the men who I was and a little bit about my background. I knew even then that what we are is usually less important than what we want to be, mostly because what we want to be so often shapes what we will become. I therefore emphasized that there were only twenty-seven 81s platoons—one for each battalion—in the entire Marine Corps, and that the 81 platoon in 3/5 was going to be the best. "And when you are," I concluded, "nobody will have to tell you, because *you'll know*. Platoon Sergeant, take charge of the formation." I moved back into the cool shade of the platoon office. As I turned I had a smile on my face I could hardly have controlled had I wanted to. I could tell by the electricity in the air as I finished that my words had found their mark. From then on we backed our words with hard-driving work.

The 81-millimeter mortar platoon was potentially a

very important weapon in the infantry battalion. Known at the time as "the battalion commander's weapon of opportunity," the 81 mortar was the heaviest indirect fire weapon in the battalion. It threw its rounds in a high toss and had an effective range of 2,000 to 3,600 meters depending upon the weather, the condition of the mortars, and the skill of the gunners.

The basic 81mm mortar weighed over 115 pounds and made a four-man load. The rounds averaged nine pounds apiece. And there was a great deal of other equipment such as sight units, aiming posts, direction stakes, and communications gear, all of which had to be carried on the march by members of the platoon. Also, like every other infantryman, these men were responsible for the personal gear they carried: weapons, ammunition, packs, helmets, entrenching tools, canteens, and flak jackets.

Except when the guns were used on "a direct lay," fire direction procedures usually operated on the principle of adjusting fire from the observer's fixed point of reference. On these occasions an observer-target azimuth would be called in by the forward observer (FO). Adjustments of range and deflection were then made from the point of impact of the marking round. On a plotting board at the fire direction center (FDC), the NCO-in-charge would mark the adjustments made by the FO, compute the firing data by use of a series of charts, and mark the target information on the plotting board. He would then generally relay the firing data to the guns, either by word of mouth or through wired headsets from the FDC to the mortar squad leaders. They in turn passed the data to their gunners.

When the gunners had the data on their mortars, they would say "Gun up," and that would be relayed back to FDC. After the correct fuse and powder charge were placed on the round, and usually on the command of the FDC, the assistant gunner placed the round at the mouth of the tube and let it drop. The round slid to the bottom of the tube where it was usually ejected when the firing pin sent the round on its way. The gunner carried the bipods, the assistant gunner the tube. Junior men in the squad handled the baseplate, ammunition, and other equipment.

Ammo was generally carried in large pouches sewn onto canvas vests that were placed over the ammo carriers' shoulders like drab, priestly garb. They were very hot. If the command "action" was given while the platoon was on the march, an incredible but eventually well-organized scramble took place to set the guns up, get the direction stakes and aiming posts in place and properly sunk, and the guns quickly dug in, if time allowed.

The mortar squad leader was usually a corporal. At the time the 81 platoon had eight guns, one gun to each squad. There were two squads to a section. Each section had its own forward observer, radio operator, ammo corporal, communications gear, and other equipment necessary to operate independently. Indeed, when the sections were "attached" to rifle companies, which they often were, the sections operated very much on their own and were supervised almost entirely by their own NCOs.

The forward observers had to have especial skills; they and their radio operators had to know how to read a map accurately, spot rounds, estimate ranges, adjust fires, request the proper types of round and fuse, and know the best means of attacking a target.

Of course the members of the fire direction center also had to be able to read a map, handle the plotting board with skill, be thoroughly familiar with communications procedures, and have a sound grasp of the mathematical computations involved in formulating the correct range, deflection, and powder charge. In addition, they had to be able to select proper fuses and advise on general attack decisions involving the guns.

Since they so often had to operate independently with fairly complicated weaponry and equipment, and considering the strength and determination required to handle the guns in the field, I knew that the mortarmen in my platoon would have to be of exceptional fortitude and ability. In my opinion, the 81 platoon in 3/5 consisted almost wholly of such men.

In the early part of December 1965 we began to increase the tempo of training; the daily physical training became steadily more strenuous. About then, too, I attended a brief supporting arms school at Pendleton.

At this school the instructors seemed particularly knowledgeable about their subjects, which they presented in a clear, semirelaxed fashion. Moreover, unlike most military schools I had attended, classes did not last all day, so I had enough time after class to get back to platoon headquarters to lead the men in vigorous afternoon PT sessions capped by a run up goat-shit. I was also able to keep abreast of personnel problems and developments by perusing service record books and talking to my NCOs in the evenings.

With the information from supporting arms school fresh in mind, I was keen to lecture my platoon on the mission and function of the battalion's fire-support coordination center. This I reasoned would allow me to introduce the troops to "the big picture" at the battalion level, to explain each of the supporting arms and its special capabilities, and to indicate the important part I believed the 81s would play in our battalion's schemes of action.

With the view to using them as attention-getters, I drove over to the PX at mainside and purchased in the toy section a plastic 60-millimeter mortar (there were, alas, no 81s for sale) and a dozen or so plastic rounds. The morning of the day I was scheduled to give the class, I instructed my radio operator, PFC Jim Zlatunich, to sneak up on the platoon as soon as the Gunny had assembled the men on the lawn behind platoon headquarters. When I mentioned the word "mortars" in my introduction, Zlatunich was to bombard the men with rounds from the toy weapon (we even had a clandestine early-morning rehearsal).

I expected the men to find the tactic as amusing as I did; of course they did not. After one or two uncomfortable chuckles there was deathly silence. With no small sense of unease I launched into my formal lecture by explaining that the term "shrapnel" was named after a British lieutenant of artillery who more than two hundred years ago discovered that one could inflict casualties upon the enemy by placing high explosive charges within the metal casings of the rounds, a procedure which would cause the round to burst into fragments when it detonated. I went on to explain that had I lived several hundred years ago and made a similar discovery, then NVA might be getting killed and wounded by tiny pieces of flying *kirschke*. In the silence that followed, one could, as the French say, "hear the flies fly." And the rest of my lecture proved only a bit more successful. After that lecture I was determined to leave most of the classes on technical subjects to my NCOs, who usually did a better job of teaching.

After Christmas I attended embarkation school at Camp Pendleton to learn how to load ships. About two dozen students—officers and enlisted men—were huddled together at long desks on two sides of a one-room building.

I found planning a combat load to be especially difficult. Ammunition, pyrotechnics, troops, gasoline, C rations, water, and vehicles had to be loaded so everything could be unloaded in proper order in the event of an opposed landing. Drawing plans for such a load always seemed to me like trying to stuff six pounds of clothing into a five-pound bag. I am quite sure I was one of the worst students in the class, yet I was selected company embarkation officer for the ship on which we sailed, a rusty tub called the USS *Renville*. *Renville* carried most of the troops and equipment for our battalion landing team; our H&S company had by far the most of both.

As far as I was concerned there were three fortunate aspects of my experience as embark officer: (1) it was not my primary duty; (2) it was short-lived (someone had the sense to relieve me of the position before we sailed for Vietnam); (3) Lieutenant Mirgeaux was our battalion embarkation officer. Joe Mirgeaux was almost certainly the best student in our embark school class and had clearly learned ten times more about embarkation procedures than I had. Since he also sailed on *Renville*, Joe did most of my work and did a heroic job of unscrambling the incredibly garbled loading plans I put together. In addition to providing me with his indispensable help, Joe managed what seemed an excellent job of overseeing the loading of the other ships that sailed with us, and aided the embark officers for those ships whenever they seemed to need his assistance.

Joe Mirgeaux was a former enlisted man and had been commissioned under the NESEP program (Naval Engineering and Scientific Educational Program). Like all the NESEP lieutenants I met in the Corps, he was extremely bright, a fact he did not advertise. Since he and I had gotten drunk together several times in Oceanside before we sailed, Joe had no illusions about my embark abilities and must have known from the first that I would need assistance in drawing up our company's loading plan.

About five feet eight inches tall and with a sprinter's build, Joe had keen, flashing eyes, dark blond hair in a brush cut, and a distant Tennessee drawl. He was probably in his late twenties at the time and was one of the nicest people I have ever met.

Joe was not only a reliable embarkation officer and a good friend. When the opportunity presented itself, he showed he could lead a rifle platoon the way he did everything else. On our fourth operation, Hastings, within hours of taking command of a platoon in Company M, Joe was wounded—paralyzed from the neck down—after being shot in the chest and then falling on a grenade while leading an assault on a machine gun position.

From January of that year until just before our third operation, my platoon sergeant was a staff sergeant (soon promoted to gunnery sergeant, "Gunny") named Verona. A veteran of eighteen years' service, Gunny Verona had been wounded in Korea. He also possessed an impressive set of educational credentials and had attended several foreign language training schools while in the Corps.

Sergeant Rockdale was first section leader until after our second operation. "Gunny Rock" as the troops referred to Rockdale was probably in his early thirties when he joined our platoon. Like most career Marines he had traveled over much of the globe during his previous tours. He considered western Pennsylvania his home of record.

Among Gunny Rockdale's former duty stations he had served at Parris Island Recruit Depot as drill instructor for the "motivation platoon," a Marine Corps euphemism for the unit where physically and emotionally unsatisfactory recruits were "recycled," trimmed down, toughened up, and "made proud" before being sent back to regular recruit platoons.

Rockdale had done such a fine job in those duties that he had in his SRB a letter of commendation written by General Ryan himself, who had been CO of the recruit depot when Rockdale was there. Rockdale and the second-section leader, Gunny Killinger, had the soundest knowledge of indirect-fire weapons of any Marines I have met in the Corps. Needless to say, both men knew more about 81s than me.

Gunnery Sergeant Killinger's specialty had previously been artillery. He had evidently had some disagreement with one or more of his seniors in the artillery battery he had been serving with on the coast, and had requested transfer to an infantry battalion. Thus we received Killinger into our platoon. Like Rockdale, he was very capable in fire direction procedures and had mastered all aspects of military communications.

Like Rockdale, Verona, and my fourth-section leader, Killinger was a veteran of several tours in the Corps. He was probably in his late twenties or early thirties when he joined us, but had a weather-beaten appearance that made him look several years older. Killinger's voice was in the lower-middle register and had a strong resonance, so that listening to him speak was like tuning into a "music for quiet listening" station on the FM radio. I did not learn until we were in-country that Killinger had had a back problem for some time that should have prevented his going overseas, yet he not only went through all of the training with us but also did outstandingly in handling his section in combat.

Our third section was led by a hardworking sergeant named Wesley Thomas. He too had been a DI at Parris Island. Although he did not know the guns as well as Rockdale or Killinger, he made up in enthusiasm for what he lacked in field experience and technical knowledge. Sergeant Thomas was about twenty-four years old when he joined the platoon. He came from Evansville, Indiana, and had the friendly "country" way of speaking often heard in people from southern Illinois and Indiana.

Our fourth-section leader was a staff sergeant named Oliver. A quiet man with a likable manner, he had a pockmarked complexion and a deep, gravelly voice. Sergeant Oliver lacked the technical competence of the other three section leaders but was well liked by the men in his section, and fourth-section's morale was always high. Sergeant Oliver's home was East St. Louis.

By January 1966 we obtained a sergeant forward observer for each section. In time those men all became extremely capable FOs. I will say a bit more about them later.

Our ammo sergeant was a former football player and overall good athlete named Brice. Our communications chief was Sergeant Wilson, a bear of an NCO in his early twenties, whose native state was Idaho. He was scheduled to complete his six-year enlistment about the time our Vietnam tour was to end. Wilson was one of a number of Marines in the platoon who had volunteered to go to Vietnam.

"The scuttlebutt" (which concerning personnel matters on the platoon level was almost always accurate) was that a handful of the men in the platoon had been convicted of felonies in the States and given the choice by their judges to either do time behind bars or join the Corps.

It was rumored that one of the men had been convicted of armed robbery in Utah and told that time spent overseas would be taken from his jail sentence, and that as long as he stayed in Vietnam he would be a free man. This man, who joined us as a private, was such a pleasant-looking individual that at first I found the rumors about him hard to believe. Before long, however, I noticed that most of the men in the platoon, which was not known for lack of playful aggressiveness, gave Private D an especially wide berth. That the rumors about him were true was further indicated by the fact that, long after I had retired from the service and enrolled in graduate school, while visiting wounded men at the naval hospital, I met a second lieutenant who told me that a sergeant in Vietnam had said, "If I ever met a captain named Kirschke in Philadelphia to tell him that Sergeant D in Vietnam said to say hello, and tell him he wishes him the best!" Sergeant D had remained in Vietnam most of the time from 1966 until he was seriously injured in close combat in 1970.

In many ways Cpl. Michael Williams typified the spirit

of the 81 platoon in 3/5. With the exception of a gigantic farmboy from Washington State, Corporal Williams was the tallest man in our platoon. He was a fine singer with a wide range of pitch and a strong tone. His voice was deep baritone and he often spoke with a slight stammer, except when he was angry. Not long after we formed as a platoon, Williams composed what to me and, I feel sure, to the rest of the platoon was a great platoon song, a chain-gang melody with a rhythmic cadence that made it well suited for marching. "Big Mike" sang the lead for this song, all of whose words I do not recall, whenever in our training sessions the platoon seemed in need of a special lift.

Williams also designed a snappy-looking platoon flag. And under his supervision several men in the platoon painted a five-by-fifteen-foot sign which they placed in front of platoon headquarters at Margarita. Larger by half than the one outside the 1st Marine Division headquarters, the sign was decorated by a crimson-and-gold Marine Corps emblem, along with an 81-millimeter mortar painted in black, with "81s, 3/5" in gold letters beneath it.

Corporal Williams was probably the strongest man in the platoon. He threw hand grenades as if they were eggs and had courage and endurance.

It was our practice to arrange to have hot chow sent to the men in the field as often as was practicable, so long as that did not interfere with training. A galley-prepared hot meal every now and then did wonders for morale and effectiveness in training. On our first extended week of field training at Pendleton, a truck with hot chow came out the first morning to the range where we were firing. Due to a miscalculation on someone's part at the mess hall we had insufficient food so that the men were not able to "load up" like they would have wished. By the time my turn in line came virtually all the food and all the milk and coffee had disappeared. As always, I lined up last for chow when we were in the field. Anticipating the shortage, Sergeants Killinger, Rockdale, and Verona urged me to move ahead in line.

Virtually all the troops seemed to notice right away that I refused to move up. Not moving up was the only just thing to do, yet many such small decencies over a period of months have a healthy effect on the morale of the men.

As I found to be true, the small things one does for one's troops often are promptly rewarded in ways that one can hardly repay. The entire time I was a platoon commander in the Corps, for example, interesting items continually showed up at our CP. Within a few weeks of my taking over the 81 platoon, for instance, the troops had obtained for me an electric coffeepot along with all the fixings, a freshly painted double wall-locker, and a complete set of comfortable furniture for the platoon office. One day I mentioned, almost to myself, that the platoon seemed a little short of communications wire for training, and the next morning when I came in, I found enough wire outside platoon headquarters to serve a regiment in combat for a year. Another day, late in the afternoon, and with hardly anybody around, I broke my coffee cup. When I came in next morning I found a new one on my desk, painted bright crimson, with a lieutenant's bar on one side and *Lt. Kirschke* lettered boldly in black on the other.

Early in our period at Margarita, I took advantage of our lunch hour breaks in garrison to pack each of the four mortar parts, one per day at a time, in what I had thought were surreptitious solitary jogs up and down goat-shit. On Friday of that week I carried the entire base plate as an assembled unit, i.e., with the outer and inner rings already locked together, much as my men often had to in training and in combat. I did those runs to get a small sense of the discomfort and endurance demanded of my men daily in the boondocks. The jaunts served to reinforce my already high respect for all of the members of my eight squads. Even so, I made the trips that week in a rested state. Moreover, on these jogs I wore only my skivvies, trousers, and combat boots. I did not, in other words, have to carry up goat-shit all of the other gear, weapons and ammunition, flak jacket, and helmet that my men had to hump whenever they served in the field.

In making those trips I had hoped to get out and back from camp without being noticed, and for that reason I did not wear any rank insignia. In addition, I found what I thought was an observation-free route to the plateau and back. And, since the men were at lunch, I figured I would not be seen by anyone. Like everything else I did as a platoon commander, I now suspect, the jogs were not only "spotted" by my hyperalert platoon, but quickly figured out, and before long the men's knowledge, through various means, got back to me with a finely understated sense of appreciation.

An amusing incident took place one weekend, well into our Stateside training cycle, when in civilian clothes Colonel Bronars picked up Sergeant Brice hitchhiking in "civvies" from Oceanside to San Diego. Brice did not know who the distinguished-looking gentleman in civilian clothes was, but the colonel soon established who Brice was and where he worked. For the better part of the next hour, as I pieced together from several sources, "the inquisitive civilian" learned a great deal of inside scoop about the 81 platoon in 3/5, "the bastard it had for a platoon commander" (why, the men even referred to the lieutenant as "J.J. Squared Away," a nickname he did not learn about until many years later), and the manner in which the crazy officer "drove" his men in training.

It was not until the colonel made a pre-embarkation inspection of the battalion that Sergeant Brice first learned the identity of the curious questioner who had driven him all the way into San Diego. The colonel never mentioned the incident to me, yet I understand now why, after that approximate date, he often regarded me with a faint yet discernible twinkle in his eyes.

One Friday night in early February a Basic School classmate obtained front row tickets for us to an Itzhak Perlman concert at the San Diego Symphony Hall. Perlman was by then in a wheelchair himself, but he played violin like an angel. The Marine lieutenant was a Naval Academy graduate I will call Dave Harbor. He was on the coast at the time to attend an intensive Vietnamese language course.

Dave was an interesting young man, and it may be worthwhile to say a few things about him. He was the shortest Marine of any rank I have ever met. In addition, he was perhaps the most soft-spoken. He looked to be seventeen when he was twenty-four and had a gentle manner. Having such apparent handicaps as those, that he was able to graduate so easily from the academy and also become an outstanding Marine officer says something important about his qualities.

At Vietnamese language school he graduated first in his class. And unlike most individuals who had studied the language far longer, by the time he had been in-country several weeks, Lieutenant Harbor could converse with Vietnamese of any background and be readily understood. That was no mean achievement.

Since the seventeenth century the Vietnamese language has had a Roman script drawn up by Catholic missionaries that is known as *quoc-ngu*. Overlaid by a complicated system of suprascript characters, *quoc-ngu* indicates not only the sounds of the language but also its six tones. In order to converse with facility in Vietnamese, one must have an exceptionally fine ear and be able to reproduce sounds faithfully. In Vietnamese the same syllable pronounced with a different tone may undergo a complete change of meaning, so that the wrong tone often renders a word unintelligible to a native or changes its meaning altogether. When *ca*, for example, is uttered with a low rising tone, it means "all," but when it is pronounced with a high rising tone it means "fish." Moreover, each of the five or more southern dialects presents special pronunciation problems.

The Vietnamese vocabulary is basically monosyllabic but the grammatical categories are nearly as complex as those in English. Like Chinese and Thai, Vietnamese makes frequent use of compound words and patterned grammatical constructions. The best opinion I was able to obtain at the time indicated that the closest tongue to Vietnamese was Mon-Khmer, of Cambodia, another language few Americans had mastered. More recent opinion tends to group the Vietnamese language with some of the Chinese dialects and with Thai (Siamese). But the point here is that the Vietnamese language, like the people themselves, was not simple.

Yet Dave had done an astonishing job of mastering the language in a very short time. Probably the combination of his external characteristics and the inner drive

that should have been obvious to all but the most igno-
rant served to induce some of the problems he developed
not long after he went overseas.

At the 1st MP Battalion in Da Nang he had evidently
worked so assiduously at his duties as translator and civic
action officer—important duties, particularly in Vietnam—
that he suffered a serious nervous collapse and had to be
evacuated to the States and then be retired from the service.
But there was more to his situation than would be obvious
to someone merely scanning his medical records.

Dave was an outcast at 1st MP Battalion, as I came to
see in the few days I stayed there, because he worked very
hard in the midst of a group of officers who were among
the most worthless I have encountered in the Corps.

The few weeks before our battalion sailed passed very
quickly. In the midst of field training I received "permanent change of station orders" indicating that, "effective
commencing on or about 25 February 1966," I would be
assigned "to duty in a restricted area" with "Battalion
Landing Team 3/5," the new official designation for our
unit. From that time on activity really picked up since we
had to complete field training and tactical drills and also
be sure our men were prepared to go overseas in other
ways, including having their personal affairs wrapped up.

In early 1966, I checked out of my apartment and drove
down to San Diego to begin supervising the loading of our
ship. Already there when I arrived were our likable supply
officer, First Lieutenant Jassems, who later died in a skydiv-
ing mishap, Joe Mirgeaux, and the embarkation officers for
the other two ships. Along with *Renville* (APA 227), the
BLT sailed with USS *Winston* (AKA-94), and USS *Tortuga*
(LSD-27). The embark officer for the *Winston* was Roger
Pullis and for the *Tortuga*, Mike Carey. Both were second
lieutenants who had been enlisted men before receiving
their commissions. Like almost all of the lieutenants in our
battalion, they were also several years older than me.

In August 1966, Roger Pullis, now a stockbroker
in south Florida, was seriously wounded in a "hot" landing zone. He wears a brace on his right arm, which

he is lucky still to have. After a tour as an enlisted man, he worked at various jobs and eventually graduated from St. Peter's College in Jersey City, where he majored in English and starred in water polo on a good team.

Roger always reminded me of a funny Manhattan bartender, which in fact he was for a time after he retired from the Corps. Along with five or six other pals ("the good guys"), he almost continually told jokes, clowned around in a Bronx fashion, and made wisecracks out of the side of his mouth. There was a serious side to Roger but at the time I did not see it. I thought him so hilarious that I imagined being in his platoon must have been like having a red-haired, Irish version of Jay Leno as platoon commander.

When Roger was about to load his footlocker aboard ship, he hailed two of his troops to lug it aboard. The locker box was heavy, I know, since I had helped him haul it from his car to pierside. When his troops picked it up he warned them not to drop it, since the footlocker held "two hundred pounds of Hershey's—with nuts—And I don't want you to break them!" His timing as always was beautiful. The men laughed so hard when he uttered the punch line that they nearly stumbled down the ladder, footlocker and all.

Mike Carey, the other embarkation officer, was one of the three saltiest lieutenants I met while in the Corps. Like the other two rifle platoon commanders in his company, Mike had not yet gone to college; he had received a meritorious commission. All three of the I Company lieutenants were savvy, although they all were, I think, unduly self-conscious about not having obtained a college degree. Mike is now a chaplain in the prison system in Guam and has his own congregation in Agana.

Along with the other members of the advance party, my job was to see that the loading went as smoothly as possible. *Renville* was to carry a combat load, including ninety-four vehicles and twelve hundred troops—far more men and equipment than she had ever taken aboard at one time before. As indicated earlier, thanks largely to Joe Mirgeaux's assistance, the loading of our ship went smoothly.

Not long after we arrived the docks came alive with the activity involved in loading the ships. The 81 platoon and two of the four rifle companies acted as stevedores, and the ship's officers and NCOs (except for one Marine first lieutenant, all were Navy men) bustled around giving directions to assist in the loading.

Most of the battalion actually headed overseas from Long Beach, but most of the advance party left with the ship when it sailed north from San Diego. We left Long Beach destined for Camp Schwab, Okinawa, in late winter, 1966. Our overseas tour began the day we sailed. We would therefore have "a short tour"—less than the thirteen months standard at that time in the Corps—but most of us soon saw far more than thirteen months' worth of action. The Marine Corps has always had a way of getting its money's worth out of its infantry battalions in combat.

The U.S. had deployed its military forces overseas to implement foreign policy decisions on over 150 occasions before we sailed for Vietnam. Rarely if ever did any of the previous engagements seem so difficult of attainment as our mission. When we sailed from Long Beach on that pastel-colored evening there were no brass bands braying in our tribute, no pipes skirling tunes of farewell, and no large crowds cheering our departure. To my best recollection, the only civilians on the pier to wave good-bye were the *Renville* skipper's small family and the girlfriend of a rotund sailor. The latter pair kissed good-bye at length. After several minutes the ship's whistle tooted and the sailor jogged heavily up the gangplank and came aboard.

Instantly it seemed that the gangplank was up and the vessel was drawing away from the pier. With a poignant sense of relief I watched first the pier and then the land itself recede from view. As *Renville* shuddered into a turn, I wondered what lay ahead for me and the other men in our battalion landing team.

For many of the men, the view they had that evening would be the last they would have of their native land. Few of those men were rich or "well-connected" socially, nor did many have impressive educational credentials. But almost all of them were willing to give everything they had to assure that a nation of sixteen million people would not be forced to live under an unwanted communist regime.

The sea the first few days out was almost as rough as the North Atlantic I had experienced the previous October. Almost everyone aboard except me seemed seasick. Despite the weather I ate as well as always, exercised almost as vigorously, and began to prepare the classes I would be giving aboard ship.

Every morning after breakfast I went to the troop compartment to visit my platoon. On days when the weather was especially rough I went below several times and stayed much longer. As on all the ships on which the BLT sailed, on *Renville* the enlisted men lived in incredibly difficult conditions. The racks were five or six high and jammed very closely together.

In high seas, with so many men in such little space belowdecks, the atmosphere soon grew fetid in the extreme. Many men seemed to become ill as much from the compartment smells as from seasickness itself. On Hans Haupt's sage advice, I therefore had our NCOs hustle their men topside as many times a day as possible those first few days at sea; the fresh air could only help. Despite their living conditions, the men's morale remained incredibly high. I do not recall overhearing a single complaint the entire time we were aboard ship on our tour.

All forty-two Marine lieutenants and most of the captains in our landing team were quartered in one large compartment that the troops referred to as the "bull pen." On *Renville* I found shipboard living for the most part enjoyable: there was a steady routine, excellent food, and interesting company.

Few people who have been to sea for any length of time have not been moved by its majesty. In the several weeks we spent crossing the Pacific, I took special delight in the mornings. Often I arose at dawn, moved quietly in to shave and wash up, put on my field boots, khakis, and field jacket, and stood uncovered for an hour or so at the railing on our level. Leaning over the slick, taut wire, I watched the sun rise out of purple waters, listened to the steady piping of the breeze, and inhaled the sharp tang of the salty sea air.

From the third day out the 81s platoon followed a schedule that usually included three hours of classes on the fantail every morning except Sundays. In the afternoons we usually had another class or two, physical training, and inspections. Some of the classes were "Communicating by Wire," "Forward Observation Techniques" (by Cpl. Hilario Asocar), "Jungle Survival," "Okinawan People and Culture," "Self-Help and Buddy Aid," and "Medical Aspects of Service in Vietnam" (the latter two were delivered by our platoon corpsman).

In our second week at sea I began a series of formal lectures on Southeast Asia, with particular emphasis on Vietnam, that occupied more than fifteen hours of training time during the next two months. Among the topics covered were Vietnam's terrain, people, and climate as well as the economic and political aspects of that country. The last subject set out our reasons for fighting the war. I believed it to be "the most important class on the schedule," as I indicated in a letter I wrote my family on St. Patrick's Day at sea.

About two or three days a week we held inspections on the fantail. Since my platoon was so large I had to inspect one section at a time. As the section leaders were forming up their sections, I would listen to the creaking noises of the ship and the cries of the seabirds whirling and diving some twenty-five meters off our stern. PT sessions aboard *Renville* were generally furious, each unit in the small exercise area seemingly doing its best to outwork and outshout the others.

In the evenings I often changed into field boots and sweat clothes and went topside near the bridge, where it was usually not crowded, and tried to duplicate the PT I had done with each of the four sections in our afternoon workout. I would also charge up the four flights of ladder to the bridge several times to try to keep my legs and wind in shape. On several dashes I nearly knocked over naval officers taking sightings with the sextant. And after I almost collided with the ship's captain, who was descending the ladder as I was sprinting up, I slackened a bit on that routine. One evening, as I recorded in a letter I wrote shortly after we left Hawaii, I did an especially rigorous PT session, capped by 220 push-ups. The workout seemed to leave the Navy j.g. I had been talking to intermittently during my calisthenics totally astonished, which was of course half the fun.

In a letter home on the seventeenth I mentioned that we would be having a platoon PT contest and that competition for it had really been building. I remarked that I would like all four sections to do well and end up in a tie, but I knew that was not possible.

We cast anchor in Buckner Bay, Okinawa, on March 26. It rained that day like never before. The entire BLT did "wet-net drills"—go over the side, then clamber down cargo nets into landing boats, then come back up again, several times—before the actual off-loading began.

I watched the 81 platoon go over the side the last time, their green utility uniforms soaked black by the beating rain. But I had to stay aboard to supervise the off-loading. One of the rifle companies—I cannot recall which—remained aboard to do the stevedoring. From the lethargic way the company handled the operation, it seemed clear that their minds were already ashore on liberty. After twenty-six days aboard *Renville*, who could blame them? The off-loading throughout the early part of that day went so painfully slowly that someone, probably Colonel Bronars, suggested we exchange that company for a group of fresh Marines, and this order was conveyed by me to the battalion CP already set up at Camp Schwab in northern Okinawa.

About 9:30 P.M. civilian time I boarded an LCM to make the mile or so trip to shore to meet the new working party and escort it back to the ship. The storm had passed by then, and as I waited on the beach a fine, cold, misty rain began to fall. Soon several long, green buses approached the edge of the beach and the replacement stevedores filed out. These men were so quiet as they got off the bus that one could hear the faintest cough.

To my deep disappointment I soon made out that this replacement unit was my 81 platoon. That made me sad, since I knew they must have been pulled off their first night's liberty overseas in order to do this off-loading. The next thought which occurred to me was, they must think that I had requested them specifically, a belief their uncharacteristic silence served to reinforce. Silently they formed ranks for roll call, then boarded the mike boat in absolute quiet. As the ramp went up, Gunny Verona came to stand alongside me at the bow and the rest of the platoon gathered in the noiseless darkness at the stern. I never again heard the 81s so silent in the eleven months I served with them. Needless to say, I felt awful.

No sooner had the engines started than Corporal Williams began singing the proem to our platoon song. Then the rest of the platoon joined in with full-throated chorus. And could they sing! They had anticipated how badly I would feel and prepared this welcome surprise.

Their voices reverberated around the bulkheads of the LCM and warmed the chill night air all around us. They sang so loudly and well that the mike boat itself seemed to rock with the steady rhythm. As we came within sight of *Renville*, what appeared to be the entire ship's company came to the rail to watch us draw alongside. I can hear the melody even as I write, more than thirty-three years later.

As we drew alongside the ship, the platoon let out an enormous cheer, charged up the ladder, and worked furiously all night. The off-loading was finished by early the next morning. Before we disembarked, seemingly every officer in the large ship's company congratulated me on the vigor and good spirits of my men, and said they had never worked with a unit that labored so hard for so many hours at such full speed. And yet the men laughed, sang, joked all night, and kept everyone's spirits high.

Need I say I was proud of them?

Around mid-morning the next day we boarded trucks and moved north to Camp Schwab. Schwab, in the northern third of Okinawa, was laid out much like Margarita except that the Okinawan camp seemed larger. Neither I nor my men, however, had much time aboard the base; perhaps 85 percent of our time from then on was in "the boonies."

Our aim was to work the platoon harder in training than it would be worked in combat, and in that we may almost have succeeded. In the field all week and in garrison on Friday afternoons and Saturday mornings, we did exercise after exercise, and the harder we worked the more the men seemed to prosper. To me, few jobs have been so directly rewarding as training that platoon for combat. No matter what I planned and did for them, they always seemed to give back more.

During the month or so on Okinawa, we almost never took vehicle transportation anywhere; we marched to nearly every training area and firing range. The marching in itself was a great conditioner, especially since we "packed" all our own gear on every exercise. A fairly typical pattern would be to march to one firing range, set up the guns, fire missions for several hours, do some gun drill, have chow, then disassemble the guns and march to another range, where we would go through a similar routine.

On the breaks that we usually took every hour or so on marches, I sometimes lectured briefly on ways to move more easily in hilly terrain. I demonstrated, for example, "mountain-walking" and traversing techniques that I had learned at the Mountain Operations Course in California's High Sierras the previous summer. On night marches in particular I sometimes gave the men brief, morale-building speeches. I have reason to believe the men not only listened but deeply absorbed the import of the brief talks. On one night as we marched I recited a brief list of the actions for which the Marine Corps has reason to be proud: Belleau Wood, Wake Island, Guadalcanal, Tarawa, Iwo Jima, the Okinawa we were then traversing, the Chosin Reservoir, and Inchon. I exhorted the men to give their best to assure that Vietnam would be added to the list that Marines in future years would try to live up to.

On another night, when we marched until the sky grew rose-colored with dawn, I kept morale up by stressing that each man in our platoon would have to carry his own load, and that in 81s if you were too tired to walk you would crawl but never give your equipment to someone else to carry. When tactical silence was not called for on our many long marches, the men laughed and joked continuously. When I gave my brief pep talks, however, all was silent save for the clanking of equipment and the sounds the platoon made as it tramped along the roadway or pushed through heavy brush.

One thing I did aboard *Renville* was go through the platoon's SRBs to discover areas where NCOs had special knowledge which might prove relevant. After that, I discussed the areas with the NCOs and advised them to prepare brief lectures on their subjects. They had to be ready to deliver their lectures on-call as fillers when we found ourselves waiting for any extended period with nothing to do. In brief talks the men received fine, informal classes on camouflage, hand-to-hand combat, range estimation, marksmanship techniques, field-craft, rock climbing, and emergency first aid—subjects in some cases not as well covered in the larger classes arranged by the battalion operations section. The filler lectures moreover virtually guaranteed that our platoon never had that "hurry up and wait" feeling that is so often destructive of morale in the armed forces.

One of the most interesting lectures during those first weeks on Okinawa was on "night noises," by Gunny Rockdale, held in the middle of the boondocks on an exceptionally dark night. Before the lecture Gunny Rock was silent for five to ten minutes to allow the men to listen themselves to the sounds of the jungle. Gunny introduced his lecture with a joke about a young man and his date who found themselves in the woods one night. The substance of the joke I cannot recall, but the punch line was: "Them's not crickets, honey; them's zippers!"

Rockdale then had men from his section make "night noises" at various distances: clanging the bolt of an M-14, whispering, digging, crawling, walking, and running through the bush. After each noise, Gunny would ask someone in the audience what the sound was, how far away it was, and how many people were making it. All in all it was a very instructive class.

On Okinawa I continued the practice I had begun at Pendleton of reminding the section leaders to remember their men's birthdays that occurred when we were in the field. On those days we "did-up" a C rations pound cake, often with a disk of C rat chocolate melted over it, and stuck matches on top in lieu of candles. We always made a big show of marching up to the man whose birthday it was and singing a vigorous "Happy Birthday." The troops seemed to enjoy the festivities almost as much as their platoon commander. When we were actually training, however, it was serious work. In gun drill and live firing we paid the greatest attention to details; even small errors or delays there could cost friendly lives in combat. During live-firing exercises I usually moved from the fire direction center to the guns, to the FOs, and back again, passing along useful small tips in each area when possible.

When we were not doing live fire, we often had gun drill. Gun drill was accomplished in two basic ways: on the march, I would often have the Gunny call, "Action!" The sections would then scramble to set their guns up from scratch. In the other method, when the guns were already in place, we would provide different sets of "dope"—elevations and deflections—for the gunners to put on the guns. When the "dope" was correctly applied and the sights aligned properly with the aiming poles, the gunner would say "Up!" and they would be ready to fire.

The first kind of gun drill especially required much coordination, precision, and teamwork since in setting up the guns in combat, often every second was important. In adjusting, aligning, sinking, and realigning direction stakes and aiming posts, the gunners gave their ammo carriers hand and arm signals that were very similar to those employed by civilian land surveyors. In training we timed the platoon at various stages for setting up, both when we were on the march and for getting the guns "up" after they were already emplaced. As with virtually every aspect of our military training, the men competed against the stopwatch. The section leaders held competitions for speed and accuracy between their squads. Of course, we also held periodic competitions among the four sections. And we timed the entire platoon with the watch. I regret that I did not make a record of the times for those competitions; by the day we sailed for Vietnam we were incredibly fast—I doubt that any platoon has ever been faster or more reliable.

In order to simulate combat conditions and enliven our drills, the section leaders, myself, and the platoon sergeant often designated different men as casualties, so that the next senior Marines could take over. "Your gunner and A-gunner are dead," we might say, and the next two Marines in the chain of command would scramble from wherever they were to take up new positions. At times the drills became amusing. On several occasions a pair of Marines would come from different positions to man their gun—and slide headfirst through the mud and ram each other head-on, helmet to helmet. On occasions like that, I often remarked, "If you can't level the bubbles, kick the baseplate," a comment that soon became the platoon joke whenever things did not go just as planned.

To help reinforce the habit of instantaneous response we sometimes had the "Action!" command given when the men had been relaxing for a half hour or so after eating. On occasion, too, we held surprise reveilles for the whole platoon—sometimes for selected sections—so the men would get used to coming to their positions rapidly and alertly at all times, just as they would have to do in combat. A certain amount of confusion is probably a necessary adjunct of war, but we wanted, through constant and efficient training, to reduce confusion as much as possible. Many of our "Action" drills reminded me of the "miracle" drills we used to do in receiver practice in football—diving, leaping, and sliding after deliberately poorly thrown balls—with our Marines sprinting, jumping, and sliding here and there in a rapid movement that by mid-April was no longer confusion.

One Friday morning I received a radio message to report to the S-3 office as soon as we got in. As I entered the "Three-shop" as it was called, Major Monfort arose with a smile, crossed the room, and asked if I would like to take my platoon to Japan for a couple of weeks. We sailed out of Naha on Monday.

We sailed to Japan aboard a greasy old LST. The "T" had a broad, nearly flat prow and a shallow draft forward to allow landing craft to exit directly. Because of this design and the fact that the LST bowed up in the middle in heavy seas, its ride was uncomfortable in rough weather. The exercise area on our LST was just forward of amidships, and during "last-man-up drills" (a form of tag-team race) the first day out of Naha we nearly lost several men overboard when the amidships portion of the ship bowed up and then slammed down. And that was in comparatively tranquil waters.

Sergeant Thomas had already served in Japan for two full tours so I asked him to lecture to the platoon about Japanese culture, language, and traditions. I especially enjoyed the simplified way that Sergeant Thomas went over the rudiments of the Japanese spoken language. He explained the styles of address and levels of respect, and how they were combined in speaking in different situations. With an infectious enthusiasm he emphasized how delighted the Japanese are if a foreigner attempts to speak to them in their own language. Sergeant Thomas also pronounced and explained the ways of saying "please" and "thank you," how to order food and drink in different circumstances, and how to use the various salutations in the language. After each explanation he held several pronunciation exercises so by the time we arrived, most of the men knew at least the basics of polite greetings in the language.

By the second day at sea a typhoon came our way full force. For some reason I felt that might be the only chance I would have to witness a typhoon at sea, and decided to make the most of it. I found a place near the superstructure, just aft of amidships, where I was able to brace myself between a pair of bulkheads, and watched most of the storm.

About two hours before the typhoon struck, dark ragged clouds scudded swiftly overhead and the water turned from blue to an ominous gray. The clouds increased and seemed to coalesce as the wind came up. Suddenly, low-flying, anvil-shaped clouds came over us and a torrential rain began, drenching my utilities. The torrent continued for about two hours before, for a half an hour or so, the sky suddenly cleared. Then, accompanied by heavy rain, low-flying long clouds appeared as the typhoon's tail passed. As the storm receded, these broke up and dark, low-flying clouds reappeared as the sea slowly turned blue again. Then came more anvil-shaped clouds, which spun past higher up and stayed overhead until twilight. Soon all I could hear were the swift sounds of the nearby pulling sea and the intermittent thudding of our prow as it slammed into wave after wave.

When I went below I found the troop compartments to be as foul-smelling as those aboard *Renville*. All section leaders were already down there with their troops, and the platoon seemed in its usual incredibly good spirits. As almost always, everyone evidently knew where I had been and what I had been doing. After a brief chat with the men I excused myself to change into a dry uniform, but before I left, Gunny Rockdale asked if I would join him, Gunny Killinger, and Gunny Verona in the chief's mess.

I was the only officer there. Rockdale and Killinger introduced me, somewhat proudly, to the Navy chiefs. At wooden tables we had fresh coffee in thick mugs, freshly baked hot rolls, and a long stretch of mostly sentimental conversation about our families and homes. I went to sleep that night with a bittersweet feeling such as I have seldom felt before or since.

We came to a rocky beach on Numazu on a bright Thursday morning. When the vehicles had been off-loaded, the 81s formed a chain-gang working party to hustle the seabags and other gear ashore. They performed the chore in what had become their typical fashion—whistling, laughing, and joking as they moved the gear so swiftly ashore that it actually seemed to be riding on a high-speed conveyor belt. Sergeant Brice, myself, and a Navy chief watched this process, and with a heavy note of affection in his voice Brice turned to the chief with a smile and said, "These 81s make a *game* out of *every* goddamned thing."

From Numazu we went by truck column to the training camp at the base of Mount Fuji, a drive of about twenty miles. We had two full weeks of training at Fuji. The ground we operated on there generally was either covered by black volcanic ash or mostly dark mud; a cold rain fell steadily most of the seventeen days we were there.

With our general situation at Fuji in mind, I set up a platoon training schedule for six days a week as follows: Reveille, 0600, followed by hot breakfast. Two hours of classes, then a forced march to the training area (the closest one was several miles away). Training till 1 P.M., a C rations meal for lunch, then field training until around 5 P.M. At that time we made another stiff, forced march (actually a double-time) back to camp. After a hot meal we returned by tactical movement to the field, where we held night maneuvers until around midnight. We then usually returned to the base for five or six hours' sleep. Despite the chilly weather, the steady rain, and so little sleep, I feel we were able to accomplish so much in training at least partly because two good, hot meals a day will do a lot for a platoon of well-motivated Marines.

At Fuji we continued to have a lot of gun drill and numerous displacement exercises, night and day. On those maneuvers I often had the sections wind over hills and through valleys as I watched them with my binoculars, to make sure they remained sufficiently well dispersed. During daytime displacements I often had the forward observers come with me up the mountainside so they could get a better idea of what different-size units look like at various distances.

On the night displacements I moved closer to the platoon and listened for unnecessary noises while I checked the men's dispersion. Before long they had gotten into the habit of moving well spread out, and became able to move and set up their guns remarkably quietly in almost total darkness—habits and abilities I believe helped save us many casualties in Vietnam. In addition, we did a great deal of work on setting up security around the guns, and worked extensively on challenge and password, such as we would use in Vietnam.

In the morning classes I delivered, I reinforced the shipboard lectures I had given on Southeast Asia and reemphasized the most important points about our commitment to South Vietnam. I reminded the men that 80 percent of the people of South Vietnam were concentrated on 15 percent of the land, and one of our primary missions was to protect those people.

One evening I went to a club in Gotemba and drank sake that was much stronger than any I have ever tasted anywhere else. It was brought out by a waitress in a blue kimono, who placed the drink in front of me on a low table and poured it into a warm cup. After each drink a new cup was placed on my table. When I was finished drinking, my bill was settled by the waitress, who simply counted the number of cups that I had in front of me.

My attempts at speaking Japanese led to at least one amusing incident. As do many Asian peoples, the Japanese sometimes use hyperbolical forms of polite address. One drizzly, gray evening I entered a modest-looking shop on the narrow main street in Gotemba. Using Sergeant Thomas's lessons in good fashion, I ordered a pot of tea and a piece of cake. Then I asked the proprietor, a lovely *mama-san,* if she could tell me where the men's room was. Smiling a wide smile of approval at my attempts to use her language, she led me to the door of the room. Before I entered, I turned to say what I meant to be an *arigato*, the informal Japanese equivalent to our "thanks." Mistakenly, though, in an attempt to be extra polite, I used the expression *makato ni go shinsetsu de gozaimas*, whereupon the elderly lady bubbled over with uncontrollable laughter. When I emerged from the men's room, she had already summoned her husband and, still smiling, indicated that she would like me to repeat to him what I had just said to her. When I did, my performance elicited a near-hysterical response from both. I later asked Sergeant Thomas why, and he told me with a broad "country" grin that the phrase I had used translates literally: "In truth, an august, special lordly amiability is here honorably placed."

At Fuji again I felt the same desire for consuming experience that I had felt most of the time I was in California. In town I carried a camera with me almost all the time. Most of the time I was away from the camp I moved around the hilly territory on the outskirts of Gotemba "at the double quick," taking in as much as I possibly could see, pausing now and then to take pictures of the many beautiful, apple-cheeked Japanese children, then, after thanking them, their parents, and grandparents, jogging off.

In the midst of one such day's breathless activity, I spent an idyllic hour or two rowing a rented boat around the center of a tranquil lake. It was a Sunday, and many families were out around the lake, which was surrounded by cherry blossom trees, *sakura* as they are known by the Japanese. By the near edge of the lake, a dozen or so families were enjoying what seemed to be a marvelously bibulous picnic, several small families were rowing around on the lake, and a half-dozen or so mothers were out bicycling with chubby-cheeked infants propped up on the handlebars of the bikes. After a few tranquil hours by the lake, I jogged away, passing as I did the party I had seen earlier. By that time almost all the adults were very intoxicated and the children roamed around mostly unattended.

For the benefit of the rifle companies that accompanied us to Fuji, one afternoon we held a fire-support demonstration. The companies sat in bleacher seats. During most of the demonstration I used a mechanical bullhorn to make myself heard. For the last fifteen minutes of our scheduled lecture, Gunny Rockdale took over and made some valuable points about the 81s' capabilities. To my embarrassment, when I offered him the bullhorn he not only declined but seemed to make himself better heard without it than I had with it.

At Fuji our FOs used every standard forward observation technique and added their own occasional efficient twists. All four 81s FOs were excellent, but Cpl. Hilario Asocar from San Antonio was perhaps the best. He was what was known in Corps parlance as "a good field Marine." That is, he was great in the field but always in trouble when not. As late as 1970, after more than twelve years in the Corps, Asocar was still a corporal, yet he was the best FO of any rank I have seen. An amusing incident took place about midway through our training at Fuji that tended to confirm this view of Asocar.

The colonel had come to observe our Japan training for several days during the second week we were there. At one time, when he went out to check on our FOs, Colonel Bronars had apparently crawled up behind Asocar, who was lying in concealment to observe and adjust a fire mission he had just called in. When the colonel asked what target Asocar was shooting at, the latter handed the colonel his field glasses and pointed to a fifty-five-gallon drum on a hill at almost the maximum distance our guns were capable of firing. Just as the colonel got the field glasses on the target, the first "adjusting round" whistled in: a direct hit. Colonel Bronars returned the binoculars to Asocar, moved back through the brush, and left without saying a word.

By mid-April 1966 we were back on Okinawa and resumed the same sort of training we had before we left. More than twenty hours of it included instruction on land mines, booby traps, and demolitions. As I look back upon those classes, I see that they could have been far better. The information passed out was correct enough; the problem was mainly with the instructors and the thrust of the emphasis. The instructors were all young and fairly immature enlisted men, most of whom had already been wounded three times in Vietnam on one tour alone (at that time in the Corps, three Purple Hearts on one tour meant you had to leave the country). The absence of officers or even staff noncommisioned officers (SNCOs) anywhere on staff at that instructional site proved evidence of deficient good sense in leadership.

Perhaps because they had been wounded so often, or perhaps because by nature they were sadistic—or perhaps both—the instructors presented their information in the most grisly and cynical fashion imaginable. Mines and booby traps, especially as employed in that war, are awful things, and because they are I believe the instructors who teach how to use and dismantle them must have patience with and sympathy for the potential fears of those who have to deal with them.

It also seemed to me that in our training on mines and booby traps, too much emphasis was placed on the more exotic items—Malayan gates, man traps, Malayan whips, Venus flytraps, swinging maces, dead falls, and other devices which mainly involved punji stakes—and too little on the standard explosive devices that were usually not so easily detected but did far more injury. In my opinion we should have had less dramatic presentations that more thoroughly covered the more mundane and practical business of detecting and clearing mines, booby-trapped mines, and high explosives, including everything from hand grenades to booby-trapped five-hundred-pound bombs, items that we found ourselves clearing, always without mine detectors, regularly on our Vietnam patrols.

Our Saturday morning PT sessions continued to be quite demanding. Usually we began with loosening-up exercises, followed by twenty-foot rope climbs and several "last man up" drills. Then we often had section competitions in the fireman's carry, each man sprinting to lift and "rescue" a squadmate who was on the deck. Sometimes we held intersquad tag team races and several times we had combatives, such as "horse and rider fights." In the latter I usually teamed up with Zlatunich. I was usually the horse and Jim Zlatunich the rider—a formidable enough looking pair—but I do not believe we were ever the last ones standing. When we fell, the troops shouted with great delight. All of the competitions were undertaken with more hustle and spirit than one sees in professional sports, and perhaps rightly so—for us, the stakes were higher.

On perhaps three occasions in our pre-Vietnam deployment, I tested the men's endurance by following the above-mentioned exercises with a jog several times around the camp. How far we ran I do not remember, but we double-timed until there were just four or five men left. These remaining few seemed likely on all occasions to keep going as long as their platoon commander.

When a Marine in my command performed especially well during training, I sometimes wrote his parents or wife to apprise them of the accomplishment. I have doubts now about the wisdom of that approach since I believe it potentially can undercut the section leader's authority. Nevertheless, at the time I believed I was doing the right thing. I did not make copies of the letters, but I do have the letters that were written in response to them. I include a few of them not because they say anything significant about myself, but because they are typical of the letters I received, and, I believe, reveal something of the quality of the families from which the young men came:

May 17, 1966

Dear l/Lt. Kirschke,

It is people like you who help uplift heavy hearts at home when loved ones are separated.

Thank you a million times, and God Bless.

Sincerely,
Emma L. Williams
Michael's Mother

May 17, 1966
El Paso, Texas

Lt. Kirschke,

I am David Lopez' father and am very glad to hear that he is doing excellent in his training.

Both his mother and I appreciate your taking the time to write and let us know of our Son's progress.

We are very proud of him as he has always been a good boy. To me he is the finest boy in the world. He has always been very respectful to his superiors and I hope he continues being a good and brave boy.

We would appreciate very much if you would keep us informed of his progress.

I hope he continues to be in your platoon. Although we haven't the honor of knowing you personally, we think you are one of the few platoon leaders who really appreciates what the boys under your command are doing. We hope and pray that you and the rest of the boys will be home soon.

Well Sir, once again I thank you for your wonderful letter and I hope my son won't let you down.

Respectfully,
Joe Lopez

These letters arrived, with many others expressing similar sentiments, virtually on the day we sailed for Vietnam. Needless to say, they made me want to be a far better platoon commander than by my nature I tended to be. For that inspiration alone I am most grateful.

For about a week on Okinawa we trained at the Northern Training Area (NTA). There we worked on various aspects of field-craft such as building shelters, moving in various kinds of terrain, and "living off the land." We did day and night compass work, practiced stream-crossing techniques, crossed over one-, two-, and three-rope bridges in the jungle, and fired small arms at pop-up targets in a jungle lane. We also did rappelling down rain-slick, orange-mud cliffs and sailed down a two-hundred-foot "slide for life"—a hook rigged onto a spinner cable—which we jumped from into a pond that, from the jumping-off point, looked like a small, brown puddle.

When we completed the course at NTA we received a brief speech from Brigadier General Ryan, who I believe was the commanding officer of all Marines in that part of the Pacific who were not deployed in Vietnam. As a junior officer on Tarawa in World War II, he had earned the Navy Cross. The day he spoke to us was damp and close with a low cloud cover, as it often was at NTA. The general, a soft-spoken, modest-seeming man, had a compact build, clear blue eyes, and white hair. His speech recapped some of the things we had learned in our recent training and emphasized in a sensible way the challenges before us. I had drawn the platoon up into formation for the speech. When it was over, I prepared to salute General Ryan and dismiss the platoon, but he asked me if I minded if he spoke to one of my NCOs.

"Not at all, Sir."

The general walked over and spoke briefly to Gunny Rockdale, whom I later remembered had served under Ryan's command when the latter was a colonel at the recruit depot on Parris Island. When the general finished talking to Gunny Rock, he shook his hand and patted him on the shoulder. The gesture remains typical to me of the gentlemanliness I encountered among every Marine general I encountered in the Corps.

Saturday nights at Camp Schwab, I usually went to the O Club, where I drank several bottles of the good, inexpensive San Miguel beer sold there. On several occasions late in the evening, Captain Haupt came in and sat next to me at the bar. Always on duty, Haupt was able to retain his military scowl even after he had put away a good number of drinks. During those hours at the O Club bar, Haupt passed along several worthwhile tips about ammunition requests and personnel-handling techniques. More often, however, after he was sure I was half-crocked, he would ask me for the lowdown on men in my platoon who had the resolution of disciplinary problems pending (most involved fights with men from other units while on liberty). I wish I had a dollar for every time I told Haupt, for example, "Corporal Asocar's a good man, Sir, he just has some trouble now and then on liberty," or, "Sergeant Wilson's an outstanding Marine, Sir, it's just that . . ." I believe that by maintaining my composure and speaking honestly in these bar-rail sessions with Captain Haupt, I was often able to persuade Hans to go easy on my men when meting out company commander's disciplinary actions.

Our training on Okinawa ended in late April. In early May the entire BLT had a technical, weapons, and personnel inspection by the 9th Marine Amphibious Brigade staff, accompanied by General Krulak, whose son, Chuck, a Basic School classmate, decades later became a fine commandant of the Marine Corps.

General Krulak's was the last inspection we had before our mount-out to the Philippines, our base of operations for the Special Landing Force operations we conducted in South Vietnam. The evening before we sailed for the Philippines, after all our gear was packed and ready, I jogged up a long stretch of beach alongside Schwab. About the time I decided to turn back, the tide came in so quickly that I was not able to jog on the beach but had to pick my way back over shining coral. In the pastel twilight, wave upon wave burst into powder over the rocks and coral. I was happy not to get washed in and to be able to get back to my quarters before night fell altogether. Nevertheless, I enjoyed those last few hours of time by myself since they gave me valuable moments in which to sort out my thoughts before we made our first landing.

I learned the next morning that about the time I was picking my way back along the coral, my men were having an Okinawa farewell party at the EM Club. After that, they apparently marched back in platoon formation to the battalion area, singing the 81s' song the whole way.

As they moved below the I Company area, the troops from Company I began harassing them—yelling, "The 81s suck!", "H&S pogues!", and several other remarks—and then rolled several trash cans down the hill to buttress their opinions. The casualties from the uphill assault were I Company, eight men hospitalized, numerous walking wounded; 81s, no casualties.

The late Capt. Sam Glaize, CO of I Company, was magnanimous about the incident, and acknowledged to me right away the next day that he had heard the whole story and that his men had been in the wrong. The colonel and Major Monfort, however, were not at all pleased. The major let me know that sort of thing was not to happen again. On the one hand, I was proud of the men's having done such good work, yet I knew that we could not allow that kind of incident to recur. I told the men and there were no others.

That afternoon our truck convoy drove out of Schwab, heading for the ship-loading area from which we would sail to the Philippines, briefly, and then to Vietnam. As we drove out of Schwab we passed several dozen base enlisted Marines. As each one saw us, he paused, uncovered, and bowed his head in silence as we rumbled past. On the long green bus I was on, not one man laughed or said a word.

We sailed for Subic Bay aboard LPH-5 *Princeton*. Much of the time we were on the LPH (landing port helicopter) I passed time by doing PT with the platoon, lifting weights, and tossing the football around on the hangar deck with a friend, Lt. John W. Keker. John was seriously wounded on our fourth operation in Vietnam, recovered, and then graduated with distinction from Yale law school.

An LPH was always a good ship to work out on; the *Princeton*, a converted fixed-wing aircraft carrier, was used as a helicopter launching-pad and thus had plenty of deck space. It also had ample space for classes, and I used it on our short trip mainly to give the troops a lecture on how they were to conduct themselves on liberty in the Philippines.

I was officer of the day our first day in port. As it turned out, that proved a benefit since I had a jeep at my disposal all day and had, as part of my duties, to tour the nearby town. Always in Olongapo the smell of the privy was seldom far from one's nostrils. As I crossed the bridge to the town with my driver we were greeted by several dozen youngsters, mostly in small canoes in the water below us, proffering their sisters, brothers, mothers, and girlfriends. My driver and I were wearing our pistol belts and red MP armbands, yet we were greeted by comments such as "I love you, Lieutenant, no shit! Hey, Marine, you wanna ___ my sister? I have cute sister, Joe, no shit!" Both on Luzon (where Olongapo was) and later on Mindoro, we encountered such poverty as I doubt I will ever see again. I believe we all found it disturbing, especially in a supposedly free-world country that was our ally.

Shortly after this our battalion went on Operation Hilltop, the last major training exercise before Vietnam. The exercise took place on Mindoro and lasted three days. Through most of it the wind and rain came in sudden, violent gusts. For the operation, each of my sections was attached to one of our rifle companies, so I saw the sections only when I went on patrols to do so. For most of the operation I stayed at the fire-support coordination center, where I plotted the locations of friendly units and monitored and coordinated the delivery of dummy fire missions to support them. As I would do in Vietnam, on the FSCC exercise, if a helicopter medevac was called into an area at the same time a fire mission was scheduled for the same coordinates, I had to make sure the 81s did not hit the helo. Generally I did that either by shifting the mission elsewhere or by having the guns check—halt—fire until the helo had lifted out. Also, I did map surveys of the patrol routes of friendly units to assure that our guns did not inadvertently fire on them. And with the air liaison officer and artillery liaison officers in the FSCC, I made recommendations to the colonel and Major Monfort concerning the best ways to cover different targets with supporting arms fires.

An incident occurred when I was out of the battalion CP on Hilltop that tells much about my own character, as well as that of Jim Zlatunich. At first light on the morning of the second day of our operation, Zlatunich and I went out on what was to be an all-day patrol. Our intent was to visit with each of the four rifle companies in the battalion. While there, we planned to see how the guns were being employed and to discuss their disposition with the company commanders or the ExOs to whom they were attached.

Zlatunich and I had been up most of the previous night monitoring radio transmissions in the FSCC. We went on patrol with at least one C ration meal apiece. We moved out in heavy mist along a trail no wider than a man's body. The trail ran along a sheer cliff face: to our right was a slick, mud cliffside that went up at a steep angle for several hundred feet; to our left the cliff dropped off at approximately the same incline for what appeared to be at least four hundred feet. Zlatunich and I were moving Indian file along the narrow path and the mist was so thick, I did not see the boy until I was almost on top of him. I lifted my hand to signal Zlatunich to hold up.

Before us on that narrow, muddy, godforsaken cliffside trail was a naked, skinny boy who appeared to be about seven. He was squatting, huddled back against the wall of mud, and shivering, his head on his arms, which were folded across bony knees. It must have been nearly a minute before he became aware of our presence and looked up. I recall wondering to myself where he had come from. Zlatunich right away insisted that we take the boy with us, which we should have done. But I said no. "But we can't just leave him here, Lieutenant," Zlatunich responded, a mixture of impatience and incredulity in his voice. My reasoning, if one could call it that, was that since we would have to be on patrol all day, we would not be able to take the boy with us. Besides, I thought to myself, if the boy had gotten into these straits already, no one would come to claim him anyway, so that our assistance would only be temporarily good for him. Needless to say, I am sorry for having thought that way.

Reluctantly, Zlatunich assented to my judgment. But before he left, he bent over, said some kind words, grasped the boy on the shoulder, opened every can of C rations he had with him, and left each one on the trail next to the bewildered youngster.

After a few days back at Subic after Hilltop, I received a message from the "Three-shop" asking me to stop by their office. As I entered, Lt. D.N.T. Perkins, originally from Oregon and now a successful consultant and author, stood up to say hello and shook my hand in his warm and low-key Northwestern manner. He asked how I was doing, then asked if I would like to take my platoon to train several days on Zambales Island. My smile must have been answer enough.

We left Subic the next morning on foot and marched some distance to the embarkation point. From there we went by mike boat to the island. Zambales, a few miles out in Subic Bay, was at that time an uncultivated island. As I wrote my mother, it had "wild pigs and chickens, beautiful lagoons, high ridges and thick jungles . . . It was warm and beautiful . . ." When we arrived perhaps two dozen naked children supervised by their mothers were bathing and playing in a natural saltwater pool that was sequestered from the headwinds by a graceful arc of sand dune. Shortly after we landed I passed a young Filipino mother with her chubby infant lying beside her on the slope of the sheltering dune. The baby was holding her hand with both of his, gripping her forearm at the same time with both his feet, and cooing and gurgling as loudly as could be.

We had taken with us a great number of illumination and HE (high explosive) rounds with various types of fuses. We fired at one range the first day and displaced early next morning to another range on the other side of a steep ridge. The keenness of the inter-Section competition and innate pride had so sharpened the sections that by then the platoon was in fine fighting form. We fired night and day each day we were on Zambales and our morale was indescribably high the entire time. One technique we brought to near perfection on the island was firing illumination rounds to allow adjustment of HE rounds. The long, wavering incandescence of the illumination rounds lit the terrain on the hills and in the valleys like stage lighting in a vast amphitheater. Into that eerie setting the HE rounds came whistling, a series of rapidly blossoming orange flowers. At dawn on Zambales a bar of gold always formed on the horizon, and the afternoon soon grew brutally hot. After noon chow we secured firing to hold a swim call. The beach was unspoiled and beautiful, the water so clear that we could see the rocks on the bottom even when standing waist-deep.

On our last day on the island the birds that began chattering at first light were silenced by the rising sun. As I think back on my tour I do not remember hearing any birds sing when I was in Vietnam. I wonder if they sing there today? That afternoon we loaded onto the mike boat that took us back to the mainland.

The mike boat skipper was a large, swinish-looking Navy chief. Bare from the waist up and sweating profusely, he ambled forward on the deck to watch our platoon move aboard. As I almost always did when we were in the field, I had removed my lieutenant's bars that day. Just barely within hearing distance the chief strode up to Gunny Killinger and began to run on at length about the worthlessness of Navy officers, what a fool this ensign was, how incompetent that lieutenant was, and how glad he was to have his own mike boat to skipper.

Killinger was a salty-seeming staff NCO and in him the chief seemed sure he had found both ally and confidant. When he finished, the chief squinted at the gunny, expecting affirmation. I feel sure that Killinger never knew I overheard his answer. After a long silence, he replied: "I don't know what kind of officers you have in the *Navy*, but the lieutenant we have is fine."

"What's that?" the chief asked uncomprehendingly.

"I said," Killinger repeated, "the platoon commander we have is just fine. He's a good man," he added in a matter-of-fact way, looking at the chief as if he were defending his home state. I moved several steps farther away and asked Gunny Verona a meaningless question. I felt much complimented.

When we reached the mainland we formed for a long, hot march back to the LPH. When our formation swung onto the main boulevard leading to the pier, we reached a several blocks' stretch where palm trees arched above the roadway. A gentle breeze then fanned us as we moved, whispering through the branches high overhead. I called the platoon to attention and sounded the cadence several times so the men could get in step.

For a brief second I heard only the sounds of the clanking equipment and the steady tramp of the men's feet on the roadway. At my request Corporal Williams sang the proem to our platoon song. All who were within the sound of the men's voices—military and civilian alike—ceased what they were doing and walked to the side of the boulevard to watch the 81s platoon swinging in. Eighty-nine men: dirty, tired, hungry, and proud—the best 81 platoon in the Marine Corps—the men knew this even before they had the chance to prove it in combat. "If there is a Heaven," I thought to myself, "and if I should have the good fortune to get there, I will have just one request: that I find the 81s platoon, 3/5, all present. Perhaps it will be a late spring day such as this, and Corporal Williams will be prepared to sing the cadence."

We sailed for Vietnam the next morning.

THREE

3d Battalion, 5th Marines: Special Landing Force and In-Country

We sailed on USS *Princeton*. On the few evenings before our first Vietnam landing I walked the deck briskly with Lieutenants Mosby G. Perrow III and J. Starns Kopfler. Mosby came from the Blue Ridge Mountains of Virginia and Starns from Mississippi, and I think they rather liked befriending this "lone Yankee" on our voyage. On our walks we had conversations about home, of course, but we also discussed philosophical questions such as men our age at that time perhaps seldom considered, and those conversations I have always considered a permanent part of my youthful education.

Aside from the few evening walks, I especially recall the hours I spent those last few days on the ship's forecastle. There I always felt secluded even when others were present. On the forecastle I felt ahead of the ship and above the sea. The large black links of cable, the squat gray winches, the rushing water in the hawse pipes, the beating wind, the slickness of the deck and rails, and the flying fish skimming the sea before us combined with the ancient smell to make it seem as though we had gone back many centuries in time.

As we neared the Vietnam coast the officers in our landing team received briefings in the wardroom, then received the maps for our first operation, Deckhouse I. One of the most important briefings came from a sloppy-looking thirtyish major, an intelligence officer from regimental headquarters. His was also the most misleading intelligence briefing I received before any of our operations in Vietnam.

He began by saying, casually, that we would probably have just a little sporadic enemy contact. On that point our experience soon showed he was very wrong. He indicated offhandedly that we could also expect to "lose a few people—maybe ten or twelve—from mines and booby traps," which he said "were scattered throughout our area of operations." On that subject he was indeed right, but one presumes that, if he'd had to make the landing with us, and continually face being blown up himself by one of these horrible devices, he would not have almost yawned through his land mine information. Needless to say, on D day the major remained aboard ship. The day before the landing we made pre–D day transfers so that the 81s section going in with Company K, along with Zlatunich and me, moved to a landing ship that carried amphibious craft. The other sections from my platoon landed by helicopter several kilometers inland, along with rifle companies L, M, and I. Deckhouse I took place during the hottest time of year near Song Cau in Phu Yen Province. We awoke before dawn to have a steak-and-eggs breakfast that in my state tasted like paper. In near-total darkness we stumbled around somewhat to find the amphibious tractor (formally LVTP-5) we had been assigned.

Inside the amtrac it was almost totally quiet, the close air still except for the hum of the ship's motors and the occasional rough sound of the engines as we vibrated into a turn. Desultory conversation came in whispers, and there was little of it on the landing craft I went in on. I know that from the time I arose that day, my heart beat very fast and my mouth seemed lined with cotton. I would be very surprised to learn that any men in our BLT were more afraid than I was. I did my best to try to conceal my emotions.

I was not so much afraid of the physical enemy. I had already been under fire in the Dominican Republic, was sufficiently used to being shot at, and I felt that all my training had prepared me as well as possible for combat against other fighting men. But I was most concerned about the booby traps and mines we had been told to expect. Not long before our first landing I learned that one of my best lieutenant-friends, Tyrone Pannell, had been killed in Vietnam by a land mine. Ty was the first black

Marine officer killed in Vietnam. He was such a great person—so dynamic a personality, such a great athlete, and so full of life—I found it hard to conceive of a mine powerful enough to kill him. The realization that Ty Pannell had been slain by one of those devices made me more nervous than I might have otherwise been.

Soon after dawn, through the peephole in our LVTP-5, I watched the light sea mist begin to lift. Soon our landing craft stopped circling, tugged once, and churned for shore. As we did, naval gunfire screamed overhead and threw up portions of the beach that drew steadily closer.

Our landing craft came in just behind Capt. Dick Maresco's Company K. Apprehension mingled with fear to make my senses very keen when we landed; for most of the rest of our tour, in fact, the colors and features surrounding us I usually saw in very clear relief, the details and colors almost always seemingly accentuated. I believe even my sense of smell was sharper most of the time I was in action. That heightened sense of one's world was one of the primary experiences I have taken with me from my year in combat.

Beyond the beach was a narrow forest and then a series of steep cliffs up which we moved most of our first morning. Like every day for most of the five or so of the operation, D day was one of brilliant sunshine and fierce heat. Zlatunich and I moved with difficulty up a rocky defile, in trace of Sergeant Killinger's section. In the spaces between the boulders where we moved, the heat seemed to rise and strike us from the rocks. In spite of my fine condition I felt wobbly from the intensity of the heat, yet there was not a word of complaint from the 81s, who moved with far heavier loads steadily uphill in front of us.

After a battalion CP site was decided on, Zlatunich and I scrambled up to a high shoulder of ground to set up an observation post (OP). About three-fourths of the way up I fell into a very well camouflaged pit about waist-deep which had roughly a dozen sharpened punji stakes. The pit was not large around—a perimeter of about two feet by two feet—yet my feet landed in about the only place they could where I would not be touched by a stake. Moreover, my legs were just long enough that my genitals were not impaled. In addition, six snakes were in the bottom of the pit, slithering rapidly around my boots. As a precaution, Zlatunich carefully hacked all six in two with his machete. After I photographed Jim holding the twelve half snakes draped over both arms, we continued our hot climb.

In many ways that OP was the most beautiful spot we occupied our entire tour. No sooner had we caught our breath from the climb than Zlatunich and I smelled the salty sea air mingled with a faint scent of areca flowers. We looked at each other and smiled.

The atmosphere was clear and the view exhilarating. To our east was a vast stretch of the South China Sea on which a handful of our ships still floated. To the south and north we had splendid fields of observation of the valleys below.

On Deckhouse I, before we took up our OP position, I was told that all the friendly villagers in the province had been explicitly warned that they were under no circumstances to move north across a river roughly eight hundred meters south of us. Our troops were told that any Vietnamese seen moving in our direction across that river must be presumed to be enemy and taken under fire. Throughout the operation we had patrols from our battalion moving not far from that river. Enemy troops moving north of it might well be ambush forces sent to attack our men.

Zlatunich and I had soon settled into a narrow trench and I promptly scanned the riverbank to look for signs of crossing. I soon spotted several small boats south of the river quickly loading with Vietnamese, seemingly heading to our side. But at our not inconsiderable distance, the people appeared to be women and children, and to this day that is what I still believe most of them were. Before I called in the first fire mission meant to kill, I double-checked with battalion operations to make sure I understood my orders correctly. I had no time to say anything more. Then I had our artillery fire a warning shot, deliberately short, to induce the boats to turn around in the event they did carry civilians who were not crossing to do us harm.

Rather than stop, the boats moved across even faster. I felt I had no choice but to have the artillery fire "for effect." There seemed something more than a little incongruous about calling artillery and naval gunfire missions on boats full of people crossing such a peaceful-looking river on such a beautiful day, but it appeared that I had no choice. Several reasons for their movement of course existed. First, they may have been women and children, as they appeared to Zlatunich and me from our OP some eight hundred meters away, but even if they were that did not preclude their being unfriendly. On our Vietnam tour, hundreds—perhaps thousands—of Marines were known to have been killed or wounded by seemingly innocent civilians. In addition, I came to know firsthand of several incidents later in our tour in which North Vietnamese Communist regular soldiers forced apparently unwilling, unarmed civilians—men, women, and children—to do suicide or near-suicide missions such as clear minefields and booby traps, act as diversionary forces at the point of a gun, and scout our troop positions after dark and, sometimes, even during daylight hours.

On Deckhouse I, of course, the unfortunate and perhaps likely possibility existed that the Vietnamese we saw crossing in the heavily loaded boats were not women and children but NVA males disguised as noncombatants and carrying concealed weapons—a situation we likewise encountered many times afterward on tour. Moreover, as I reasoned at the time, if the people crossing were "friendlies," they had already been instructed not to cross; and our orders were to fire on anyone who attempted to move north of the river. How could we know their political sympathies or why they were crossing? Nevertheless, even as the rounds were on the way, Zlatunich and I prayed sincerely that what we were doing was right.

As the deadly volleys were about to explode, I raised my field glasses to observe and adjust the fires. No adjustment was needed. Since there were no trees unduly close to either bank of the river, I had requested airbursts. They went off in a series of gray-black puffs above the stream, apparently raining down hail upon hail of shrapnel. The casualties were many—I doubt that many of the dozens who tried to cross managed to do so without being hit or sunk—yet they continued to come for several boat waves. After the first several nightmare ferries, few attempts to cross the river were made during daylight on that operation. But those first fire missions nearly made Zlatunich and me physically ill. It was not the most pleasant first exposure to combat in Vietnam, but there was soon more.

That the weather was so clear and the terrain visually so pleasing made the tactical decisions we had faced even more difficult. In many ways those decisions were the hardest I had to make on my Vietnam tour. I am glad to say that subsequent operations presented few such moments. After Deckhouse I, whenever I had to fire on the enemy, he clearly was one; most of the time the enemy soldiers we encountered were either fully armed and uniformed North Vietnamese regulars or non-uniformed Communist soldiers who fired on us first.

Since a rifle figured to be more useful on the observation post than a pistol, I soon obtained an M-14 for the remainder of that operation. Every night when we were on that OP, Zlatunich and I ran our rear sights down at dusk so that we could fire more accurately after dark if we had to. After dawn, listening carefully to count the clicks, we put battle sights back on our weapons. Each soldier had a setting he preferred and knew by heart. We would manually adjust the sights in the dark by listening for each click. In order to be able to "spot" our rifle fire better during the daytime we put tracer rounds in our magazines when we were on the OP. During my Vietnam tour I fired a rifle only twice. Both times were early on this operation.

One way to control movement around our positions after sundown was to have a curfew in effect at dusk. As with the river crossing so also with the curfew: all the non-Communists in the area had reportedly been clearly told they should not be out after dusk on the north side of the river. On one of the first evenings of the operation, Zlatunich and I saw two young men walking slowly across the valley south of us, carrying what seemed to be farm implements on their shoulders. It was not long after sundown and they were roughly five hundred meters away.

I am fairly certain I called our battalion command post to ask if I should take them under fire. If I did, the answer was affirmative. With the controlled excitement of the hunter, I lined up one young man in my sights. Since I fired a tracer, Zlatunich was able to report that the first round had just missed, something I saw myself. The second struck the Vietnamese in the legs; he thrashed around a bit in the paddy before his friend hauled him out of sight.

At first Zlatunich and I were both elated, but how can one stay happy long over shooting someone like that? Neither of us could. The looks we exchanged soon made it clear that each of us felt sad and disgusted.

Throughout the first few nights of this first operation the 3/5 rifle companies' fire discipline was utterly lacking. For most of that time, three of the four companies engaged in nearly continuous firefights—most seemingly among each other. Throughout those nights dust from the companies' fires rained almost continually into the trench where Zlatunich and I had stretched out. Tracers erratically speared the darkness overhead with orange flashes as small-arms fire hissed and cracked steadily above us. Through most of those early nights on Deckhouse I, after dark a raised hand would almost surely be shattered at once. As we lay almost head to head in that too-narrow trench, Zlatunich and I reflected more than once that "if ours was a crack battalion . . . !" Miraculously, apparently we incurred no friendly casualties from the intercompany battles. And fortunately, 3/5 soon got the unsteadiness out of its system.

In contrast to the human scene we experienced at the time, the first mornings on Deckhouse I were among the freshest I recall in Vietnam. There was comparatively little humidity and dawn arrived slowly—a suffused pink and rust.

In order to pass the time on our OP between fire missions, Zlatunich and I talked about home. Like characters out of Samuel Beckett, we played word games and did quizzes and puzzles to pass the time while we scanned the terrain below. I did not win most of those contests. Occasionally I tested Zlatunich's retentiveness by giving him long messages phrased in elaborate sentences mostly to see if he could repeat the essence of what I had told him. He almost always did.

After several weeks on Deckhouse I our landing team

was joined by elements of the U.S. Army's 1st Air Cavalry Division, and we stayed ashore with them to conduct a second operation, Nathan Hale. Like Deckhouse I, that operation lasted several weeks.

On Nathan Hale I had little contact with Army personnel; most of the 1st Air Cav outfit operated the next few weeks several miles south of us. As the new operation began, however, Zlatunich and I were joined by an Army naval gunfire spotter team—a sergeant FO and his radio operator. The sergeant told us he had been in Vietnam seven months and that, operating out of Tuy Hoa, he had been a naval gunfire spotter the entire time. After he arrived the first occasion we had to use naval gunfire was on a fire team of uniformed NVA who were hustling, bent over, through brush in the valley south of us. The sergeant hastily read the observer-target relationship off the degree scale on his compass rather than from the mil scale, and misread the map coordinates of his target. His radio operator proceeded to transmit the mission in a jumbled and excited fashion.

I "checked" (that is, stopped) the mission and gave the correct target information as well as the accurate compass reading. Had I not done so our naval gunfire mission might well have struck a K Company patrol moving through the valley.

Before long Zlatunich learned that the radio operator who worked with the sergeant was totally unaware of fire-adjustment procedures. Small wonder.

Through most of our first two operations I had little direct contact with our 81s. For most of my tour as 81s platoon commander in Vietnam, in fact, I was unable to witness firsthand the men's best performances. On Nathan Hale, Zlatunich and I saw little action ourselves. We mostly sat in observation posts from which we saw few signs of the enemy and monitored incoming fire-support requests at the FSCC.

On Nathan Hale we were often not far from the camouflaged squad tent that served as the battalion command post. To me the most memorable and instructive events on Nathan Hale involved Colonel Bronars and happened not far from the CP tent.

Early in the operation a thatched-roof dwelling had been set up as an enemy-suspect screening headquarters. The headquarters received perhaps a half-dozen Communist suspects a day through the first few days of Nathan Hale. All the suspects were fighting-age adult males who wore skimpy black pajamas; most were hustled into the area by Marine guards. Inside the detention headquarters was a slim, mean-looking South Vietnamese Army interrogator. From the sounds we overheard he apparently slapped, beat, berated, and otherwise abused the men brought before him. I heard the slaps, what sounded like kicks, and what definitely were threats directed by the interrogator at the prisoners.

What kept me from intervening, I am ashamed to say, was a combination of callow weakness mingled with the limp rationale that we must allow our allies scope for action in what was more properly their sphere than ours, or so I might have phrased it at the time. I suppose it was the evening of the second day of Nathan Hale that Colonel Bronars apparently overheard the procedures in the interrogation quarters. Without hesitation he moved in and abruptly put an end to the torture. I recall my feeling of relief as I watched him move into the house, and the even greater feeling of the same emotion when he came back out. I like to believe that had I encountered the same scene later in my tour, Colonel Bronars's example alone would have provided me with sufficient guidance so that I would promptly intervene. But who knows? Regardless, Colonel Bronars acted with the manfulness I should have liked to be able to claim for myself.

Another example of Colonel Bronars's moral qualities occurred toward the end of either Deckhouse I or Nathan Hale. Our battalion executive officer who, until then, many had thought a good officer, within earshot of me suggested to Bronars that we carry as a battle casualty one man who had actually been shot and killed accidentally by a careless sentry. Colonel Bronars responded with the vigorous "no" one would hope for from any officer in the service of one's country. Those two examples are typical of the way Colonel Bronars conducted himself the entire time I served under him in 3/5. Small wonder he rose to three-star general before his retirement.

At the conclusion of Nathan Hale, from a landing zone (LZ) aswirl with dust, we boarded helicopters and flew over miles of deep-green South China Sea to our troopships. From there we steamed back to the Philippines.

On the way to Subic we had memorial services on the *Princeton* flight deck for the Marines from our landing team who had been killed on the two operations. It was a bright, clear morning. The landing team chaplain led the prayers, including the Psalm that begins, "The Lord is my shepherd." After that came a benediction, a rifle salute, taps, and the presentation of the flag. In the steadily beating wind on deck, the open flags made stuttering, popping sounds as they were presented. The services were moving but brief, which seemed fitting since we would have many more on our tour. All of us, I believe, were already aware of that. Intelligence reports from higher headquarters notwithstanding, even on those two operations, enemy contact, which was supposed to be negligible, proved quite otherwise.

Mainly on the strength of the many reports I received from the officers in the rifle companies, I gathered that my men had been outstanding on the first two operations. Right away it became evident that the physical conditioning had paid off. Our battalion landing team suffered 150 heat casualties in all. But in the 81s, who carried more gear and ammo per man than anyone, there was only one, a Marine who had just come off mess duty, carried seventy-five pounds of equipment most of his time ashore, stood five-feet six-inches tall and weighed at most 135 pounds. On our way to Subic several Marines who were close to him told me he became so dizzy and faint he could not see his rifle to pick it up, nor could he remember his serial number, yet when the corpsman told him he had to be evacuated he protested vehemently.

Virtually every officer in our battalion complimented my men's courage and conduct in the field. "The 81 platoon is tops in my book"; "My hat is off to the 81s"; and, "Your men are in better condition than any platoon I've ever seen" were typical remarks from officers in the rifle companies with which our 81s sections had moved. At least three of the sections fired very well, and our platoon had been responsible for a sizable number of enemy killed and wounded.

We remained in Subic Bay eight days. During that time we did a little training and partying. On one of my first evenings ashore I went to the Cubi Point Naval Officer's Club for dinner. As I crunched down the gravel walkway to the entrance, loud, drunken laughter carried from inside. The club was mostly filled with clean-cut-looking Navy pilots in their mid to late twenties, and few women were present, which in itself I found depressing. There seemed to be at least one pilot in every gathering—at the bar, at a table, or standing in casual groups—making flying-maneuver motions with both hands in ways that have become cliches in war movies involving pilots.

At Cubi, primarily an air base, the jet traffic—coming and going—was nearly continual, and from the club I had a splendid view of the runways. After dark the activity on the strip became almost hypnotic as the parti-colored lights on the runways steadily crossed the different-colored lights of the incoming jets. On my way out of the club that evening I passed a bibulous table of naval aviators laughing heartily as several repeated what one had evidently just said: "If they're dead, they're VC. That's right! If they're dead, they're VC!" Even in my semi-inebriated state I did not smile at the gathering; I felt that a widespread attitude such as that among our military would soon diminish the already small chance of success we had. Moreover, the comment recalled to mind with a rush the carnage I myself had recently unleashed during Deckhouse I.

There was a surreal quality to those last, swift days of liberty before our special landing force operations resumed. Although I would not have thought it possible before our first Vietnam operations, I did not much enjoy the few days' respite in Subic; despite the similar climate, the contrast between the unmenaced human scene in the PI and the one we had just left proved almost too painful. Of our last week's training all I can recall now are some furious platoon PT sessions followed by several trips over the obstacle course for myself, and at least one for each of our sections.

At the edge of the steamy PT field, as we gulped water from a hose, I noticed some troops from I Company practicing with a map and compass nearby. Within hearing distance the I Company Gunny strolled up behind one of the troops, who was fumbling with a map and compass, and declared, "If you see an azimuth, shoot it!" The comment seemed lost on the confused PFC to whom it was addressed, yet seemingly all the 81s picked it up right away and our platoon cascaded into laughter.

The day before our last recall the platoon had a beer party at a beach on the base. Shortly before the party broke up the troops captured me and carried their struggling lieutenant into the ocean for a friendly dunk. The section leaders also soon hit the surf the same way. After that the whole platoon had a relaxing saltwater swim. Recall came shortly before sundown, when we rode bumpy, open sixbys swiftly back to the ship in the face of a glorious sunset.

Sometime after I was dunked and before our recall order I had wanted to go waterskiing. A Filipino base employee had been hired by the Navy to drive a motorboat offshore that was rigged for waterskiing. For a rather long time I lounged patiently in the warm water, awaiting what would have been my first turn ever on water skis. I was supposed to be next when the messenger from battalion came bumping and honking down to the beach in his jeep toward our party. By the serious look on the Marine driver's face as he pulled up, I sensed his message. By the way his wheels scattered stones as he took off to his next stop, I knew we had to go.

I have never had before and have seldom had since a desire to water-ski, yet I felt strongly compelled to stay in the water just a bit longer because my turn to water-ski would have come next. I could not, however, since that would have shown a bad example to my men. When I headed up the beach to board the trucks, I had a strong premonition that I had just missed my last chance at that water sport. But mine has been a very full life, and waterskiing is one of the few things I had really wanted to do that I probably never will be able to.

The scuttlebutt I heard as soon as I came back aboard ship was apparently accurate, since I had written my mother that we were supposedly heading for a landing about five miles south of North Vietnam within a few thousand meters of the so-called DMZ. I closed by writing, "Don't worry—by the time you get this letter I'll be back aboard ship."

Almost as soon as our ship was under way we came under blackout conditions. In the evenings there were no flight operations, so after dinner Lt. Mosby Perrow, Lt. Starns Kopfler, and I resumed our walks on the deck for an hour or so. Those times are difficult to describe yet they were special hours for me. We had a chance to wonder aloud about our ultimate destinies, reflect on our lives thus far, and discuss other important questions.

Around the edges of the flight deck the troops lounged and talked quietly among themselves—perhaps about some of the same questions. Near the tail of the deck the three of us sometimes paused to stare at the South China Sea disappearing behind us. Often a moon the color of an apricot reflected off the water in our wake, swirling through the mist in phosphorescent showers of stars.

I did not have time to get to know Starns well, but I recall that he had a philosophical disposition and seemed prepared for combat. Mosby G. Perrow III was about six-feet tall and solidly built. He had graduated from Washington and Lee University, where he returned after his tour to attend law school. He had light-brown hair, a dignified Virginia drawl, and large, light-blue, *lemur catta* eyes of a shape and color I have never seen before or since.

As a diversion from our philosophical discussions we sometimes passed the time by trying to identify constellations and name the brightest stars in them. Once I thought I saw Regulus, an especially bright star in the constellation Leo, but Starns contended I was wrong.

"Well, what is it, Starns?" I demanded in mock-serious fashion. Standing near the prow, we heard the sea rushing inexorably beneath us.

"Donno, Jim," Starns answered darkly, "but ahl faand out before y'all do." He was killed within the week.

The operation we headed for next was Deckhouse II. The 81s platoon was helilifted off LPH *Princeton*. On the morning of the landing I briefed our section leaders, and they summoned their squad leaders to convey the orders. Those NCOs were: 1st Section, Corporals Hill and Watson; 2d Section, Corporals Rivera and Whitehead; 3d Section, Corporals Howells and Williams; 4th Section, Corporals Harrison and Poole. No 81s platoon commander could have wished for better squad leaders.

Before the squads picked up their ammunition I asked Gunny Rockdale where the Willie Peter (white phosphorous) ammo was. The Gunny extended the tip of his boot to several boxes at the bottom of one pile on the hangar deck next to him, smiled, and said, "Them's them, Lieutenant"—an efficient gesture very typical of the Gunny.

Not long after the matter-of-fact sounding "Land the landing force" command echoed from the loudspeaker, our ship turned gracefully into the wind. The naval deck officer, wearing a gold, iridescent zip-up jersey, signaled his crew chief and he alerted his men. About eight tightly built sailors wearing snug blue shirts, goggles, and caps with holes cut around the ears hustled out to positions fifteen yards in front of the helicopters on the carrier's launching pad.

The choppers on deck began turning their rotors with an uproar of wind and splashing water (it had rained briefly that morning). In front of each helo stood one of the deck crew sailors, goggles secured over eyes, wrists crossed overhead, signaling the helos to hold down for our embarking men. On another sign from the deck officer, a handful of sailors who had been loitering on cargo boxes pulled their goggles down and walked casually aft to the Marine heli-team leaders, each of whom held green assignment tags. After quick head counting, the teams raced out behind their blue-shirted guides to a position at the center of the deck, from which they split, running single file into a curling pattern toward the interior of the choppers.

After the troops in our helo were buckled into low canvas seats, the helos took off, tugging slightly a few times at first under the strain of their load and the unlifted curtain of weather. In a moment our wave of helos was airborne, droning rapidly in the direction of the coast.

Deckhouse II was the first operation we made in what had been designated I Corps (pronounced "Eye"), the northernmost of the four tactical regions then in South Vietnam, where the Marines did virtually all their fighting throughout the war. From then on, all the operations and patrols I went on in Vietnam took place in I Corps's area. During the year I served in Vietnam, 50 percent of the American casualties and at least 55 percent of the enemy casualties were inflicted in that part of South Vietnam.

We landed at 0630, four thousand meters south of the DMZ. We made no enemy contact our first hours ashore. Until nearly twilight we set in a defensive perimeter on a sand spit twenty-five-hundred meters north of the mouth of the Cua Viet River, in the coastal area of Quang Tri, the northernmost province of I Corps. Throughout the next month we operated within a few thousand meters of the so-called DMZ—a zone by then considered "demilitarized" by the allied Forces only; for at least a month the North Vietnamese had been pouring infantry battalions through it as rapidly as they could.

Before evening the battalion command post displaced to a bombed-out village on the edge of a pine forest. There the 81s CP set up across the road from a well, where most of us washed that evening. Entrenching tools rasped in the damp twilight air as we dug fighting holes in the gravelly soil. From wood he had gotten someplace Zlatunich built a pair of wooden racks so we could sleep off the deck that evening. He also came up with several dozen green bananas, which we had to abandon long before they ripened.

For the few days we were on Deckhouse II, our battalion's main objective was to block the NVA routes of advance through the DMZ into Quang Tri province east of

Route 1. We had little activity on that brief operation and there were few fire missions by 81s.

In mid-July 1966, our landing force displaced westward by helicopter to the Cam Lo area of the same province, where we began Operation Hastings. For that operation we landed not far north of the Cam Lo River. Under steadily cracking sniper fire we hustled northward to a CP site. The first place considered was an abandoned stone plantation house surrounded by light vegetation. As soon as Captain Haupt saw it, however, he strode swiftly away with a sour expression on his face. To Major Monfort the colonel said something like, "No. I agree with Hans. We don't want that," as he moved away. The major promptly added: "I imagine that house is the registration point for every NVA mortar south of the DMZ." Later in my tour I learned he was right.

Fortunately perhaps for all of us, we moved the command post five hundred meters or so east of the abandoned plantation site, in a gentle ravine on lower, much less exposed ground, and were altogether better concealed by the vegetation surrounding us.

That part of Cam Lo consisted largely of uncultivated, heavily vegetated, rolling valleys and steep, thickly vegetated mountains. For most of the operation I worked out of the battalion fire-support coordination center, at that time under the command of a Naval Academy friend of mine, a fine artillery officer named Lt. Dale Lux.

One of my first missions on Hastings was adjusting artillery and 81s fire onto the nose of a heavily wooded ridge— later named Mutter Ridge—twenty-five-hundred meters north of our CP. Since the jungle cover appeared very thick I used fuse delay, as I always did when firing into a tree cover.

That night I had to move quite far outside our lines to adjust artillery and 81s concentrations on likely avenues of approach for the NVA. It was a pale, moonless night when Zlatunich and I left the defensive perimeter. We moved cautiously as far as we could, staying in wood lines and under cover. The only place from which I could adjust the fire, however, was from atop a bare knoll five hundred meters north of our perimeter.

To do that I left Zlatunich in the brush behind me, took his radio, and crawled as fast as I could atop the knoll. When I got there I lay still for a moment to catch my breath. The air was very clear, the stars brilliant and flashing such as I have seen only in the High Sierras and aboard ship when crossing the ocean. After I called the adjusting rounds, I strained my eyes down the long valley north of me. It was the most confusing hour of the night, when the last clearness from the upper sky merges with the encroaching blackness in a blur that tends to disguise terrain features and falsify apparent distances. I could not hear the artillery round go "on the way," but the 81s fired from comparatively nearby so in the still air I could hear the *punk* of the round as it left the tube.

"*Whoosh-blam! Whoosh-blam!*" The 81 and 105 adjusting rounds whistled in just where I wanted them. I whispered hoarsely into the handset to mark those missions as concentrations and crawled hastily down to Zlatunich. I think we were both relieved when I rejoined him.

Fairly early on this operation our 106 (recoilless rifle) platoon commander, Lt. Marv Christians, took a long security patrol west of our positions and discovered an apparent NVA rallying place. He brought back a sizable cache of weapons, equipment, and other matériel. As I recall, Lieutenant Christians and his unit made a similar seizure again later on the same operation.

In the first two weeks of Hastings alone our battalion made over thirty major contacts with the NVA and inflicted many casualties. During the operation our landing team discovered and destroyed eight major enemy installations, each of which could have accommodated a battalion-size unit or larger, and a number of smaller living areas for NVA troops. The schematic summary in our unit diary of enemy killed and wounded and weapons and equipment captured on that operation covers five typed, single-spaced pages.

Also on that operation at least eight of our platoon commanders were wounded, and Starns Kopfler was killed. Around midway into the operation his company made contact with three NVA on a well-used trail running north and south near Hill 362, just south of what soon came to be known as Mutter Ridge. Shortly thereafter I Company came under small-arms crossfire along with a concentrated, heavy, 82-mortar barrage. The attack continued for at least an hour and inflicted numerous Marine casualties. A sizable enemy force then assaulted I Company and got within thirty yards before they were repulsed. In leading the I Company counterattack, Starns was killed.

Also around that time an I Company lance corporal named Richard A. Pittman earned the eleventh Medal of Honor in Vietnam. When I Company came under the heaviest fire he exchanged his rifle for a machine gun, ran forward and shot up a group of NVA hidden in the nearby brush, then moved forward again and stood in the middle of the jungle trail where he fired his machine gun at about forty NVA who had been massing for an assault. He reportedly killed over half of them before diving to safety. With a captured submachine gun and a .45-caliber pistol he killed three more NVA before hurling a grenade into the midst of the remnants of the NVA as they fled.

While I stayed continually aware of the action going on all around our CP, my main duties during that operation were monitoring fire missions, helping to plot others, and providing advice to the colonel and Major Monfort, our battalion operations officer. Probably my single major contribution on Hastings was one which may have saved many Marine lives and inflicted at least a few enemy casualties. Around 2000—8 P.M. civilian time—on August 1, after I Company had already been under coordinated attack for nearly a full day, it again received heavy shelling from NVA 82 mortars. At that time Major Monfort asked me where I would position my 81s were I an enemy platoon commander attacking I Company. After a quick map check I gave Major Monfort map coordinates 021 628, for several reasons. Major Monfort promptly directed fire onto that point, which produced a pair of large secondary explosions. The incoming mortar fire suddenly ceased. It seems likely that the artillery concentration both silenced the mortar fire and blew up the enemy's ammunition piles. I am glad to say that I Company received no additional mortar attacks on that operation.

On Hastings one of the most difficult but necessary of my duties was reprimanding Gunny Rockdale. Early one evening I had canceled a fire mission submitted to me by the Gunny, since I knew from the company patrol overlays for that night that a patrol from Company M would be going through the same area where harassing and interdicting ("H&I") fires were planned and at approximately the same time the 81s mission was to be fired. Later, urged on by a premonition of disaster, I made my way the several hundred meters down to the 81s in pitch darkness and checked the firing charts. As the guns were about to fire an H&I mission, I glanced at the charts by penlight and immediately noticed that it was the same mission I had canceled earlier that evening. Needless to say I canceled this mission again right away. Steaming with anger, I moved swiftly to the fire direction center.

Gunny Killinger, on duty then, told me that Gunny Rockdale was asleep. Rather than awaken him and dress him down within earshot of the troops, I left a message for him to report to me first thing in the morning. Early the next day as I squatted between Zlatunich and Wilson over a small breakfast fare, Gunny strode deliberately up to me with my note in hand and said, "Lieutenant, I don't like to receive notes for me to report to anybody."

With a building fury I have seldom ever felt, I responded, "Shut up, Gunny."

But he continued till I leapt to my feet, knocking over the C rations cans I had been opening as I did. As I stood, my mouth flared into an uncontrollable sneer.

Seeing my anger, the Gunny apologized profusely. I told him briefly the reason I had canceled the mission and said what I believed, that he would have done the same thing had he been in my position. I then ordered him back to the guns. Though painful, such incidents, I suspect, confront every officer. I have included this incident because I believe that virtually every junior officer has to fight, in some way or other, to earn the respect of his senior NCOs. In the Marine Corps this is especially true on the company and platoon levels since here the platoon commanders are often younger and frequently in many ways less experienced than the NCOs they command.

Operation Hastings ended for us in early August 1966. During the operation our battalion fought five freshly trained and rested North Vietnamese battalions, all well equipped with Russian- and Chinese-made 82mm mortars, rocket launchers, automatic weapons, and Chinese-made assault rifles. NVA casualties for the operation were in excess of two thousand. Of North Vietnamese killed alone there were at least 824, with 14 enemy soldiers captured. The Marines' casualties were 126 killed in action and 448 wounded. As usual there were no Marine POWs. In fact, on the more than one dozen operations and hundreds of patrols and ambushes I accompanied in combat, we did not have a single Marine captured or missing in action. Considering the amount of action we saw and the number of enemy casualties we inflicted, that says a great deal about the premier strengths of the United States Marine Corps: loyalty and tenacity.

After Operation Hastings we returned aboard ship briefly before we moved in-country. When we were about to disembark and move inland we were officially relieved as special landing force by another battalion which had just moved into the South China Sea to serve as our offshore replacement.

When we moved in-country we went first to a camp called Reasoner (named after another Medal of Honor winner, a Marine lieutenant killed in action the previous year). At Reasoner, where we stayed only a few days before we made our fifth operation, our official mission was standby reserve, meaning we had to be ready to go out again as soon as called, just as on special landing force.

After inspecting our men's cramped tent quarters, I learned that the Marines' NVA POW retention camp was set up just across a small bog from where we stayed. Out of curiosity I walked over to see how the prisoners were being handled. It became readily apparent that these NVA prisoners lived and ate much better than our own infantry-men in Vietnam. They billeted in reinforced squad tents, had three warm meals a day (not C rations), and did not seem restricted to their quarters during the daytime but were free to roam at will within the rather large confines of their barbed-wire encampment. Moreover, they had no laboring duties whatsoever as far as I could ascertain from my casual conversations with the Marine enlisted men who were their guards. And, I was assured, they suffered absolutely no torture or any other harassment. To me, the gulf between our treatment of their prisoners and the *Bridge on the River Kwai*–style of cruelty routinely inflicted on our POWs remains an eloquent statement on behalf of our values.

Our battalion stayed across the water-filled crater from the POWs for several days in early August, yet during this time just before Operation Colorado, a call went out to our battalion to donate blood for the Marines wounded on Hastings.

When I heard that my first reaction was startled outrage. Asking for blood from men in an infantry battalion, and one on standby reserve! I thought to myself, Can't they draw from any other donors? As I watched the steady stream of men moving in the direction of the aid station where the blood was to be donated, I said out loud, "Now this is too much!"

Gunny Rockdale had just passed the word to the section leaders in their sections' tents and was standing next to me when I came out with this. He turned with a puzzled look on his face and said, "Pardon, Sir?"

"Oh, nothing, Gunny, I was just thinking out loud," I said, and moved in the direction of the straggling lineup of Marines and corpsmen.

I myself was too selfish to give blood. If the truth be known, I was even somewhat relieved when I had my first malaria attack shortly thereafter, since that provided the "official" excuse that allowed me to assuage my conscience about not contributing to the division blood bank, or whatever it was called. As the men straggled by on their way to the aid station, however, I followed them from a distance. Men of every color, creed, and ethnic background in the 81s platoon (and no doubt from many other platoons, as well) lined up in generous numbers—indeed, as far as I could tell by a quick head count, the entire 81 platoon minus their leader gave blood that day. They lined up in such a quiet manner that, had I not known otherwise, I might have thought they were queued up to receive mail. I know that their unassuming acts of charity deeply embarrassed the lieutenant, who watched them from a distance and then asked himself why he had been privileged to have men of such high caliber under his command.

I believe it was on the fifth of August that I realized I had probably gotten malaria during Hastings. As the first attack began I felt the approach of nausea that usually preceded the bouts of shivering. After the first of those I was thoroughly drenched with perspiration. As soon as I began to recover, feeling alternately feverish and chilly, I went to see Dr. Thornton. He diagnosed malaria and advised me to go on "no duty" for three days.

As long as we were in Vietnam our corpsmen distributed, weekly, orange malaria tablets which contained 300 milligrams of chloroquine base with 45 milligrams of primaquine. They evidently did not work for me. We operated most often in Vietnam in hyperendemic malaria regions where the *anopheles minimus* and *anopheles maculatus* flourished. Of the several dozen species of mosquitoes, these two are apparently among the most dangerous types of malaria carriers. Both species prefer clear, slow-moving streams and brooks with grassy edges—the type of environment we moved in daily in the hill country inland—and often proved resistant to preventive medicine.

On August 6 our battalion commenced Operation Colorado. Despite the no-duty advice of Doc Thornton, I made the operation on schedule and felt malaria-free during almost the entire operation. We began Operation Colorado in Tam Ky. Like Chu Lai, Tam Ky is in Quang Tin—a poor province fairly typical of the populated provinces we operated in.

In those areas isolated houses were rarely seen. Although the Vietnamese population was mostly rural, people tended to cluster in villages and hamlets rather than spread out on the land. In the Que Son Valley, where we moved on Operation Colorado, the population at the time was estimated to be 60,000, or more than 100 people per square mile, most of them farmers who worked small plots of family-owned land. The farms produced mainly rice—the chief crop in that part of the country. Since that was still a time of private ownership of land in South Vietnam, the farmers took great pride in their fields. Terrain permitting, the rice fields tended to be laid out in paddies roughly twenty meters square. Windrows divided one rice paddy from another. On the many operations and patrols we conducted in Quang Tin Province, it was not uncommon to see peasant farmers strolling around their land for hours on end, inspecting the dikes, while the wives and children hunted the small crabs that burrowed into and sometimes through the rice field dikes. The older boys in every family were generally entrusted the job of handling the water buffaloes, and next to the rice fields themselves the animals were the farmers' most prized possessions. They were apparently valued even more highly than the farmers' homes, especially since the latter were more easily and cheaply replaced. Very often as we moved through and around the villages in Quang Tin we glimpsed boys perched on the backs of water buffaloes seemingly in a state of mystic communion with their fearsome beasts. Often when it began to rain the farmers would come out to the rice fields to watch their dikes and windrows, to ensure they could withstand the strain of the increased volume of water and to strengthen them in the weakest places.

Most villages in Quang Tin were surrounded by a bamboo hedge; lacking this, they were almost always marked off by a hedgerow or similar natural demarcating feature. In the countryside, where we always operated, houses were generally wood frame with dried mud walls and thatched bamboo- (or sometimes palm-) leaf roofing. Many of the buildings had a small veranda, often at least partially enclosed by bamboo screens. Most houses were one story and, from my observations, seemed to be waterproof during even the worst storms.

It is difficult to recapture what it felt like on our many patrols through the fields and villages outside Chu Lai.

When the sun shone the cicadas zithered steadily in the trees. The ever-present, fecund scents of hot earth, manure, and barn fowl might not have seemed as unpleasant if we had not had to be continually alert for land mines and booby traps of every conceivable variety, as well as to the possibility of ambush. Around the villages the air was often heavy with the musky scent of areca flowers. They, too, might have seemed more pleasant in less dangerous circumstances. The areca flower, of course, produces the betel leaf chewed by the Vietnamese farmers, and the stains it left at least partially accounted for the rotted appearance of the mouths of many peasants in the remote countryside.

While moving through the villages we sometimes smelled the cooking of a Vietnamese dish such as chicken or light vegetable soup—generally speaking, the poorer the family, the lighter the broth. The latter was made with a green vegetable and rice and generally flavored with *nuoc mam*, to me a nearly unpalatable fermented sauce made of fish and salt.

When our battalion moved in-country, the dry season was ending in that part of Vietnam and dust was nearly everywhere. Within two months the climate turned and the monsoon blew with full force. When that happened, mud and water became a major problem. During the monsoon season the absolute humidity—the amount of water vapor in the air per cubic meter—becomes very high; I doubt it ever gets higher anywhere else. With the temperature and humidity high, many lower forms of life multiply rapidly. Among them, fungi and bacteria as well as insects, "weeds," and "bush" proliferate with extreme rapidity.

On the numerous operations and patrols we made by day and night, we moved through villages—both deserted and otherwise—rice fields, elephant grass, bamboo forests, tropical jungle where no sunlight seemed to have penetrated for thousands of years, thick scrub, mudflats, salt rivers, and virtually every kind of swamp. We seldom seemed to patrol flat or even gently rolling terrain; instead, we were often going up and down steep, slick, vine-covered hills and mountains. In addition to the ability to endure hardship, the Marine infantryman in Vietnam had need of no small amount of stamina; I doubt that many Americans have ever worked so hard for so many months as did the Marine infantrymen I served with that year in Vietnam.

For Operation Colorado we flew out on helicopters that picked us up in Tam Ky. Our first few days out we made no significant enemy contact but the weather proved a steady nuisance. Throughout the first few nights it rained continually. On each night before the rain came the landscape surrounding us was enveloped by rushing clouds of dust. Vivid flashes of lightning, incessant peals of thunder, loud and continuous, warned of the coming deluge. The nights were moonless and black except when lightning illuminated the scene. Then it seemed as if a dozen floodlights shone on the bushes around us. During the daytime a brutal sun blazed without remorse and there was seldom a breeze.

During Colorado the 81s had numerous fire missions, none of which I observed; the sections operated independently, one section with each of our rifle companies. On their missions during Colorado the 81s accounted for at least twelve NVA killed and eight wounded. To my recollection our squads sustained only several wounded, but at least ten of our Marines had to be evacuated because of malaria, most cases apparently contracted during our extended stay in the hills in Quang Tri Province on Operation Hastings.

In mid-August, Generals Walt and Platt, along with Arthur Godfrey, of all people, visited our positions in the field. Godfrey wore a flowered, Hawaiian-style shirt, not good camouflage at the time, and strolled amiably from foxhole to foxhole shaking hands with the troops and saying, "Hawayaa, hawayaa," just as when he appeared on TV, except that he looked and sounded at least a decade older than he had ever looked on the tube.

Arthur flew out none too soon that evening. That night there was a heavy probe on K Company's lines not far from my position. Much of the firing was apparently directed at the 81s forward observer's position, so I crawled there to see if Corporal Asocar and his radio operator, Lance Corporal Thibault, were all right. When I arrived I found Thibault sitting on the edge of their foxhole talking to

Asocar, who was wisely crouching in the hole and peering up. We made whispered small talk for several minutes.

Suddenly the enemy launched a coordinated attack using light mortars, small-arms fire, and 82 mortars simultaneously. Right away a half-dozen mortar rounds whistled in a tight circle around our position and tracer fire lit the sky above us. The first volleys landed just behind Thibault, who sat between me and the explosions—less than eight paces from me and even closer, of course, to Thibault. I grabbed his arm and Asocar pulled his leg to get the radio operator into the hole with us.

"Ooohhhh. I'm hit! Jesus Christ, it hurts!"

Assuring that we'd take care of him, I ran my hand down Thibault's back and felt a fairly large, sticky flesh wound. I did not know it right away but the young radio operator had been hit in perhaps the safest place—the backside.

The NVA timed their small-arms and machine gun fire to begin as the first mortar volleys struck, and small-arms fire hummed and cracked close above us. An 82-mortar round bursting within forty paces will normally kill or seriously injure a man. Since these rounds burst all around us, and from very close range, Thibault and I were very fortunate to be alive. That was one of many close calls on my overseas tour. If I'd been alone and had no cares other than for myself, I believe I would have been frightened by the experience, but, as so often, because I had my men to look after, I found I was able to retain my composure.

After the first volleys the NVA fired a series of airbursts, the shrapnel from those spattering around us, the rounds sucking the air out of our fighting hole as they exploded. Since Thibault continued yelling for a few minutes I thought his wound might be more serious than he said. So as soon as the small-arms fire ceased I helped him up and, against Corporal Asocar's pleas, brought Thibault to the battalion aid station—at least two hundred meters from the FO's position. Fortunately for us, the NVA did not resume their attack as I half carried, half supported the hopping lance corporal across the largely unprotected ground to battalion aid. As we neared the CP, I hoarsely asked for a corpsman. To my surprised satisfaction, in the blackness we almost stumbled over Doc Thornton, who promptly treated Thibault in the calmly expert way Jim handled all casualties.

My prompt action in getting him to the doctor did not, perhaps, diminish me in Thibault's eyes, but that bit of bravado I believe was the only unnecessary risk I took on my tour—unnecessary, since it probably would have been faster to have a corpsman come and treat Thibault where he was.

My birthday came while we were on Operation Colorado, and somehow the troops learned the date. When I went to check the first and second sections' positions that morning, someone broke out a can of C ration date pudding into which were stuck several matches for "candles." The men surrounded one of our NCOs and began singing "Happy Birthday" as they slowly approached with my lit up "cake." Of course, that gathering called for brisk shelling by the alert enemy. After a brief break in the firing our troops attempted to resume the party, but another shelling—heavier that time—prompted me to order, from a position flat on the deck, "Party canceled! Spread out and take cover!" I realize now that I should have added, "Thank you!"

From Operation Colorado until my transfer we moved in the field continually. With 3/5 we went on two more "named" operations and dozens of patrols, virtually all of them featuring at least some enemy contact. From Colorado onward I grew generally more fatigued. Because of that and the continued pace of our activities, I wrote fewer letters and kept fewer records. In addition, after we went in-country the 3/5 unit diaries became far less detailed than they had been during the operations we made on special landing force, for most of which we were fairly well rested. Thus, I have not been able to reconstruct our activities during my last few months with 3/5 with the same exactitude as for most of the rest of my tour.

The rest of the time I served with 3/5 our troop movements were generally on foot or by truck and then on foot. We of course became thoroughly familiar with the inglorious physical hardships involved in most infantry troop movements—especially in a tropical country such as Vietnam. At that period in the war the roads in the tropical regions were not all totally insecure, and in the dry season we sometimes sped dozens of miles in the open, breezy backs of six-bys over dusty, bumpy roads.

At predesignated places we scrambled out of the trucks and patrolled through every kind of terrain in South Vietnam. On these many patrols I came to appreciate the wisdom of the ancient Greek idea of measuring distance by the parasang, which varied its measurement according to the difficulty of the terrain. Surely it was far more difficult to move through swamps and streams or up and down jungle terrain than it was to walk the same distance over open ground—something that strictly staff officers seldom seem to appreciate.

Insects—mosquitoes especially—became a steady cause of annoyance, particularly in the evenings when we were in ambushes. Several evenings in late August and early September 1966, I recall lying in ambushes near trails well inland from Tam Ky. As we listened for the sounds of the enemy, one sometimes heard only the wind breathing softly through the grass, the tapping of the crickets, and the incoming hum of the attacking mosquitoes. On one especially beautiful evening as I lay in an ambush with Lieutenant Carey's platoon, the air was still warm and the sun had not yet disappeared. As we waited for the enemy, in front of me on the trail a cluster of gnats hovered in a lath of sunlight, inscribing in the air the kind of motion in stillness I had seen somewhere in movies of the human cell. Briefly my mind became transfixed by the gnats' movement. It occurred to me with a rush that probably the same kinds of cells that moved within me moved also within the men we hoped to kill soon. As rapidly as I could, though, I drove that thought from my mind. With some difficulty the soldier in me banished the philosopher; for the rest of that patrol, with some difficulty, I kept in my conscious mind the hope that we would soon find the trail in front of us strewn with Communist dead.

On another ambush patrol late that summer, just after

sunset, Staff Sgt. Oliver and I noticed a pair of Vietnamese children switching their brace of water buffaloes rapidly away as soon as they saw us emerge from the elephant grass. Feeling a twinge of anxiety, almost fear, I motioned by hand and arm signal to the men behind us to spread out even more. We had not moved a dozen steps beyond the grass line when two huge, crumpling explosions occurred some twenty-five meters behind us—land mines. One Marine howled loudly and at least one other moaned as the close air around us filled with swishing shrapnel, slumping mud, and flying body parts. Since I was the senior man on the patrol I told everyone behind us to "freeze." On my hands and knees in the fast-fading light, I gingerly stabbed the ground between the wounded men and myself. I reached them without finding any other mines, probed hastily around each of the three Marines, then told the corpsman with us to follow cautiously the same way I had come. Within seconds he reached us. When the corpsman arrived I lifted and turned the body of the man closest to me, so Doc could check the man's eyes. At first he appeared unwounded, only unconscious or sleeping. As I lifted him, however, his helmet plopped into the mud, revealing the exposed brain still throbbing through an open wound.

As hastily as we could we clambered to the other two men, assuring each other as we went that all would be okay. The young corpsman with us ably stopped the worst bleeding from these ghastly wounds, and by the beam of my penlight he started one bottle of plasma in each man before the medevac helicopter came beating mercifully toward us in the swiftly encroaching darkness.

By far the best site for a landing zone seemed to me to be a cirque we had moved through not long before. If we could reach it safely, the boulders that enclosed the "armchair valley" would provide good protection against small-arms fire in the landing zone and conceal the chopper for as long as it had to stay down.

By the time the helicopter was within earshot, we had without further incident also formed three carrying parties to the wounded men. No sooner had the stretcher-bearers lifted their men, however, than the air was filled with close-buzzing machine gun fire that cut the air around us continually until we got to the other side of the boulders enclosing the cirque. As we jogged along, tracers pinged and ricocheted weirdly amongst the rocks surrounding the landing zone. By a miracle, none of our party was hit by the fire.

As the chopper settled into the cirque, several enemy mortar shells burst among the trees and onto the rocks surrounding us; the air filled with the slashing, humming sounds of small-arms fire from God knows where. Shards of metal and splintered rock flew around us and slivers of branches tumbled down even as I called the medevac chopper to advise him to hold for another pass. As soon as we thought we had neutralized the enemy fire—not more than five minutes—we called the chopper back. Throughout the ordeal the two wounded men remained composed as if they were resting on their backs in bivouac. By the time we got them aboard the chopper, light began to disappear, the shooting ceased, and the several Marines within earshot breathed an audible sigh of relief. We all, I believe, became concerned that the chopper would not stay around for a third pass if we were not able to secure the landing zone as soon as we eventually did. And since we were all Marines, except for the Doc who served with us—and our corpsmen had all been temporarily "adopted" by us—we would never have abandoned those wounded and dead men.

As soon as our patrol resumed that evening, rain began pattering down on the leaves and into the elephant grass. For the first few hours it felt like a warm, sticky bath. Within hours it became a "bucketing" storm that turned what had been a braided stream just hours before into a rustling torrent that we were able to recross only by throwing up a single-rope bridge and then hauling ourselves across one by one.

In order to put up the bridge, I first waded, then swam across. As the men crossed over, the lightning flickered while thunder boomed and boomed. Then the rain came in squall-like sheets, making the night seem even darker between the lightning flashes and matching my mood. As I fitfully recalled the gruesome wounds sustained by my men during our recent attack, I could not help but mutter curses to myself. The work of helping to supervise the patrol's crossing, however, soon moved me out of my dark feelings, just as similar activity almost always did throughout my Vietnam tour. I believe that, for one's own morale, it is often much easier to be an officer or an NCO in combat, since the duties that come with extra responsibilities seem to make the psychological difficulties easier to bear.

The day after the land-mine explosion, we patrolled again from dawn to sunset. By mid-afternoon we had reached central Quang Tin, where I encountered a natural scene matched in my perception only by a marjelen lake of amber-colored water, held between an ice wall and a cliff that I came across suddenly in the High Sierras before I went overseas. In central Quang Tin our patrol moved along the edge of a wide expanse of sunlit lake, such as one might see in the countryside in upstate Pennsylvania. The terrain was heavily overgrown with bush almost to the lake's edge, so we had to move Indian file and well spread out along its circumference, and even then we had to be careful to keep our footing so as not to fall in. A slight breeze made ripples that caught and deflected the light so that for a time I had the illusion of a moving lane of splendor, which passed as we moved through that place on the circle of water—a small natural gift to help compensate for the horrors and difficulties of the previous two days. To me, at least, the brief sight proved temporarily sustaining.

Operation Jackson took place after Colorado. On that operation our battalion landed by helicopter approximately thirteen kilometers south of the Chu Lai airfield, west of Route 1, and north of the Song (river) Tra Bong. Through most of the operation our battalion patrolled toward blocking positions held by the 2d ARVN Division. While moving we made sporadic contact and drew steady Communist fire but sustained few casualties. Nevertheless, Operation Jackson proved significant in at least two ways.

We landed on an interfluve, a flattish area between two rivers. After half swimming across the one south of us, Gunny Rockdale and I scrambled onto a sharp, rocky peak to see if we had landed where we were supposed to. As Gunny Rockdale and I shot compass resections on an arête—a comb-ridge—which also appeared on our map, the battalion command post set up headquarters on the steep ridge beneath us. The comb-ridge was several hundred meters away, and with map and compass Gunny and I quickly determined that the battalion command post had been set up several hundred meters into the 3d Battalion, 7th Marines' supposed area of operations. When I told our battalion executive officer, he replied, "That can't be, Lieutenant Kirschke, since those coordinates are not in our zone of operations," circular reasoning if ever there was. After Gunny and I repeated our resection with the major present, he reluctantly called the battalion CP's correct coordinates to higher command, erased the Magic Marker entry on the plastic-covered operations map, and drew in the line correctly.

Throughout that operation and most of the next one, Napa, the heat and humidity had to be experienced to be believed. At nearly every stream or rivulet most of the men gulped water from their canteens, refilled them, doused faces and hair, and refilled the canteens under the brutally hot sun. We marched nearly continually up and down steep, difficult terrain and sweated furiously most of the way. In the vibrating heat the few quiet villages we moved carefully through became transformed into *pointilliste* landscapes.

On those two operations battalion heat casualties were very high, yet 81s did not sustain one such casualty until the last day of Jackson. The reason for that, I believe, is that our platoon had already "humped" steeper hills, for longer periods, in training. Thus, the men of the 81 platoon had both a physical and a psychological advantage. Moreover, as I have perhaps already indicated, our unit's morale and esprit had become outstanding, so that the will to "hang in" was not inconsiderable, as the following anecdote perhaps illustrates.

The one man in our platoon to succumb to heat exhaustion on those two operations was an ammo carrier, probably the biggest Marine in our platoon, a large-boned farmboy from the state of Washington. Yet even he did not totally succumb. Within sight of the trucks we were to ride to a more secure area in termination of Jackson, the giant PFC fell flat forward. Remembering my injunctions from our night marches in training, he began crawling so he could finish the operation on his own. Apparently he resisted many other offers of assistance. When Colonel Bronars saw him, he offered to take the man's gear and help him walk, but our Marine resisted vehemently: "No, sir! The lieutenant said the 81s have to pack their own gear!!" Although he had to crawl with full equipment the last two hundred meters or so, that is what the big Marine did. By the time I reached the road the ammo carrier was incoherent, his jungle utilities were black with perspiration, and he had to be helped aboard the truck by Lieutenant Dyke and myself, yet the young man had retained his pride.

Operation Napa is an example of one of the many "minor" and unremarked-upon operations in the Vietnam War that contained no small amount of combat, death, and injury. Conducted in early September 1966 in the western part of Quang Tin Province, inland from Tam Ky, our battalion was involved in nearly incessant patrolling, day and night, and innumerable firefights involving substantial casualties on both sides.

In the early days of the operation I moved with companies L and K, which patrolled up and down narrow, mostly dry river gorges and across "hogbacks" (narrow ridges). On one of those days, when I moved near Lieutenant Manning's platoon, an elderly man huffing heavily came toward us at a halting double time at the turn of a trail. One finger tugged on a string under his chin that held his sunhat down, and with a shaking hand and arm he pointed southwest: "Boocoo VC. Boocoo VC!" Pointing again with a trembling finger in the direction from which he had come, he said, *"High mooy lom"* and *"high mooy lom,"* gesticulating frantically, which we took to mean "twenty-five plus twenty-five."

With a kindly smile and a warm voice, John Manning ordered that the man be well taken care of, then splashed headlong down the rocky bed of a ravine that ran alongside the trail the man had come from. I told the 81s section nearest me to stand by, and along with Zlatunich I ran, bent over double, after Manning. By the time we caught up with him he was fifty meters down the dung-smelling ravine and had crawled through a hedgerow that bordered it to quickly reconnoiter the enemy position. No sooner had Zlatunich and I arrived than Manning huffed back uphill, whispering hoarsely to us that we should hurry back with him.

Promptly and coolly, he requested an 81s mission on the enemy-occupied position, then ordered an infantry assault on the position while the guns were getting up. Using fire and maneuver to good advantage, most of his men moved down the slippery terrain frontally and finally assaulted across a rice paddy or two, but not before Lieutenant Manning himself led a squad-size flanking movement that swung in the hook just after the frontal base of fire had been lifted.

Before it all began, Zlatunich and I splashed down behind a windrow to observe the envelopment as best we could. Incoming and outgoing machine gun and rifle fire sprayed the paddy water in front of us, and tracers and mortar rounds set fire to the haystacks and flammable huts in front of us and on our flanks. In addition, Manning's smoke grenade also largely obscured our view, so we saw nothing of the actual envelopment. As soon as the grenade unfurled its smoke, we heard the sound of a violent struggle at close range as Manning's men began their brief envelopment.

In moments it was over. He passed the word to us over the radio, and Zlatunich and I along with John's base of fire moved through soon afterward. Blasted or burning hooches and torn trees were all through the overgrown areas. In the muddy and bloodstained trenches we found surprisingly few enemy bodies but a great many abandoned air-cooled machine guns, AK-47 assault rifles, and packs—all either Russian- or Communist Chinese–made. Two of the NVA wounded were still more or less alive when we first saw them. One man had apparently been relieving himself when the firing began. He had been hit several times by small-arms fire and propped himself against a banana plant to die. Another Vietnamese seemed to be shot in the lungs and bowels. He had vomited gobs of blood in the fighting hole where we found him. Both men soon died of their wounds and thereby joined the roughly two dozen uniformed NVA we found elsewhere nearby. Most of these were lying spread-legged, arms akimbo, like many infantry, silent after the assault. By the time I saw them I felt no remorse. To the contrary, finding, fixing, and killing the enemy was a big part of our mission, and I believed the NVA would have felt the same absence of remorse for us had our situations been reversed. Nothing I saw on my Vietnam tour led me to think otherwise.

Toward sundown that evening, as the 3d and 4th sections dug in and began to set up their guns, they drew heavy sniper fire from a wooded ridge not far north of us. As so often in Vietnam we were unable to ascertain exactly where the enemy riflemen were, and since the fire soon grew very close, the mortarmen began getting jumpy, which made it difficult for them to set up their guns.

In order to distract the enemy gunners, therefore, I pinned my large, silver first lieutenant's bars on my jungle utilities (to my recollection, that was the only time I wore these bars in the field in Vietnam) and paraded up and down in front of the guns "to provide a well-paid moving target" as I said to the troops. In addition, I waved my arms back and forth, whistled, and made not very nice comments about the parentage of the snipers who meanwhile zinged dozens of rounds at me, rounds that hummed past or kicked up dust around me as I moved and gesticulated. Of course, exposing myself to the enemy delighted our sections and provided the relief the men needed to get our guns up in good order. With accurate fire missions that night the 81s immediately repaid their fortunate platoon commander.

The very next evening just before sundown, as 3d Section was attempting to set up its guns, they drew heavy, close sniper fire again, yet on that occasion for no reason I can explain my nerve utterly failed me. Zlatunich and I hugged the dusty ground beneath us as bullets swished steadily through the leaves overhead and beat back the foliage around us. For some reason I felt more exposed than I had the previous day. The one time I looked up hastily, however, I saw Corporal Williams, his hands clenched into fists on both sides, long legs scissoring through the tall grass: "Let's get these fucking guns set up!" he said clearly and deliberately. In a second a well-organized scramble took place; both squad leaders soon hoarsely reported: "Gun five up." "Gun six up." My heart sang.

The next day we moved out on patrol as the first gray light began to drive away the stars. We had not moved far when the patrol I was with moved past our battalion command post. Captain Vorreyer evidently knew we were coming. Through most of our predeployment training he had had steadily running Batman–Robin dialogues with Lieutenant Cullen. As the latter neared, the captain stepped out from the brush near a trail junction to caution Larry about a punji trap in the trail ahead. After solemnly pointing to the slightly camouflaged punji pit, Vorreyer whispered with a smile: "Forewarned is forearmed, Robin."

"Yes, Master," Cullen deadpanned in response.

On a patrol that same day, a big corporal had not been so forewarned; he was struck chest-high by a booby-trapped grenade that flew at him across a trail. The corporal had been wounded so badly that I was astonished to learn years later that our Dr. Jim Thornton had not only kept the man alive then but helped him pull through all the way.

Near twilight on that operation, perhaps unwisely, I decided to go to the top of a small hill to relieve myself and ponder the view over the rice paddies as a large sun set in a blaze of orange. The recollection of this sunset remains more vivid than it might have because the following incident anchored it in my memory.

A sergeant from the communications section, whose name I am quite sure is Ross, soon squatted next to me, about five paces away. Suddenly he hurled himself full-length backwards beyond his pile of manure, screaming "Oh! Oh! Oh!" loudly, clutching his chest with both hands, and kicking his legs. Since I had neither heard the report of the rifle (as is often the case when you're under accurate fire) nor heard the bullet, I at first briefly thought the sergeant was clowning—a strange act, indeed. As soon as I realized he was not, I must have set a world record for end of toilet.

Fortunately for Sergeant Ross, Dr. Thornton was again not far away. Running bent over double across the hill toward us, medical kit in hand, Doc Thornton soon reached Ross and helped drag him below the brow of the hill. I learned from Jim years afterward that the bullet had passed through the young sergeant's chest and collapsed one lung, but otherwise did little serious damage. Reassuringly, Doc Thornton patched the pneumothorax wound; within ten minutes Sergeant Ross was on a helicopter and safely off the hill.

Several other incidents on Napa make the operation worth remembering. One was overhearing the following story after K Company had just overrun an NVA-held village. Shortly after the assault, Capt. Dick Maresco reportedly stopped a squad leader who had drawn his bayonet in bloodlust, prepared to slice off an ear of a dead NVA. Holding out his hand in a gesture indicating "stop," Captain Maresco said: "There'll be none of that in my company." I felt proud to hold a commission in the same service as that officer.

Another incident soon afterward produced a similar feeling. This one, too, involved an early-twentyish NCO—a sergeant from an Ontos* unit who had been ordered to drive the lead vehicle in a night convoy. The convoy was to move an artillery battery from our infantry battalion's position to another artillery unit at least ten miles away. During the night I was awakened by a runner from Colonel Bronars, who told me the colonel said to choose a light platoon to provide an infantry escort, in case of an ambush, to accompany the artillery battery as far as it had to go, then return immediately with my men to our battalion area in the jungle.

The artillery colonel looked hard at me and then said in a determined way: "Lieutenant, now listen to me."

"Yes, sir." He then ordered the movement as follows: the Ontos, myself in a jeep with a radioman and driver, the artillery colonel in another jeep with radio and driver, and then the light platoon of infantry and the artillery battery interspersed in irregular order behind us. Had he not dictated the order of movement, I believe he

---

* A small, tracked, lightly armored vehicle which carried six 106mm recoilless rifles as its armament.

thought I'd have gone first, in an open, unarmored jeep. If so, then he'd have surmised correctly.

It was almost totally dark when I issued the order to move out. As soon as I did, the sergeant exclaimed, "I'm not going to go! It's suicide," he said, flapping his arms and stalking several paces away. For the only time in my career I felt disposed to shoot or pistol-whip one of our own men, but the stocky colonel, who stood ready as I issued my order, handled the situation in a better way.

In the darkness I barely made out the squat figure as he moved abruptly to the sergeant, turned him quickly by the shoulder, grabbed his arm, and led him several paces away from where we stood. In muffled words, which I was unable to make out (but wished I could hear), the colonel addressed his man ferociously. His words quickly found their mark. The sergeant responded with a docile, "Yes, sir." The colonel muttered something else and the sergeant said again, "Yes, sir," and stood motionless for an instant before the colonel pointed at the Ontos and said in an undertone something that sounded to me like, "Now get up into that vehicle." The sergeant moved swiftly away.

Promptly I gave the order and all of us mounted up. As the vehicles coughed into warm-up, the blackout lights were turned on for what proved a long, chilly, but uneventful ride to the artillery outpost.

The last significant incident on Napa occurred on the final day of the operation; a few moments when I felt conscious of a promise having been honored. On a combat patrol we moved through an abandoned village I strongly felt I had moved through before, although I knew it could not have been in this life—a strange sensation I have felt on several other occasions.

On either side of us, skeleton roofs and pierced walls heaved out of the earth. Despite a few signs in Vietnamese on the fronts of the abandoned houses and shops, the desolation told us the war had visited that isolated village, too.

As we had almost moved through the ville, K Company came under small-arms and semiautomatic weapons fire from across a large, clear field on their right flank. Running through the outskirts of the village, I could hear the bullets cracking and slashing through the leaves overhead. I arrived at the 81s' position just in time to see Sergeant Killinger's section go into action. Hurrying forward under fire, in the same way they had done so often in training, the 2d Section splashed and slid through the mud and got its guns up and rounds on the way as fast as one can read these words. Within minutes the enemy fire was completely silenced by several volleys of well-placed mortar rounds.

After Operation Napa our battalion moved back to the Chu Lai area, where we provided security for a village that contained perhaps two hundred families. For the remainder of my tour with 3d Battalion, 5th Marines, that security mission served as our primary duty, and there I had my closest glimpses of Vietnamese civilian life.

Even by that early time in the war (1966), approximately 80 percent of the friendly (that is, Allied) Vietnamese had been forced to live on less than 20 percent of the land; namely, on the fairly narrow strip of land along the seacoast from south of the DMZ to just south of Cam Ranh Bay, and from Bien Hoa, just north of Saigon (now known as Ho Chi Minh City), to Ba Xuyen, roughly one hundred miles south of the capital. That was the only area where Allied military forces could provide anything resembling adequate security.

The ville I billeted closest to comprised a pleasant-seeming series of single-family, thatch-roof huts interconnected by meandering dirt paths. Beyond the ville were rolling hills and well-tended rice paddies where entire families along with their water buffalo often worked from morning until dusk. With no exceptions I can recall, the people seemed very happy to have us around.

In the evenings, when on patrol around the village, we often saw families squatting outside their hootches, playing quietly and talking. Many of the men smoked typical Vietnamese pipes, among them an old, slender, quiet-seeming gentleman. His pipe, well over a foot long, was made of bamboo perhaps two inches in diameter. At Sergeant Wilson's polite request the man filled his pipe to show us how it was done: he fit a pinch of tobacco in a bowl into the side of a tube near the bottom; the upper part he filled with water. The old man then drew two puffs through the water, making a sucking noise, then exhaled great clouds of smoke. Soon he refilled the bowl with a bit of tobacco and lit it again. As he did he offered the pipe to Wilson and Zlatunich, both of whom refused, but in typically generous fashion, urged on the man cans of C rations and other goodies they could well have used themselves. He courteously accepted.

Just before we took up positions around the village, Colonel Bronars appointed Lt. D.N.T. Perkins the battalion S-5 (civic action officer). "Perks" was a real gentleman and had more sense and tact than any man his age I have ever met. During the time I remained with the battalion, Lieutenant Perkins did everything possible to make sure relations between our battalion and the people in the ville we protected remained as amicable as possible. "Perks" established a liaison with the leading citizens in the village and tried to learn "how things went" there. He also found out what, within reason, we might do to help the villagers.

Mainly the people seemed to want physical protection from the Communists and courteous behavior from the Marines. Lieutenant Perkins communicated those needs to all of the battalion's officers who, in turn, made the same things clear to the men.

Observing these village families at work and play gave all of us a great sense of satisfaction, I believe, but providing the security necessary to allow life to go along for the South Vietnamese with any degree of normalcy proved no small job, even with the full-strength battalion we had at that time in 3/5. For one thing, not only did we patrol incessantly around the village, we also mounted frequent long-range patrols to make sure we were not caught off-guard by one of the many large NVA forces then in-country. In doing that, our battalion had to operate virtually unassisted by other Allied units in the area, which apparently had all they could do to handle their own responsibilities.

As even North Vietnamese propaganda writings from the war years I have examined repeatedly state, American military forces could not adequately cover the territory, perform the numerous other missions higher headquarters continually ordered for our infantry battalions, and protect the South Vietnamese people at the same time.

And that was especially true for the Marines, who had more of the most difficult missions than any other service during the conflict and who, as far as I have been able to ascertain, worked and fought by far the hardest and best, and suffered proportionally the most casualties. Had any other civilian or military leaders at the highest echelons in our governmental service during that time attempted to travel for even one month with either of the two battalions I served with on my Vietnam tour, the extent of our difficulties might have been appreciated. Should our nation contemplate similar long-range military missions in the future, it seems to me that some members of our highest military and civilian offices should try to do just that; spend at least a month in the field with some of the active units; *that* might give the higher decision-makers some idea of the challenges faced by the men who do the hardest and most important work during wartime. Surely in a democratic nation some people in our highest commands could be spared from their desks for at least a month; by serving with the men in the field, I believe they would find that many mistakes could be avoided.

By the time we went in-country even the protection of the people in our peaceful village proved no small challenge. Intelligence reports I have seen since returning from Vietnam (reports whose accuracy, however, I have been unable to corroborate and crosscheck) indicate that when our battalion landed, although the enemy did not yet control any of the provincial capitals, he did control a majority of the villages and hamlets in South Vietnam. I personally do not believe the situation was that difficult by spring 1966, but surely it was possible.

In the words of the British author Sir Robert Thompson, probably the most knowledgeable expert on counterinsurgency, "Of all the United States forces, the Marine Corps alone made a serious attempt to achieve permanent and lasting results in their tactical area of responsibility by seeking to protect the rural population." Thompson is also quoted in David McKay's *No Exit from Vietnam* as saying: "It was a great pity that, because the

Marines were the most readily available forces and therefore the first to arrive in Vietnam, they were allocated to the northern provinces and not to the populated areas of the Mekong Delta where this type of operation would have had the greatest and the most enduring effect."

As it happened, then, we operated primarily in the northernmost provinces and, since those were the ones most readily subject to infiltration, we had the work not only of continually protecting the people in the villages but also of fighting the regular North Vietnamese regiments which had come south as part of the large-scale invasion.

On my tour, when we were not on one of our more than one dozen named operations, the two battalions I served with in Vietnam were generally on patrol. Except for the named operations, most of our enemy contact was made while we were on those patrols since the NVA who swarmed around our positions had the good sense rarely to attack an alert and dug-in Marine unit in the field.

It seemed to me that the battle might have been better prosecuted by the Allies had we sometimes used slightly different terms for our essential maneuvers. Higher headquarters frequently designated these essential patrol missions as "sweeps" and somewhat less often as "search and clear" missions. The word "sweep" implies a fairly effortless movement performed smoothly and easily, yet as one who has gone on many such missions in Vietnam, I know the term "sweep" hardly ever described the way good infantry units moved when they were in the field. Surely the term had been coined by a staff officer who had seen too little time in the field and had become overused to making thick red crayon arrows on large map boards. The term "search and clear" seems a bit more accurate, but even that left out what we hoped for on every operation or patrol I went on in Vietnam. As uncivilized as it sounds to a civilian who has never served in the infantry, "search for, capture, clear, or kill" or "search for and kill" would be terms that more precisely describe the types of missions we were generally assigned.

As long as I was with 3/5, at least, the 81s went on many such missions. The mortars generally proved effective weapons to have along on the patrols; they could place fire on the reverse slopes of hills and, when well aimed, penetrate narrow ravines. In addition, the guns had greater range and destructive power than any other weapon in the rifle company's arsenal at that time.

At virtually every battalion-level briefing I attended in 3/5, the company commanders asked to have at least one 81s section travel with them in the field. And after virtually every tactical mission, the rifle company commanders told Colonel Bronars and myself how glad they were to have the 81s with them. The immediate, heavy firepower of course proved a great asset, but the companies would not have been able to bring our guns along were our men not able to carry their own gear on the arduous patrols and operations. And the 81s in 3/5, as many fellow officers told me, nearly always fired accurately and "could really hump," comments that made me beam whenever I heard them.

When I served with 3/5 and later with 2/5, our battalions sustained many casualties. It is of course possible to fight defensively without incurring casualties, but that cannot be done when one is continually on the tactical offensive and strategic defensive—a dangerous combination that applied to our forces our entire tour. In that year in Vietnam the Marine forces in-country nearly doubled in numbers, yet our casualties grew proportionally even higher. For the entire war the Marines' officially recorded casualties alone were more than 105,000—far more Marine Corps casualties than in any other war in our nation's history, World War II not excepted (in the latter the Corps sustained 90,000 casualties). Moreover, I can say absolutely that many of our casualties in 3/5 and 2/5 refused to allow themselves to be reported, and no doubt those two units were not unique.

Regarding enemy casualties, the percentages inflicted throughout the conflict remained at least comparable to the relative figures included in this narrative, but the possibility exists that they sustained many more casualties than we had proved since the enemy had a vital stake in keeping us from knowing how many we had actually killed. Unlike our nation, from the outset the Vietnamese Communists appeared to be prepared for a long struggle. And in their strategic plans and assessments the NVA took elaborate care to assure that most of the propaganda during the conflict reflected unfavorably on the Allies. One way they maintained their morale was to retain, whenever possible, the bodies of their KIAs and WIAs by rapidly removing them from where they fell. They did so by slinging ropes around the casualties' limbs to drag them away, thus denying us, as often as possible, both information and satisfaction. Of course, we left no bodies behind either.

Not too long before I transferred to 2/5, Lieutenant Manning, who had become one of my best buddies in the battalion, was hit several times in the torso by enemy small-arms fire. Being the powerful giant he was, he pulled through well. An indication of his morale not long after he was shot probably comes across in the following anecdote. After John had been sent to a rear-area hospital in Vietnam, Captain Vorreyer managed to get back to see him. When Vorreyer arrived, Manning was about to be taken to a plane to fly to a hospital outside Vietnam. Thus, Vorreyer did not have much time to visit. While John waited to have his stretcher carried aboard the plane, a piece of plaster fell off the ceiling overhead and struck him in the eye. He grinned, wiped it away, and said in mock-heroic tones to Vorreyer: "The whole *world* is falling in on me!"

Toward the end of September, Colonel Bronars called me into the battalion headquarters where he told me I had an outstanding platoon and he was very pleased, indeed, with our performance. He said he wanted me to stay in the Marine Corps, and felt a change of billet would be to my advantage. He offered me the command of H&S Company, if I wanted it. He said he had already checked with all of the rifle company commanders, all of whom had asked to have me come to their outfit as company executive officer. The colonel said I could of course stay where I was as long as I wanted to remain with 81s. And lastly, he said, if I wanted a rifle company of my own, he felt certain he could get one for me in another battalion.

By that time in my tour, Gunny Rockdale and I had gotten the 81s into very fine shape, but I saw less and less of them since the sections almost always served attached to our companies and were seldom under my direct operational control in the field. I thought I had helped the platoon just about as much as I could as long as we were in Vietnam. For that reason alone, then, by early autumn 1966 I felt it was time for me to assume a new billet.

As H&S Company commander I would have nominal command of more men—at least 275 at that time—but the command was always very widely dispersed. Moreover, the H&S Company constituted a disparate group of men, most of whom hardly ever went on patrols or saw much fighting.

The rifle company executive officer's job would more than likely have been somewhat more dangerous and physically challenging than H&S Company commander, but as the former I would have been second-in-command and therefore circumscribed in my activities by the company commander. As much as I liked and admired the four rifle company commanders in our battalion at that time, I did not relish the idea of being ExO under anyone.

Of the choices, the idea of commanding a rifle company appealed to me by far the most. The passion that has predominated through most of my life thus far has been pride. Pride rather than timidity has invariably been the source of my major successes and failures. While I might have served the Corps better at that time as rifle company exec than as a company commander, the higher position appealed to my sense of pride.

Moreover, I have always been a fundamentally independent person who enjoys operating, as much as possible, on his own. As commander of a rifle company I would have a large, fairly independent command. Moreover, I would be living in the field with the men and would probably remain fairly steadily in combat, which is what I wanted most at that time.

After he had explained the options, Colonel Bronars said I could have as much time as I wanted to think over what I wanted to do. I think at this time he also communicated again, at least tacitly, that he wanted me to stay with our battalion, but would let me go if I was sure I wanted something else.

I pondered the choices for perhaps a day. Before deciding,

I spoke to Gunny Rockdale mainly about the condition of our men, equipment, and replacements. As soon as he learned my intentions, the Gunny, in typical fashion, concentrated all his powers on appealing to me either to stay with the platoon or remain with the battalion in some capacity. Captain Haupt also brought his well-focused powers to bear in trying to talk me into staying with 3/5. As I look back upon it, I see that their having done so was a sincere compliment, but I had made up my mind and was too set in my thinking to change it. Would I have been better off if I had stayed with 3/5? In some ways, perhaps, but if I had, I would not be the same person I am now. That much seems certain.

Regardless, I made up my mind and told the Gunny I was going to ask the colonel for command of the rifle company in 2/5 he had mentioned as a strong possibility. When I entered to see Colonel Bronars the next day, he seemed to know why. As I walked in, he rose to his feet and received me with sturdy politeness. As I began to tell him what I wanted, it occurred to me with a heavy rush of emotion that my decision would entail leaving once and for all a battalion I had really come to love. I believe I barely had the words out when I broke down in heaving sobs. That clearly affected the colonel deeply; he asked me to sit down, gave me his own hankie after I had thoroughly soaked mine, and told me I could have all the time I wanted to think about my decision. As soon as I regained my composure—it took several minutes—I drew myself up and told the colonel, as steadily as I could, that I still wanted the rifle company; I knew "it would be good for my career," I believe I said. With sad reluctance, Colonel Bronars assented. He said he would be in touch with 2/5 as soon as possible. As I left his presence I felt a hollow feeling inside that signified the immediate sense of loss of the almost palpable camaraderie that had grown strong within 3/5 by that time on our tour. Several more weeks would pass before I began to feel the same emotion within the next battalion I served in Vietnam.

As soon as I could, I packed my meager gear, notified Gunny Rockdale I would be leaving right away, and moved to the battalion CP, where soon I boarded an uncovered six-by for the long, sad ride to join my new battalion.

FOUR

2d Battalion, 5th Marines: Operation Prairie

The day I boarded the truck to ride to the 2/5 command post, Gunny Killinger and Zlatunich passed as I was climbing onto the back of the truck. Killinger asked, "Are you leaving us, Lieutenant?" I was too choked up to respond and just stared at both of them. As the 3/5 CP receded in a swirl of dust behind our six-by truck, I leaned against the bumping side-boards and ran through my mind the accomplishments of the 81 platoon during the year I had been its commander. For that period, as for all the others when I was in combat in the Corps, Colonel Bronars's Change of Command fitness report on me, which was not seen by me until many years later, probably represented my performance more favorably than it deserved. Yet the appraisal almost does justice to the 81 platoon I felt privileged to command:

Lieutenant Kirschke is a highly dedicated young Marine officer. His performance as the 81mm Mortar-Platoon Commander is best indicated by the reputation his unit gained in combat. During Operations Deckhouse I, Nathan Hale, Deckhouse II, Hastings, Colorado, Jackson and Napa, experienced Marines acknowledged that the supporting 81s delivered some of the most effective and responsive fires they could recall. Lt. Kirschke fully demonstrated good organizational ability in allocating and coordinating his resources in complicated operations. He is enthusiastic, aggressive and highly motivated. His personal appearance has always set the example for his Platoon. Lt. Kirschke has excellent growth potential and is capable of assuming positions of greater command and/or staff responsibility.

Sad as I was when I left 3/5 that day, I had made a decision I believed was right. I knew somewhere inside that the move was to be of great importance in the years ahead. I appreciated Colonel Bronars's implying that he really wanted me to stay with the battalion and offering me virtually any lieutenant-level position in it, not to mention the offer to have me either stay with 81s or become CO of H&S Company. But the time seemed ripe for me to leave; I wanted to continue commanding troops, and I felt I could contribute best in that capacity if I had command of a rifle company. If I had it to do over again I would not do it differently. The decades have not shown that my decision was ill-made, nor have they lessened the regret I felt on leaving.

When I reported to 2/5, their CP was on Hill 69 near Chu Lai. I reported to the battalion commander, Maj. Lawrence Steel. He was a wiry, low-key, keen-eyed, and intelligent-looking officer. When I entered his CP, he received me with warm courtesy, indicated that I had been preceded by a very commendatory report from Colonel Bronars, and said that if I liked I could have command of Hotel Company. I assented with enthusiasm.

A reinforced rifle company in combat was supposed to have approximately 280 men. The organization included three maneuver or rifle platoons, a weapons platoon, a headquarters section to handle paperwork, a detachment from H&S Company including a forward observer team, often a section of 81s, a forward air controller, a naval gunfire spotter team, and sometimes a detachment of engineers as well as translators and scout-dog teams. The weapons platoon at the time had M-60 machine guns, rockets (3.5s and LAWs [light antitank weapons]), and 60mm mortars. In the field the weapons platoon was usually integrated with the rifle platoons, and the Marines in the weapons platoon were then under the command of the rifle platoon commander.

At the H Company CP I was met by the company first sergeant, a colorful Boston Irishman who had approximately twenty years' service when I joined the company. "Top" Peabody was as good a company first sergeant as any company commander could hope to have. He had been with the company since it had formed in the early fall of 1965 and obviously took great pride in the unit.

The first sergeant in any Marine company is a very important man. He is seldom in the field with the men, but he is the senior member of the unit who does not hold a commission. He runs the office staff, supervises most of the paperwork and, if he is good—as Top Peabody was—inspires all the company NCOs and enlisted men by the force of his example. I have never seen a Marine company that had an inefficient first sergeant yet was a first-rate outfit. There is no small correlation between the two.

When I reported aboard, the CO of Hotel Company was Don H. Vogelgesang, an outstanding officer. Perhaps five years older than me, he was a second lieutenant and therefore junior to me. Our company clerk, Sergeant Smith, whose comments on most things were accurate, told me later that Don had a master's degree in psychology from Ohio State and that he had played center on his college football team. The latter fact I at first found hard to believe, since Don was slightly smaller and perhaps lighter than me, but after I got to know him and appreciate how tenacious he was, I could believe almost anything positive about him.

One of Don's last official acts as CO was to hold company commander's office hours (disciplinary action) on a PFC who I will refer to as Spain. Both Don and Top Peabody were in my opinion excellent judges of men. About Spain, however, I think they were wrong.

Before he entered, Don told me the Marine was "a real shitbird, worthless as hell," or words to that effect. Top Peabody also commented, "he's got a Page 11 (where disciplinary offenses are recorded) as long as your arm." About that, Top was not wrong. Soon Spain entered. He was uncovered, wearing crumpled utilities, under handcuff, and under guard. His guard, or "chaser," was Cpl. Arthur Desclos, who I later came to know much better. Corporal D carried a nightstick and wore a .45-caliber pistol in holster. Spain looked up for just a second, exchanged glances with me, then looked down at the deck to await his sentencing. As I recall, his handcuffs were not removed throughout the brief proceedings. In the moment that we briefly exchanged looks, I had the distinct feeling that Spain was a man who was worth something.

PFC Spain had black hair, keen dark eyes, and a solid build. The boxer Oscar De La Hoya most resembled Spain, except that Spain if anything looked 20 percent stronger and meaner. At the time he served with us, PFC Spain was about twenty-six years old and had been in and out of trouble for years. He was found guilty of whatever offense he was charged with during that fall of 1966 and sent off again for the time being to the brig. He would be back with us before long, however, I am glad to say.

When I became CO, Don moved down to take command of 1st Platoon. The 2d Platoon commander was another old friend from 3/5, Lieutenant Christians. The 3d Platoon was commanded by a mid- to late-twentyish staff sergeant whose name I will not mention. He had very little active duty experience related to commanding an infantry platoon in combat, but was the senior company staff sergeant and we more or less had to put him in that position. His lack of experience cost us dearly during the next two weeks. The weapons platoon commander was a chunky, volatile, likable Mexican-American gunnery sergeant named Gonzalez.

After our first two landings with the Special Landing Force in 3/5, most of the rifle companies did not have an executive officer; almost none had a lieutenant as weapons platoon commander. Seldom were there even three lieutenants commanding the rifle platoons. Moreover, the companies I saw and served with in the field were all severely understrength. For example, the ones I operated with almost continually had less than one-third the complement they were supposed to have, and very often had less. In the year that I was wounded, 1967, General Giap, the North Vietnamese defense minister, remarked in a Hanoi-based armed services newspaper that "the Marines are being stretched as taut as a bowstring." He was not wrong.

A man of Top Peabody's caliber tended to gather about him NCOs whose loyalty was absolute. Chief among his was our company gunnery sergeant, "Gunny" Husak. Husak was a large-framed, amiable, blue-eyed man of about thirty-five. He had a brush haircut, a modest, self-effacing manner, and the courage of a bull. He spoke with a slight lisp but was always able to make himself clearly understood, and the men in Hotel Company soon thought the world of him. With good reason. He kept our supplies and replacements coming in and more often than not made sure our casualties got out quickly and safely. Were it not for him I would almost certainly not be alive today.

Husak risked his life many times to get our wounded men out safely. Less than two weeks after he helped me when I was wounded, he took a round through the arm while performing the same rescue service for other wounded Marines in our company. At the time Gunny was wounded the company was still heavily engaged, and he managed to disguise his wound for nearly twelve hours. Before anyone discovered that he was hit, he had gotten all our other wounded and killed aboard choppers. He stayed with our company that night and allowed himself to be put aboard an outgoing chopper only the next morning.

An outstanding company gunny and sharp platoon sergeants were vital in that war, especially. The company gunny was the second senior NCO in the company, and the platoon sergeant the senior NCO in the platoon. On their different levels they saw to it that their units received the ammo, chow, and gear they needed in the field, that the heliteam wave and serial assignments and landing craft assignment tables were in order, that casualties were evacuated in good fashion, and that troop strength was reported accurately and properly. None are easy tasks in daily combat, as we were in almost from the hour I joined the battalion.

At midnight of my first day with the company I was shaken awake by the looming figure of Maj. James L. Cooper, our S-3, who told me to get my company ready to move out: we were heading on an operation. I alerted Top Peabody and moved to our battalion command bunker to receive the attack order. There I met for the first time the other company commanders in the battalion; together we received our five-paragraph order from big Jim Cooper.

Major Cooper was perhaps six-feet five-inches tall and weighed about 220 pounds. At the time he had a deep Southern drawl that made him sound like a cross between

Lyndon B. Johnson and former Alabama football coach Bear Bryant. With his swarthy complexion, Jim always reminded me of a large brown bear. He almost always had a big cigar. Once he got to know me he comported himself toward me in the gruffly friendly manner one might expect from a kindly and concerned older brother.

The operation we were going on was Prairie. It would begin in the same area that we had covered with 3/5 during most of Hastings. Our mission was to search for and kill NVA. We would go in by helicopters with three rifle companies—H, F, and G—and the battalion CP group. Hotel Company would be the assault company, provide landing zone security, and then security for the battalion CP. We received radio frequencies for medevac, resupply, and supporting-arms requests. We would also be given information about target designation systems as well as air and artillery prep fires on the LZ just before we landed.

I briefed my platoon commanders along with our company command group at the mess hall after an early morning hot meal. When it was still dark we moved out under blackout conditions by trucks from Hill 69 to the Chu Lai airstrip. From there we were flown north to Dong Ha, where the battalion staff and the four company commanders present on the operation received a series of sobering briefings from concerned-looking members of the division staff at the headquarters there. The essence of the briefings was that the NVA had begun large-scale infiltration through the DMZ and the Marine battalions already there had had numerous recent contacts with NVA units. The board that listed such contacts was filled with red marks indicating enemy contacts and sightings during the past few weeks. Our battalion's first mission was to land at coordinates 080 600 (in the vicinity of what was then Kho Xa) and reconnoiter in force the area to our north and west.

On the day we were at Dong Ha, Major Steel ordered two observation helicopters so that he, the S-3, and the three rifle company commanders could look over the LZ and do a preliminary visual inspection of the terrain in which we were to operate. In my opinion that was a grave error. The recon helicopters circled too long (it seemed to me close to forty-five minutes) over our imminent landing zone. Like virtually every tactical error I recall being made in Vietnam, that one cost us almost right away.

After our helicopter prerun I distributed maps to our company. As usual we had enough maps of the area to go down to all of the squad leaders. As nearly always when we operated in Vietnam the maps were excellent. The importance of good maps to the infantry commander in combat cannot be too much emphasized; in Vietnam the maps did a great deal to offset the enemy's evident firsthand knowledge of the terrain on which we operated. At the company CP, radio sets were calibrated to the assigned frequencies, and ammo, C rations, and water were distributed.

Since I had been in the area before, I briefed the company on what might be expected and how the men were to conduct themselves on the operation. That may have been my least successful speech as a Marine officer, yet I believe I managed to get across that we could expect some hard fighting in the days ahead. I endeavored also to inspire some extra spirit by my speech. I see now, though, that Hotel Company was a veteran outfit and that my efforts added only a small degree to the company's morale.

I slept that night in a French concrete pillbox erected probably at least a decade earlier. We awoke on the morning of October 2 to a brindled sky, gulped a hasty C rations breakfast, and hustled aboard choppers to jump off on the operation.

After landing in almost precisely the same LZ we had used on Hastings with 3/5, we were greeted by semi-automatic weapons fire from the southeast quadrant of the LZ. The platoon that landed in that area—I believe it was Don's—returned fire nicely, and we had the LZ under control by the time the rest of the battalion whirred in over the treetops.

Major Steel then made what I think was a second tactical error: he set up the battalion CP in a two-story, stone plantation house—probably the only one within miles, and the same one of which Major Monfort had said, "[it's] probably the registration point for every NVA mortar this side of the DMZ."

The house itself was surrounded by trees, and a trail that had once probably been a driveway led up to it. Near the edge of the trees, perhaps seventy-five meters or so from the battalion CP, we set up our company CP. That afternoon I took a two-platoon-size combat patrol to scout the high ground southwest of us. We made no enemy contact. On our way back in, however, I saw that the battalion CP was in nearly full view from the high ground that we had traversed. When we landed I considered suggesting to the battalion CO that we change our position. But as a new company commander, I knew my suggestion would be disregarded. Before we left on our patrol I ordered the platoon that stayed behind to dig defensive positions for the whole company. The platoon, Don's, I believe, did its job well, and I am sure this saved us many casualties.

The only passage over the ridge was a narrow, north-south ravine enclosed on the right by a steeply rising slab of earth and on the left by thick shrubs impossible to cut through. As our patrol moved out I had the 81s FO call a fire mission on the reverse slope of the one-hundred-meter ridgeline we were about to cross. Due to the terrain, both platoons had to be strung out single file, so I had air strikes delivered in the draws on either side of us. But instead of coming in from the north, as I had indicated they should, the planes flew in from the west, perpendicular to our advance. Moreover, while the first flight dropped its bombs in the ravine west of us, the next released its ordnance in the draw *we* were in.

I would not have thought it possible for so many tons of high-explosive bombs to land in that ravine without our sustaining even one casualty, but that is what happened. At the side of the narrow trail we were moving up, there was a single, shallow, presumably water-made trench, in most places just large enough to provide protection for a single man. When the jets zoomed in, releasing their bombs in our direction, every man among us tried to squeeze into that one shallow trench. The bombs hit so close that the concussion lifted my radio operator and me off the deck, and they exploded even closer to our point platoon, which must have bounced very high indeed.

I think that if friendly troops are in danger of being hit in an air strike, the CO should have the FAC specify not only the direction of approach but also the heading for the attack aircraft to approach. Moreover, popping smoke grenades to indicate the boundaries of friendly units should probably be done *just before* each strike, since smoke tends to drift after several seconds. These are not new suggestions, but they were often not followed in Vietnam.

Another thought borne out by this experience is that, in the kind of terrain we traversed in Vietnam, an airplane delivering bombs is often an ineffective way to cut off supplies and destroy enemy forces. Even when the rounds are "on target," as these must have appeared to be from the air, there is the possibility that many or all of the enemy will get through unharmed. This is what apparently happened, not only when we were fighting in Vietnam but also, as the reports have shown, in World War II Germany, and in Korea.

At about the same time we were being bombed by our own aircraft, Company G of our battalion, commanded by the now deceased Capt. John M. Gruner from Colorado, found twenty-eight fighting holes, all freshly dug, less than fifteen hundred meters from our new battalion CP. The holes were too small to have been dug by Americans, and no South Vietnamese forces were operating in our vicinity at that time. At 4 P.M. our patrol reached the top of the ridge we were reconnoitering and discovered fighting holes and North Vietnamese newspapers at a freshly abandoned campsite. We reconned the reverse slope of the ridge as far as the Cam Lo River but found no additional traces of the enemy and returned to the battalion CP just before evening.

Before sunset I began receiving the night defensive fire plans from each of my three platoon commanders. When they were in, I had our artillery and mortar FOs register their fires on terrain from which the enemy could bring accurate fire to bear on our positions, and wherever there were "dead spaces" in our lines not well covered by individual platoons. I instructed the FOs in particular what they were to do if we were attacked and briefed the company CP group just before sundown. That evening I made a special point to remind the platoon commanders about checking posts.

Before 10 P.M. all three platoon commanders reported their positions secure and I turned in. It was a warm night yet strangely silent. Something told me I should sleep in my fighting hole with my flak jacket on. I lay down without even a poncho cover and slipped into a deep sleep.

The first rounds I could hear only as they were coming in—a dozen or so sickening shrieks culminating in numerous explosions all around us. Thereafter I could hear the *ssspunk, ssspunk, ssspunk* as the NVA 82 mortar volleys fired. Several seconds after the rounds ejected they came in: *Sssshhh-Blam! Crack-Blam! Crack-Blam!* The air around us filled with rushing sounds, smoke, chunks of flying metal and earth, and the screams of the wounded.

Lying on my stomach, I hoped against hope that the next rounds would not land on my back. I said the Act of Contrition several times in rapid succession.

Somewhere at the edge of my consciousness I overheard the orders of the 81s squad leaders summoning their men to the guns amidst the incoming shells. I looked up once or twice between volleys. As I did, several mortarmen were axed down by the explosions just as they approached their guns. Under a hail of flying metal the next men in the command tried to reach the guns; they, too, were struck down before they could get counterbattery fire under way. As they had been instructed to do, our artillery and 60mm mortars began returning fire as soon as the NVA opened up; the 81s were so badly hit, I do not believe they got any rounds under way.

The attack was over in perhaps five minutes. For a short while afterward several men cried out for help, and dust and smoke lingered in the air. The area around the company CP had a sweet, almond smell from the high explosives and the sap of the blasted trees. After dawn I counted ten rounds that had landed within six feet of where I was lying. At the time of the attack I was more scared than I have ever been. The night was warm when I turned in, yet I was so frightened by the attack that my teeth chattered as I told the radio operator to request casualty reports from the platoons.

By this time both the wounded men and their buddies were calling for corpsmen, a sound that during the previous months I had come to dislike very much. I was more rattled on that occasion than at any other time in Vietnam, but the mind is privileged to regain possession of itself, and this I was determined to do by walking the company lines. This way, I could at the same time note the men's morale, alert them to expect another attack when the medevac choppers came in, warm myself up, regain my composure, and perhaps cheer the men up somewhat as well. My tour of our positions may have contributed to all of these objectives. I know that by the time I had gotten perhaps one-third of the way around our lines I had regained my composure completely.

I reached Marv Christians's platoon just when our only man to die in the field in that attack actually perished (I have no way to know if any died after they were evacuated, although it seems likely some did). The almond smell of HE was still faintly in the air as I approached a corpsman leaning over an unconscious Marine who looked to be no more than nineteen. "Robby," Chris's platoon sergeant, flashed his light off and on quickly to give the corpsman the light he needed to see while trying not to call undue attention to our position. Shortly after I arrived, the corpsman said, "Aw, hell, Sarn't. Just keep the flashlight on; I can't see well enough like this."

The corpsman appeared to be giving the man mouth-to-mouth resuscitation and then crouching down to listen for a heartbeat. Within moments of my arrival, when the Doc moved down to the man's chest, a long, dry rattle issued from the pale face; the wounded man shuddered briefly, then relaxed for good. The corpsman worked on the body for a few more minutes and then stood up with a sigh. He continued looking at the corpse, as if still trying to think of ways to revive it. Sergeant Robinson asked, "Is that it?"

"That's it," the corpsman said without expression.

"Sheeitt!" Sergeant Robinson whispered as he walked a few yards away, then came back just long enough to tell the men to cover the body up and take it to the LZ.

We had arranged an artillery strike to come in just before the medevac helos, but I reminded the men at each fighting hole to keep their heads up, especially when the choppers came in. Even that early in the war it was routine for the

NVA to try to shoot down our medevac choppers. That was in fact the most consistent time when the enemy attacked.

The smell of open flesh wounds and human blood was heavy on the edge of the LZ where our casualties waited. Father Ed Kane, Catholic priest and battalion chaplain, and I moved around whispering words of comfort and encouragement to the more badly wounded men. Among those I soon learned was Major Steel. Other than from Father Kane and me there was not a sound to be heard. The wounded knew that the enemy was watching and listening, and had discipline enough even though badly hurt not to make noise. The official casualty figures for the attack were thirty-four but that was the number evacuated only.

Gunny Husak used strobe lights to guide the choppers in. The medevacs were loaded aboard so rapidly and calmly and the choppers lifted off again so swiftly that I at first thought the choppers had not stayed down long enough to get all our casualties aboard.

Before we moved out on patrol that morning a chunky major from regimental headquarters came down to look around and presumably assess whether we needed replacements right away. When he greeted me as "captain" I told him I was a first lieutenant. I could see the wheels turning right away, since companies were supposed to be commanded by captains although often they were not.

Just after the major from regimental flew out—around 9:15—Marv's platoon received several rounds of small-arms fire from a pair of NVA snipers who had bushes on their backs. 2d Platoon returned fire and searched the area but found nothing. As the company began to move out again five rounds of 82-mortar fire came screeching in very near our company command group. Myself, my radio operator, Gunny Husak, Gunny Gonzalez, and at least one other Marine all jumped into the same two-man fighting hole at the same time. For several moments after the shrapnel stopped singing we lay there in a great jumble of hands, legs, boots, and arms, laughing amongst ourselves.

That day our company both patrolled and provided

battalion CP security as we moved some four thousand meters to the northwest. That evening, October 3, we set up a combat base on a one-hundred-meter knoll that had heavy vine and thorn scrub leading up to it. Our leading platoons had to cut through the growth with bush knives to get to the summit. At the top the terrain flattened out and there was a broad clearing, perhaps seventy-five meters in diameter. As our platoons dug in with entrenching tools for the night, a helo came in that carried our new battalion commander and my replacement, Capt. James A. Getchell. When Jim Getchell came in I moved down to company executive officer.

To say I was depressed about this demotion would be an understatement. I had transferred from a battalion where I was well known and happy to take command of a rifle company. In less than four days I found myself among strangers and with no command at all. As company exec I would be expected to stay back and remain as safe as possible so I could take over in the event the Skipper was killed. Needless to say I was not comfortable in that position. Fortunately, I would not have to stay in it long.

What we think we are may be at least as important as what we are, since what we think we are influences so much what we will become. After I was demoted I went through several agonizing hours of despondency, and probably showed it. As I look back I see now that there was little I could have done to prevent the attack and the casualties that followed. Nevertheless, as soon as I was demoted the words "relieved of command" stuck in my mind, and I felt very bleak indeed. Jim Cooper noticed my despondency and came up to me at the CP that evening. With an unlit cigar in the side of his mouth, he said something like, "Well, 'tenant Kirschke, looks laak you 'n me 'r out of a *job* at the same tahm. You lost yoaa *compana*, 'n ah lost ma battalion." Then he smiled my way and stalked off, but not before he seemed sure that his words had had the seemingly desired effect. This was all the boost I needed to get me through the next few days.

The first sight I had of Colonel Airheart was that evening of the third when I went to the battalion CP to deliver our company's night defensive fire plans to the S-3. In the gathering darkness, as I walked past the colonel's tall, slim, straight figure, he was standing in front of a tree to which he had affixed a small field mirror. As I passed he was carefully combing his well-trimmed, white hair. This glimpse made it seem to me as if he were primping, and I "sized up" the colonel too quickly; with his spare, upright carriage, neat appearance, and dignified manner of speaking, I had misread his character completely; within two weeks I came to see that William Airheart was as good a battalion commander as Colonel Bronars was—in my eyes no mean achievement.

Jim Getchell was a senior captain when he reported to our company. As I recall, he was promoted to major not long after Jim Cooper, and that was, I believe, before the end of October. Slowly but steadily I developed a strong fondness for Getchell both as a leader and as a person. When he assumed command of Hotel, he was perhaps thirty-two years old. Except for his sunburned face and hands he had very light skin, light brown hair that bordered on blond, and large, blue eyes. He was a fairly big man and a bit overweight when he reported aboard, and like many courageous people I have known he was modest and soft-spoken.

From the start he moved well in the field and showed that he knew what he was doing. He used the map and compass well, knew how to use supporting arms, and maneuvered the platoons effectively. Moreover, he "looked after" his platoon commanders in what I thought was just the right way. His home state was Washington. Jim had a calm, quiet, somewhat dignified aspect that I always found pleasant. Of course, I resented him somewhat at first—he *had* taken over "my" company—but I got over that quickly. Before long I appreciated that he was handling the company much better than I could have.

On the evening of the third we had no contacts, but as if to remind us that "the bad guys" were still around, Golf Company, operating less than five hundred meters northeast of us, received several rounds of 82-mortar fire, sustaining no casualties.

The next day we relinquished our duties as battalion CP security to Capt. George Burgett's Company F. Our company then reconnoitered in force from a combat base roughly one thousand meters southeast of where we had spent the previous night. To get to the position where we spent the night of the fourth, a 124-meter hill, we had to break trail through thick elephant grass and bamboo forest the whole way. Breaking trail was slower and more difficult than taking a more obvious route but presented the enemy with a much less predictable target.

On the way to that hill, Chris's platoon alternated with 3d Platoon on the point. In the course of their maneuvers, two men from 3d Platoon sustained injuries—one man a badly sprained ankle and the other an injured shoulder (by the time we reached the summit, the latter, his arm in a grubby-looking sling, appeared to be in considerable pain).

By that night, the only such one I can recall in Vietnam, the entire company had run out of water. The day had been blisteringly hot and we were all thirsty. With the CO's permission, before sunset I went outside our lines quite far northward without a radio or an RTO to try to find water in one of the ravines so our men could fill their canteens, but found no water, only a pair of naked skeletons (ah, Vietnam) in the undergrowth. Captain Getchell's depressing twilight order was that we were to sleep with our helmets off and turned upside down to catch whatever moisture might come during the night. By morning most of us felt much more refreshed even though no rain had fallen during the night. That morning water cans came in by helicopter, but the two 3d Platoon casualties, maybe out of pure orneriness or a ferocious sense of loyalty, refused evacuation.

On the fifth our company patrolled perhaps two thousand meters to the north and then moved seven hundred meters south. There, near a trail juncture not far from the Cam Lo District borders, we set in a night ambush but made no contact. Both Cam Lo Province and the one we operated in next, Gio Linh, were very sparsely populated. We had not seen a civilian since our landing; the only man-made structure we observed for about the first ten days of the operation was the now almost fully demolished stone plantation house we had used for the battalion CP the day we started Prairie.

In the two days that I was ExO the only duties I had were to call fire missions in on the areas we had just moved through, help put together the night defensive fire plans, and assist the stubborn Marines from 3d Platoon as they stumbled along at the rear of the company. The man with the balloon-shaped ankle had fashioned a stout cane out of heavy bamboo stalk and limped along on that. The other man, whose shoulder seemed to be dislocated, looked by then to be numb with pain; he staggered along zombie-like with his eyes fixed straight ahead. The only way I was able to get him to abandon his "hundred-yard stare" was by suggesting every few hundred meters that he be evacuated. Then he protested he was "not gwine to leave this company, Sir. No, Sir. I'm not leavin' . . . Sir." They made a formidable rearguard: I joked with them that if the NVA attacked, they were to turn around and scare the enemy while I used my forty-five. Neither Marine smiled; my radio operator chuckled.

On the morning of the sixth, the three maneuver platoons moved out on patrol to the northeast again. My orders were to stay at a "patrol base" with my radio operator along with the two men injured the previous day. The main body of the company was barely out of sight of the ridge we were on when our two leading platoons—Marv's and 3d Platoon—made contact with what must have been at least two reinforced squads of NVA. Typically the NVA opened up on the flank of the company, and their position, placing marshy ground between them and us, made our physical assault even more difficult. The firefight, longer than most, was over within fifteen minutes.

In this encounter our company killed at least eight NVA right away and captured several submachine guns. Third Platoon had the only casualties—one killed and four wounded. Moreover their platoon commander, a staff sergeant, had suffered "a severe malaria attack," news of which passed by radio to the Skipper. When I heard over the company tac net that the sergeant was a casualty I thought my chance had come. On the radio I asked the CO if Hotel Five (me) could take over as Hotel Three Actual.

"That's a negative," came the prompt response.

As soon as the casualty figures came in I called for medevac choppers. Not long after the firing had ceased echoing up the valley toward us, the casualties from 3d Platoon made their way up to the "patrol base," the ridge the four of us occupied. All of the WIAs were walking wounded although all had been badly hit. PFC Sinke led the way. He burst through the vine scrub with a heavy lurch. Wearing a thick, blood-soaked field dressing around his leg, he was limping and leading a pair of others who came behind him, holding hands to give each other mutual support. Crimson bandages covered almost each man's entire head; one man had only one eye and a small portion of cheek showing. The fourth WIA was a lanky lance corporal—I think his name was Jackson—who had a Tennessee drawl. This man had a mean-looking gunshot wound to the arm. The dead Marine was placed on the edge of the clearing with a green poncho as cover, and the carrying party hustled back to their platoon.

Sinke looked like the ideal recruiting poster Marine except that, unlike some I have seen who looked the part, Sinke actually belonged there. He was perhaps six-feet two-inches tall and weighed about 210 pounds. When he limped up to report to me I pointed to his thigh and said, "I guess that's your ticket home, huh, Sinke."

He responded, "No, Sir. I haven't been over here long enough for that." To our astonishment he was not wrong.

Soon after I exchanged comments with Sinke, an NVA squad circled around behind us in an evident attempt to finish off our casualties and attack the main part of our company from the high ground we occupied behind it. In assault formation, the NVA steadily moved up from their draw, firing from the hip at our group. These NVA were bigger and stronger looking than any Vietnamese I had seen before. They wore green uniforms and helmets, and had bushes tied to their backs.

With scarcely a word of command from myself, our group began a countercharge. Sinke staggered and began firing right away. One head-wounded Marine sighted and fired his rifle with his one good eye. The other, who had looked dazed before, promptly passed his grenades for my radio operator and me to hurl. The Marine from the Deep South who had the arm wound ran out in front of us all, firing and yelling madly. Sinke, the man with one eye, my radio operator, myself, and the two previously injured men formed a skirmish line and moved down the hill, firing and screaming very loudly.

At least in my case, the noise was meant to make our motley force seem larger and more ferocious than it really was. It worked. Within seconds our counterattack pushed the NVA back down the same draw they had emerged from. As they retreated, the Southern Marine let loose a wild Rebel yell followed by a string of curses and started scrambling down the ravine after them; I restrained him. Reluctantly he came back and our group mostly limped, staggered, and back-stepped to the top of the ridge. Most of us were laughing as we did.

My radio operator then tuned in the medevac frequency and I talked the choppers in. As I always did whenever I called for a medevac chopper myself, I advised the pilot as to the best direction to come in from. Just then it was the southwest, an approach that would keep his bird at least temporarily out of sight of our friends in the ravine.

Much as I wanted to say so, I could not honestly tell the pilot that our landing zone was secure. There were nine bodies in it; one was dead and six were walking injured. The only healthy ones in the LZ were myself and my radio operator, and we had to carry the dead man aboard. As the CH-34 skimmed over the treetops into view I threw a smoke grenade. When the smoke began unfurling from the canisters, I said, "We popped green" (or whatever color it was).

"Roger, I see green."

Miraculously the helo was loaded and got out without a shot being fired.

As the medevac mission was taking place, Captain Getchell took a look at 3d Platoon. As soon as he did he reconsidered my request and asked me to come down to Hotel three. "Hot damn," I whispered to myself as I ran down, smiling, past Don's men. I believe I made the several hundred meters' run to 3d Platoon in seconds. The platoon I

joined was a sad-looking group. At the time a reinforced rifle platoon in combat supposedly had sixty-three men.
When I assumed command, 3d Platoon had only twenty-
five, several of whom were still wearing rust-colored battle
dressings from the mortar attack sustained on our first night
of Prairie. Moreover, many of the men looked the same way
I had felt just after that attack ended. The inexperienced
staff sergeant who had been the platoon commander was
squatting against a tree and shaking uncontrollably. It was
not malaria but fear that had him in its grip.

I cannot say it was cowardice since I felt that, had he been
able to control himself, he would have stayed with us. In fact,
after a few days' rest and some morale-boosting talk from
Top Peabody, the staff sergeant rejoined us in the field again
at Con Thien. But as soon as we got into another firefight,
his legs turned soft and he assumed the same squatting position, shaking, I believe, even more violently than before.

Because of our sparse numbers, logistical problems
prompted me to divide the platoon into two squads until
we could receive some replacements. One squad had ten
men, the other nine.

In 3d Platoon, then, one of the two maneuver-squad
leaders was Cpl. "Pancho" Villanueva. The other squad
leader was an unheroic-looking corporal named Arthur
Desclos. Villanueva, a bantamweight, did not stand tall
enough to reach my shoulder yet he was not a small man.
Short and trim, he had coal-black hair, large dark eyes,
and a calm, gentle aspect. His home state I am fairly sure
was Texas, and he spoke with a faint Hispanic accent
which grew much more distinct when he was angry.

The previous year at Camp Pendleton I served two days
as officer of the day at the 5th Marines' Camp, Margarita.
On one of those two nights there was a black-white racial
brawl at the EM Club. And on the day of that incident I had
under my command a squared-away guard detail that did
commendably in breaking up the riot. By the kind of life co-
incidence I no longer consider strange, I first served with
most of the 3d Platoon on the guard unit at Pendleton that
night we had to quell the racial disturbance.

The other maneuver squad was led by Desclos. He

was a pale, quiet, sparely built, unassuming Marine of about twenty-two. About five-feet-eleven, soft-spoken, with dark brown hair and green eyes, his home state was either Vermont or New Hampshire.

Almost from the time I joined the platoon Desclos had an angry-looking rash that covered his face and most of his body, yet not once did I hear him complain or ask for special consideration of any kind. Far from it. It was not until I had picked up the same kind of rash—my rash was on the upper trunk only—that I came to have some idea of how much fortitude Desclos possessed.

My platoon sergeant when I assumed command was Ronald Hoole, a twenty-four-year-old NCO I had also first met on guard duty that night at Margarita. A gruff-looking Italian-American, he stood about five-feet-eight with brown eyes, bushy eyebrows, and black hair. He had a raspy voice with a central New York accent and moved with the shuffling gait of a middleweight boxer.

Our platoon guide at the time, Larry E. Honeycutt, had also been with 3d Platoon for a long time and knew Hoole, Desclos, and Villanueva well. A thin, blond, rosy-cheeked, blue-eyed Marine, Honeycutt spoke with a North Carolina twang. His hometown then was Fayetteville, but last I've heard he lives in Greensboro. In 1966, Honeycutt was twenty-one or twenty-two years old and either a senior corporal or a newly promoted sergeant.

Lance Corporal Jackson was in overall charge of the weapons section, a billet that was supposed to be handled by an experienced sergeant, two ranks higher. Jackson was nineteen. The weapons detachment at the time included machine guns, rockets, and LAWs (disposable, one-shot rockets with a flip-up sight). Jackson and I had served together the previous year in 3/6. Although he was young he knew the weapons well, and when he was with us in the field he was a great help.

Our machine gun squad leader was, like Jackson, another lance corporal from the Deep South, named Chisolm. He was about the same size as me, and in our rare, quiet moments Chisolm often amused the troops by singing "Whispering Pines" in superb imitation of the

country singer Johnny Horton. As I recall he had unusual blue eyes, one of which became slightly crossed
when he spoke. I soon came to disregard this slight pe-
culiarity and concentrated instead on the steady character of the man. Sergeant Hoole, however, often
good-naturedly referred to Chisolm as "you crazy-eyed,
rebel sonofabitch." To which Chisolm, Jackson, and
Honeycutt often responded with cutting remarks about
Hoole's Italian parentage and New York accent.

Our rockets' squad leader was a tall, broad-
shouldered, and likable twenty-year-old draftee, L.Cpl.
Terry O'Connor. O'Connor was from Detroit and had a
Midwestern accent with a bit of County Mayo Irish
speech intermingled. I believe O'Connor now lives in
Culver City, California. All our squad leaders were supposed to be sergeants, yet we were happy to have these
young lance corporals along.

A rifle platoon in combat was supposed to have two
corpsmen, yet we usually had only one. When I took command our platoon corpsman was Doc Howe. Another tall,
handsome, soft-spoken young man who reminded me
somewhat of O'Connor, Howe was not so ruggedly built,
and as a corpsman he did not need to be. Howe was soon
transferred to Marv's platoon and within the week received
a severe gunshot wound in the face. After Howe left us we
had such a high turnover of corpsmen (always prime targets for Communist gunners), I was not able to keep track
of the names and faces. Howe was the last corpsman other
than Jerry Holub and Doc Washington whose name I am
able to recall.

In a letter dated March 8, 1967, one of my Marines
from 3d Platoon, PFC Marvin Redeye, wrote that "the
last few operations have taken quite a few (of 3d Platoon's) people," and many others were wounded or killed
while I was commander. Thus, I do not know how many
of these men have survived to read this book.

For the first few weeks I was with 3d Platoon, my radio
operator was PFC Thomas W. Jiminez. Jiminez was a soft-
spoken, towheaded eighteen-year-old from Sparks, Nevada.
As soon as I figured out who my squad leaders and

headquarters group were, I ascertained where the enemy fire came from that had inflicted our recent casualties. Recalling how much relief I had gotten from my fears simply by checking lines after the mortar attack the first night of Prairie, I organized our two squads for an assault over the ground the ambush had come from. I held little hope that the enemy was still nearby yet I felt it was essential to get the men up, moving, and firing so they would at least have the illusion of taking purposeful action. In our assault, we had a good "run and shoot," and I believe our demonstration perked the men's morale considerably. Moreover, when we crossed the boggy ground we found bloodstains and drag marks, indications that the enemy had suffered casualties we were not already aware of.

That evening we moved back to the patrol base on the ridge we had vacated the same morning. After our lines were well dug in, Captain Getchell had our forward air controller (FAC) call in air strikes very close to our lines. Several low passes were made by either A-4s or F-8s which "worked over" especially well the thick terrain to our northwest, the most likely avenue of approach for a large-scale attack. Several passes were made using 20mm cannon, two-hundred-pound high-explosive bombs, and napalm.

As the HE strikes came in, whizzing steel and then clods of dirt flew all around us, the ground vibrated, and there was a noise like a wild rainstorm due to the hissing sounds made by flying earth, stones, and other particles. Jiminez and I, crouching in our two-man fighting holes, narrowly missed being hit by several chunks of hot metal as large as a man's hand that flew into our position.

A tall, thin, black Marine from one of the other platoons was struck in the forehead by a long piece of shrapnel that protruded several inches above the bridge of his nose. This was a strange wound: the gray metal shard drew little blood and seemingly left the injured man fully conscious and almost without pain. As he walked to the medevac choppers he seemed perfectly calm and alert.

The napalm canisters tumbled in very close to our lines, the fires that occurred in their wake warming us as we crouched down after their explosions. As Jiminez and

I listened to the crackling noises in the woods down the hill, we hoped aloud to each other that several dozen NVA were making good kindling.

In the morning we moved out on patrol to the northeast again. Whichever platoon was on the point found two NVA bodies from the previous day's firefight so that our total for that action was ten. A half hour later, ten more enemy KIAs were seen at the coordinates where the air strike had been delivered, so the air strike might have saved us from further attacks the previous night.

By 11:30 our company had covered five thousand meters, a good clip but probably too fast as time would soon show. We followed a light trail that led over the rolling hills southwest of Nui (Hill) Con Thien. The company was moving "platoons in column," and that was the wrong formation for the terrain and tactical situation.

My platoon was moving behind Don and the CP group. The spacious landscape to either flank was a scene of distant hills and occasional trees sharply defined under an immense blue sky. The sun was shining and the wind moving up from the south, sending puffs of clouds swiftly before us. It was the kind of day on which no young man should ever have to die.

Shortly before noon Don's point came across a diagram etched in the mud by a stick on the trail we were following. After studying it, Captain Getchell ordered Don to move out on the same heading. I thought that a temporary change in direction or change in formation would have been prudent. Jim ordered neither. As CO, Jim Getchell made few mistakes, but errors in judgment cost us right away.

Within minutes Don's platoon drew abreast of a trail juncture about one thousand meters west of Thon An Hoa. Suddenly, I heard the high stutter of NVA machine guns punctuated by a succession of thudding bangs and steadily crackling small-arms fire. As soon as the firing began I jogged up behind Jim Getchell, so that when he turned to say, "Envelop to the right, Jim," I was almost within speaking distance.

As I turned to pump my arm to the platoon to

double-time, I thought to myself, "this is it." I felt sure another NVA platoon would be waiting to hit us, too, as we made our envelopment.

I later learned that the platoon that had ambushed Don's was dug into a hedgerow along his line of approach at a distance of about twenty-five meters. The NVA had an excellent field of fire, about six to eight inches above the deck so that once a man was wounded he would almost surely be struck again if he tried to crawl. As I jogged to the right with the forward elements of our platoons I could hear at least one of Don's M-60s answering the enemy's fire, some of his M-14s, and an occasional *ponk, ponk* from what must have been his platoon's M-79 grenade launchers.

Out of fear of a double ambush I held back in my running speed as we began our encirclement. What should have been a headlong dash was more a cautious trot, I am ashamed to say. Corporal Villanueva's entire squad embarrassed me right away by the zeal of their movement. As they began to run, several members of the lead fire team tried to fling themselves into the dense hedge and vine scrub in order to reach the enemy directly. Each man bounced back, cursing at this wall of bramble far too thick to penetrate.

With .45 drawn, I pursued Villanueva's bobbing helmet as his point team swung into a detour at least one hundred meters to the east, to the first place where our strung-out platoon could swing in toward the ambush force. By then it was probably already too late. Of the five or six sweating Marines in front of me, I wondered how many would still be alive in two minutes.

Several wild bursts of submachine gun fire rent the air around us. Knowing it was almost surely too late to help Don's platoon, I held up to see where the gun was firing from. I did not wish to lose half of our platoon as well. Another burst led us to believe the gunner was in an abandoned house within hand grenade distance of Villanueva's point. This man threw a grenade and we rushed the house as soon as the projectile exploded.

When we got there we saw no one, but thought we heard

movement inside the bomb shelter beneath the house. After calling for surrenders and getting no response, we shucked another frag grenade down the hole into the shelter and stepped back, prepared to shoot whomever emerged.

A tiny Vietnamese girl wearing black pajamas and aged perhaps twelve clambered up amidst the rising dust and powder. She padded noiselessly toward me, as in my dreams she has done many times since. She stopped a few feet away—close enough so I could have reached out to help her, had I chosen. One large, dark eye stared tearlessly, at me; the other lay upon her cheek, connected to the socket by the nerves only. As I turned away from her our corpsman moved swiftly to bandage her head and quietly, considerately, treat the other gruesome wounds. About this time we received the order from Jim Getchell to come back; it was too late, something I already knew.

Our corpsman (whose name I do not recall but whose hometown was Houston) and Villanueva said something like, "We're taking her back with us, aren't we, Lieutenant?"

"No, we're not."

Why I said this, I do not now know for sure. Perhaps it was my stupid, temporary misperception that the girl had volunteered to act as a diversion. Even if it was that, it does not say much for my spirit.

Human nobility does not proceed from thought alone, but is more elemental. It does not depend upon culture or breeding. It is the kind of nobility that shone forth that day from Corporal Villanueva and that has since then provided this author with no small refuge against despair. As soon as I replied, Villanueva's whole aspect grew stubborn and unyielding, his dark eyes glowing. "We *have* to take her with us, Sir," Villanueva almost shouted. "We can't leave her here. We have to take her with us."

"No, we're leaving her."

"We can't do it, Lieutenant. We have to take her with us!" In a tone of voice combining anger and incredulity, the young corporal stood stiffly and insisted. In a few seconds I relented, not out of charity or bigness of heart but mostly from weakness mingled with shame.

How hard I cried the night I thought I had learned

Sergeant Villanueva had been killed on his third tour of duty in Vietnam! The day he died, I thought the world had lost a special person. Recently, however, I found that I had learned of the wrong Villanueva. "Our" Pancho lives in Texas.

We got back to the rest of the company just before the medevac choppers came in. I walked up to Don as he was counting heads to see who was left. His reported casualties were three KIA and thirteen WIA but, as always, many men did not "turn themselves in." When I came up to apologize for not having gotten around sooner, I was surprised to see that Don was pale and somewhat shaken. I knew Don as a man of iron and did not think he could be rattled, even by this attack. "That's okay, Jim," Don replied with a wry smile; "this ambush was laid by Clausewitz."

I did not learn until later the heroic part Don had played in countering this ambush. And only when Jim Getchell had forcibly spirited him onto the last chopper out did I learn that Don had been shot in the side and managed to conceal his wound from everyone, except Captain Getchell, until the last evacuation chopper had nearly gotten off the ground.

As the chopper carrying Don lifted away, I began to get our platoon "saddled up" to move out again when Morley Safer and a network camera crew came striding toward us. Safer had a self-important, determined look on his face as he marched up to ask if he could interview some of my men for whatever evening news he was doing at the time. I agreed, but with the proviso that there be no mention of casualty figures. "Right. No casualty figures," he said, then proceeded to select Corporal Desclos, presumably because the latter usually was one of the most bewildered-looking NCOs in the platoon, an appearance that belied his true nature.

As I recall, Safer's first question, asked in doleful tones, was: "Did you know any of the Marines who were killed in this action?" Corporal Desclos nodded yes. Even more funereally, the interviewer pursued, "And how did you *feel* when you saw your buddies die?" or some such question.

At this point I ended the interview by stepping in between the cameraman, the interviewer, and Desclos. I touched my squad leader's shoulder and gestured to him to return to his squad.

Safer seemed quite miffed and attempted to argue with me about my cutting him short. He had flown out here especially to make this interview. Reluctantly he moved away. (This scene is, I have reason to believe, still on film in the CBS archives.) That evening this news crew would very likely be back in whatever comfortable place they had flown from and I would be commanding this undermanned platoon less than four thousand meters from the Demilitarized Zone. I did not want one of my only two maneuver squad leaders to say things that might adversely affect the morale of our unit right away.

That evening our company drew up defenses on the eastern boundary of an abandoned agricultural development center approximately one mile northeast of where Don's platoon had been ambushed. It was already dark by the time we were assigned our platoon sectors. As my squads began digging in at their primary positions, I went out in front of our lines as always on a quick reconnaissance to locate potential listening post and ambush sites, scout out potential avenues of approach to our main lines, walk "the dead ground" our direct fire weapons could not cover, and have a quick look at our positions as they would appear to an approaching enemy force. These reconnaissance missions involved some element of danger since the enemy was always nearby.

As always before I went, I had Sergeant Hoole alert our squads that I was heading out. But during this reconnaissance I got turned around in the elephant grass, and as I pushed through heavy undergrowth I heard the receiver of a machine gun *clang* shut. The sound came to me in the darkness from I knew not where. I went for my .45 and stopped moving. I listened for a few seconds and at first heard nothing but my own heavy breathing and the loud pounding of my heart. Then voices drifted toward me that sounded like those of our men. After another second's hesitation, I drew aside a full arm's length of tall grass and stared down the barrel of a machine gun. Some fifteen meters away lay one of Don's gunners, sighting directly at me over the bipod between his elbows on the deck. "Halt!" he barked out. "Who goes there?"

"Lieutenant Kirschke," I replied hoarsely.

"Advance and be recognized."

I moved stiffly forward several paces. After what seemed like a great many seconds, he said, "Sorry, Sir." I mumbled something like, "That's quite all right, Marine. Carry on," and exhaled a sigh of relief as I passed him to go back to my platoon.

That night, as almost always, the men who should have been sleeping were awake and alert. Sleeping on post was never a problem in our platoon, which I am convinced is one reason 3d Platoon was never caught off guard in Vietnam.

When we awoke in the morning, the hollows of the ponchos we rolled in to sleep were filled with moisture. It had not yet begun to rain that year near the DMZ, but the weather was already very damp and the monsoon winds soon began to blow in earnest at Con Thien.

On the night of the seventh, one of the darkest I recall in Vietnam, with Steve's platoon on the point, Hotel Company, the battalion command group, and Company F moved onto Nui Con Thien. G Company, I believe, moved in from another route, somewhat after us. Con Thien was 518 meters above sea level at its highest point. It was approximately three thousand meters south of the southern boundary of the Demilitarized Zone directly north of us. Less than three thousand meters west and southwest of us, however, the southern boundary of the DMZ swung more than one thousand meters south of our positions. Thus, due west of us and less than two miles away, was also North Vietnamese territory.

In the fifty-four days we operated off Con Thien, our missions were essentially threefold: to protect the ARVN western flank (the nearest South Vietnamese battalion was ten thousand meters east of us!), to conduct patrols and ambushes to push the enemy back across the DMZ, and to provide security for the Con Thien outpost itself. The latter was little more than high ground occupied by three understrength companies from our battalion, our battalion CP, a 105mm battery, and a 4.2-inch heavy mortar battery. From our position, however, in clear weather and from certain ground we could see into North Vietnam with the naked eye.

This was an audacious position to occupy and thus, I felt, an outstanding place for our battalion. The enemy, of course, knew we were there. Fortunately perhaps for us, the heavy shelling by rocket and artillery fire from North Vietnam did not begin until after our battalion had moved south to An Hoa.

We were not supposed to fire artillery into the DMZ let alone North Vietnam; such were the rules of the war current at that time. The DMZ ran approximately thirty-five miles across Vietnam. Approximately five miles deep, it extended roughly two and one half miles to the north and the same distance to the south of the Song Ben Hai (Ben Hai River), which divided the two countries in the sectors where we operated.

In October 1966 the International Control Commission, composed of personnel from India, Canada, and Poland, was formed at least partially to ensure that there was no infiltration either north or south through the DMZ. Reportedly they patrolled the southeastern front of the zone from a base at Gio Linh, just south of the zone at its eastern flank in South Vietnam, but actually I doubt very much if they ever did. In October 1966 the Allies offered to stop all bombing to allow the ICC to inspect the northern portion of the zone, but Hanoi refused to permit the inspection. Needless to say, unlike the Korean peninsula's DMZ the Vietnam DMZ was not fortified on our side.

In January 1967 our forces captured a taped speech delivered in August 1966 by Maj. Gen. Tran Do, deputy commander of Vietnamese Communist armed forces. The speech was given at a conference of representatives of the NVA's 7th Division. There, Gen. Tran Do reported Hanoi's "right" to infiltrate 5,000 to 6,000 men each month into South Vietnam. It is clear the infiltration was taking place at the time the general was speaking in 1966. In the same speech, Tran Do asserted that "the American troops have decreased in number, their spirits are low and their morale poor."

About the success of the NVA infiltration I have no accurate knowledge, although I do know the fate of many who attempted to get through the area we patrolled. As to the morale of the American troops generally, I cannot speak with authority. The morale in our battalion, however, could hardly have been higher.

The captured enemy maps and documents I have seen indicate that one of the first main rest areas south of the Ben Hai was less than 2,000 meters due west of Con Thien and 1,000 meters east of the DMZ where it dipped well south of Con Thien. This site was just a few hundred meters north of the abandoned agricultural development center where we had set in on the night of the seventh. In the documents I have studied, it is clear that the NVA routinely dragooned scouts from the south to lead their infantry units to their destinations. The maps we had at the time were excellent, yet they are no substitute for having firsthand knowledge of the operational terrain.

At Con Thien our battalion relieved D Company, 1st Battalion, 4th Marines. Their CO was a young captain named Juul who had gone through the first summer of the Platoon Leader Course at Quantico the same time I did.

Juul was about the same size as me, somewhat more angular of build, and had high cheekbones, a soft drawl, and a modest Southern aspect. At Con Thien on the morning of the eighth, when we relieved his company, he looked older and paler than the last time I had seen him at Quantico. His calm manner had not changed, but he looked at least twenty pounds lighter and seemed to have aged ten years in the past two.

It was a cool morning of heavy mist when Juul briefed us about the situation around our position. He told us that his company rarely ran patrols and that it spent almost all its time providing security for the 105mm battery on the position. His company seemed as understrength as ours, but it was responsible for a position that would normally be covered by a reinforced battalion at full strength.

Juul's exec was a tall, good-looking lieutenant from Georgia. Like his CO, his voice was low and suffused with the dignified warmth of the Deep South. The lieutenant had also played football in college—at the University of Georgia as I recall. When we moved down to An Hoa around Thanksgiving, I learned that he had already been killed while leading an assault on a series of heavily fortified positions near there. The troops in his company obviously looked up to the lieutenant. When he took Don, Marv Christians, and myself on a tour of the D Company lines, he greeted every man by name. However, early in our tour he kicked a light green trip wire that all three Hotel Company lieutenants had clearly spotted from a much farther distance. Fortunately, the wire was rigged to a grenade flare that just popped and fizzled out after a few seconds. The lieutenant laughed, walked over, pulled the spent canister off its stick, and flipped it underhanded to the rifleman in the position closest to us. Chris, Don, and I exchanged uneasy glances before resuming our tour at a safer distance behind him.

That morning I deployed my squads in our platoon sector. Third Platoon occupied the ground on the left flank of our company. Southeast of our platoon position was a finger of land that came up to a ridge. From this ridge an assaulting enemy force would have excellent fields of fire and be in a very good position to overrun the entire outpost. When we moved in we were told that the ARVN unit that defended that high ground had also mined the finger leading up to it. When they pulled out at the end of October we discovered that they had not mined it at all. Since my platoon was the only one in our battalion that could possibly get troops onto the ridge to reinforce the ARVN platoon up there, should that prove necessary, 3d Platoon held the key Marine position on Con Thien. Needless to say, it was essential that our scant forces be well deployed.

Most of the time we were at Con Thien we patrolled, day and night, an area approximately three thousand meters all around our position. On the nights when the whole platoon was not out on ambush, we set up our watches so that each man would have two hours' watch and two hours' sleep. Throughout the night from after dark until first light, each of the squad leaders, including rockets and guns, the platoon sergeant, platoon guide, and myself, all checked posts at hours assigned by me. By having someone almost continually making the rounds, we assured that the men at each post were awake and alert.

As soon as we set in our preliminary positions, I went out to "walk the dead ground" and so forth while the men began to string the little bit of wire we had those first days and put up some semblance of a defensive position with the few materials we had on hand. We were able to lay our guns so they could bring fairly good grazing, enfilade fire across most of our front. We also put out a few directional mines and booby-trapped M-26 fragmentation grenades, and as soon as possible registered the fires of our 60mm mortars. In order to do that we had to withdraw our troops from the lines, especially in October, since at that time most of our 60s ammo was very old—often from the mid to late 1950s—and we had many misfires and short rounds until early December, when we finally began receiving newer rounds.

Before long we also had to register close-in fires for 105s and 81s, in case we needed to use our final protective fires. It hardly needed to be emphasized at the time that thousands of fighting-age adult North Vietnamese, not to mention some 110,000 Chinese Army soldiers were within several miles of us.* At the time, North Vietnam had one of the largest armies in the world. All of these tactical precautions, however, would have availed us little were our men not awake and alert on post. The enemy was always moving around our positions and ready to exploit any weaknesses he might discover in them.

On the morning we set in our company's defenses, companies G and F made contact twice not far from us. As our men were digging into their positions I picked up our forward observer's field glasses to survey the area in front of our lines and saw four NVA moving south almost within rifle-shooting distance. We called in an artillery

* On the proximity of Chinese soldiers and the size of the North Vietnamese Army, see Xiaoming Zhang, "The Vietnam War, 1964–1969: A Chinese Perspective," in *The Journal of Military History* 60 no. 4 (1996): 731–62. See especially pages 753, 759, and 762.

mission fired by the battery entrenched almost within hailing distance of our platoon CP. The mission was immediately on target and appeared to kill all four.

That evening Marv's platoon made a combat patrol to a village called Thon Xuan Hoa, where they found a four-by-four-foot portable bulletin board and a great deal of anti-American propaganda in Vietnamese.

On the eighth of October the monsoon began in earnest. Thereafter, as long as we were at Con Thien, it rained hard for at least part of almost every day. And for the rest of my tour after that, it rained even more often than at Con Thien. In the areas we operated in from October through December 1966, ninety-seven inches of rain fell. In a three-month period in the field we received more rain than falls in New York or Philadelphia in an average two-year period.

On the evening of October 9, I led a heavily reinforced squad-size ambush patrol to a site just north of a trail junction not far from Nam Tan. The position seemed a likely avenue for a careless NVA unit that wanted to move speedily around our outpost. The ambush site was approximately a thousand meters southeast of our lines yet took over an hour to reach since we had to move with great stealth every step of the way. While in our ambush position for nearly four hours under a light rain, we made no contact and became thoroughly soaked. I also relearned what I had studied in preparation for my Southeast Asian lectures, and had recalled many times since: that insects form by far the largest class of invertebrates in Vietnam. Every species of ant, termite, beetle, fly, mosquito, cricket, grasshopper, stick insect, and dragonfly must have been present in abundance within the single map square of ground we covered on that night ambush patrol. During our daytime patrols it was still warm enough up north for us to encounter various kinds of wasps and bees, most of which seemed to seek us out whenever we opened a can of C rations.

On the night of the tenth it rained steadily as I made my way from one position to the next, checking posts. I often found that post-checking was a good time to get to know the men somewhat better and maybe even boost their morale. Whenever possible I tried to leave the men in each position feeling better than when I approached.

It was raining again on the night of the eleventh when I checked posts. That night I held whispered conversations with L.Cpl. Leland E. Hammond and PFC Ronald Miller, among the last words these two young men would have with anyone on this earth.

Hammond was nineteen, had pale blue eyes, and came from Sumter, South Carolina. He was a lonesome-seeming young man and liked me, I think, because I had spoken to him about the Carolinas and about 3d Battalion, 6th Marines, on the East Coast, where we had served together the previous year. A few hours before he was killed I saw him huddled by himself under a poncho in the rain and thought he looked, perhaps, twelve. A few hours later he was stopped by a machine gun bullet through the heart.

PFC Miller had turned twenty on July 15. He was a polite, solidly built, red-haired Marine. His voice had a pleasant Southern Ohio twang. He spoke to me about his mother, whom he obviously cared for deeply, about his girlfriend, and his other friends back in Pedro. Miller had many more months yet to go on his tour and I recall wondering to myself as I left him what kind of shape he would be in at the end of it. Still, I did not think his tour would end so soon.

Before we went on patrol on the eleventh our battalion was joined by a pair of first-rate professional photographers: Larry Burrows and Catherine Leroy. Burrows was at that time taking photographs for *Life* magazine. Several years after he traveled with us he was presumed killed (as of this writing, only his camera gear has been found) while covering the war in another area of the country. Burrows was tall and thin and had a slightly clipped, indeterminate British accent.

In his own way Burrows was a compassionate man. Before we went on patrol that morning he expressed to me his considerable ambivalence about taking photographs of our wounded and dying men as well as those who were helping them. Conscious of not being a member of our unit and of being able to leave us almost whenever he wanted, Burrows said he felt strangely about his role. He knew that in a few days he would be back in Saigon or someplace else relatively secure, and the men he photographed would either be slogging it out in combat, battling pain in some hospital or other, or lying in a morgue, awaiting shipment home.

One morning Burrows explained to me how he went about planning the photographs he took. As I suspect most people do who accomplish great things in life, he had a great deal of concentration and an efficient method. As he explained, he planned ahead of time the kinds of photographs he wanted to take on each assignment. Before he went to the fields he laid all his photographic equipment out, usually on his rack, and carefully stuffed each of his large pockets with the items he would need. Once he was certain where to reach for each, he laid out in his mind the types of photographs he wanted to take. In that way, he said, he took few unnecessary shots and usually came back with just the kinds of photos he wanted. When he went into the field with us, virtually all of his pockets were stuffed with gear and he looked very disorganized indeed. But as his photographs reveal, he was not. Burrows was very seldom seen taking photographs; mostly he watched and waited for the right moment.

Another cameraperson who traveled with us now and then in Vietnam is Catherine Leroy. She is alive and well now and living in southern California, but a year or two afterward in Vietnam she herself had been fairly seriously wounded. A wiry, diminutive Frenchwoman, I would estimate that she was in her mid-twenties at the time. She had large, soft, brown eyes and mouse-colored brown hair which in the field she usually drew back in a tight ponytail. She seemed to me at the time to be much "harder," more taciturn and intrepid than Burrows, the only other civilian photographer who traveled with us for any length of time. Even with her tough taciturnity, however, I came to like and admire Ms. Leroy. She stayed with us in the field longer than any other journalist or photographer, military or civilian. It may well be that, thanks to her intrepidity, I am still alive today.

As usual, before we went on patrol we got painted well with camouflage stick, placed bushes in our helmets, picked up our rations for patrol, and checked to see that we had sufficient ammunition. I also made sure that our squad leaders checked to make sure the men had run up the battle sights on their weapons.

On this day, the eleventh, we moved northwest across country until we reached the edge of a loose-surface road that ran to the northeast and came within a thousand meters of Con Thien. My platoon was on the point on the way out. Where the road intersected with a trail that connected with the DMZ, I motioned to Villanueva to begin moving northwest so as to parallel that connecting trail. At 10:10, after advancing just fifty meters to the left of the trail, our point squad encountered four NVA. Both sides exchanged fire. As I was about to move forward with my men, Jim Getchell came on the radio to order us to withdraw so he could bring an air strike in on the area.

Air was "on station" and a strike came in fairly swiftly and at what seemed like fairly close range. As it happened it probably was not close enough; afterward we found no traces of casualties from this mission.

As soon as the strike ended, I had Villanueva's squad with PFC Ybarra on the point proceed back up the trail. The sun suddenly came out after the strike and it grew quite hot. As our point was proceeding carefully up the trail, my radio operator and I sat down and leaned back against a pair of posts alongside the trail. No sooner had I removed my helmet to take a drink than a rapid exchange of gunfire occurred very close to us up the trail. In a way I do not believe I ever did thereafter, I hesitated for a few seconds after contact had been established. My head still against the post, I looked up the trail. As I did, Catherine Leroy, bent over double with her neck-slung camera held before her, zipped past me like a streak. I figured it was time for the platoon commander to move up also. "Let's go, Meyer!" I said to my new radio operator, L.Cpl. Robert J. Meyer, and we moved up the trail on the double in trace of the tiny photographer. It's good that we did: just as I moved forward an NVA bullet smacked the post where my head had rested the previous second.

As my platoon moved up, Jim Getchell ordered Marv Christians's platoon to swing in the hook. Within seconds

Marv, with .45 drawn, burst through the shrubbery about thirty-five meters to my left. The fire and movement of our two platoons side by side was executed in the manner one would hope to see from the demonstration troops at Basic School. Sometimes daring is prudence. In a matter of seconds Marv's platoon and ours had swept through the tunneled and fortified area—about 200 meters wide and 100 meters deep—that the NVA company had occupied.

As Meyer and I sprinted into the woods to the left of the trail the air must have been alive with buzzing and cracking bullets, yet I was scarcely aware of anything but the chase. Ybarra ran down an NVA rifleman and shot him in the back with several bursts of his M-14 on automatic. Villanueva disappeared into the smoke some twenty meters ahead of us, directing his squad's fire from the heavy brush there.

As Villanueva disappeared from sight I came upon a small maze of tunnels dug into dung-smelling earth. I thought I glimpsed a green-uniformed figure so I pulled a frag grenade out of its pouch, wrenched free the pin, and flung the pear-size grenade into the mouth of the hole. Soon there was a crumping noise and out came gray-brown, foul-smelling fumes, but no enemy.

I bent over to fire at whomever might come out, and heard as I did a *pop-pop* noise. An RPG (an NVA hand-held, antitank rocket launcher) flew over my left shoulder and impacted in the open field behind me. I spun around, hurled another grenade in the direction I thought the RPG round had come from, and sprinted northward up the trench line. I heard the hum of close-flying machine gun bullets from the heavy brush that Villanueva had entered with his men. A fire team from 2d Squad was moving after Villanueva. His weapon at port arms, PFC Miller ran through the mud just ahead of me. Bullets slished through the leaves all around us.

A projectile struck Miller in the head and he tumbled backwards, still clutching his weapon. Silver-white matter and blood sprayed the trench in front of me as his body slid downward and lodged in the orange mud in the narrow trench.

Sensing that fire may also have been enfilading us from the low grass to our right, I ordered Corporal Desclos to move his men up on that flank. Without first laying down a base of fire, Desclos began moving his men across the field in fire-team rushes. No sooner was the first team halfway across than the gunners firing on us also opened up on Desclos's squad. As they approached the brush lines two of Desclos's men went down. By this time, however, we had a clear glimpse of the gun position that was firing on us. Villanueva's squad assaulted it promptly and the NVA not killed by this rush left their guns and moved back north on the double.

PFC Frisby (or Frisbie) was one of those hit by small-arms fire. He sat down hard, flinging his rifle forward as though kicked in the groin. At this time the closest corpsman to my platoon was Doc Washington, a black corpsman from Baltimore who was, at the time, attached to Marv's platoon. When Corporal D's men went down, Washington raced swiftly toward them, moving hunched over with a loose, dodging motion. When he drew within ten meters or so of the wounded men, Washington coiled and sprang through the air, sliding headfirst on his middle through the mud like a clever halfback racing toward daylight. "Two emergency medevacs!" he yelled over his shoulder. "Make that one," he said after checking Hammond.

By the time the shooting stopped, the reliable Washington had gotten hasty tourniquets around Frisby's painful leg wounds and started a plasma IV to help expand the young rifleman's blood volume. With steady fingers the corpsman elevated the plasma jar above the wounded man's body.

From the time he had been wounded Frisby had uttered a series of high, flat shrieks. As the stretcher bearers began lifting him onto a poncho his cries grew in intensity, so I went out to try to comfort him. Just as the stretcher bearers began moving him back to the LZ that Don's platoon had prepared, I reached Frisby and grasped his hand. As I approached, Doc Washington bowed low over the young Marine and said, "Shush, man, the lieutenant's here." Frisby stopped his cries abruptly without a whimper. His breath came in spasmodic heaves, but he could not keep back the tears, inexorable tokens of the torment he was enduring. He squeezed my hand and kept holding it until we placed him aboard the medevac choppers that came before long into the LZ.

While we were waiting for the choppers to arrive I surveyed the wounded from Chris's platoon—five in all. Several of the men were very seriously injured, and Doc Howe had a terrible-looking face wound. Yet the morale of the men could only be described as still strong. And with good reason. The casualty figures for this brief action were two USMC KIA and six WIA; sixteen NVA KIA (confirmed by body count); thirteen KIA probable (by reason of blood marks, severed limbs, and other gruesome details), and thirteen WIA. The list of enemy weapons and equipment captured in the engagement would take several pages to enumerate.

About the time I began to feel satisfied with our unit's achievement, another flight of helicopters came in—the one that would begin lifting out our own dead as well as those of the enemy. As it did so, PFC Holloway, Sergeant Hoole, PFC Jiminez, and Lance Corporal O'Connor carried Lance Corporal Hammond steadily past. His mouth hung open, his once pink face now gray, gaunt, and drawn in the harsh mask of death. As he passed, his powder-blue eyes stared me blankly in the face. For a brief second I stared back and thought *what a bad business this is*, then turned away.

When we got back to our positions at Con Thien that evening, I spoke to Corporal Desclos about not maneuvering his fire teams once we had established contact without providing as much fire support as possible for their movement. As always, Desclos listened quietly. And as with all my young NCOs, he never made the same mistake twice.

Marv received a well-deserved Silver Star for the actions both he and his platoon performed that day. And several of his men also received decorations for heroism. As soon as possible thereafter I wrote Doc Washington up for a Silver Star for coming to Hammond and Frisby's aid while they were still under fire, but so far as I know he did not receive the medal. He probably deserved another one for coming up to save my life several months afterward, but he did not get one on that occasion either.

After I spoke to Desclos, I had the unhappy task of finding an escort home for Hammond and Miller. At that time in the war, at any rate, when a Marine died in combat his body did not go home alone. Generally, the dead man's best friend in the outfit accompanied the body home and served as a military escort who helped to console the family members of the deceased. This provision of escorts placed a strain on undermanned units in the field (the escorts would usually be gone about five days), yet the Marine Corps maintained this practice throughout my tour of duty without my hearing one word of complaint from Marines of any rank. Moreover, in the Marine infantry one knew that, however bad the situation might be, one's buddies would not allow a Marine to die alone.

Of the roughly 2.5 million American servicemen who served in Vietnam, approximately 20 percent, or roughly 600,000, were Marines. Of that number the Marines had over 28 percent of the killed in action and over 33 percent of the wounded who were hospitalized. Of the POWs, less than 5 percent—26 in all—were known to have been Marines.

In contrast the United States Marines took 4,098 prisoners—actual fighting men and not merely detainees—and captured nearly 23,000 weapons, many of which were crew-served. During the six years that Marine infantry battalions were in Vietnam, roughly seven enemy soldiers were killed by Marines for every Marine who lost his life in combat.

On the morning of the twelfth I again awoke feeling that we were headed for action of some kind, and again I was not wrong. After our usual C rations breakfast I joined the other platoon commanders at the company CP, where Captain Getchell gave us our patrol orders for the day. When I returned to my platoon area I assembled and briefed our squad leaders, platoon sergeant, corpsman, and guide. As they were returning to their positions and getting their men saddled up, I swung into my flak jacket, the inside of which in my haste I had neglected to check: *zap*, I was stung by a large scorpion as I buttoned the front of the vest. Instinctively I slapped at the place where I was first bitten and was stung again before the creature finally died. After the second bite, our platoon corpsman, a short, dark, quiet fellow from Houston who wanted to be an undertaker after he was discharged, came over. He examined the bite, looked at the scorpion, wrapped it in skivvie paper, and strongly advised me to go to the battalion aid station right away. The tone of his voice led me to believe the bites might cause a grave reaction.

Feeling woozier with every step, I retched once on the perhaps three-hundred-meter trek to the aid tent and again on the deck as soon as I got inside. I suppose I looked like death on two feet as I entered because a pair of corpsmen moved to support me around the trunk. When they asked what had happened, I presented them with the dead scorpion, about five inches long and still vicious-looking. One corpsman took the lobster-shaped scorpion and placed it in a bottle which he capped and set alongside several others equally long and mean-looking on a dressing table inside the tent. All of them, I was told, were to be shipped back to the States for study in the laboratory.

The corpsmen then urged me to lie down, warned me of the very serious reaction I could expect, and told me I would not be able to go on patrol. *Oh yes I can,* I thought and staggered outside. Near the exit flap, a pale, thin Marine from another company who had apparently sustained a chest wound smiled up from the cot on which he was lying.

I lurched dizzily across the next hundred meters or so until I came within sight of my men. With what must have been a semiconscious act of will, my head began to clear, my stomach grew under control, and my step became surer. I reached the platoon about the time my 1st Squad began moving through the wire on the way out. I gave Sergeant Hoole a "thumbs-up" signal from some distance away and moved him back to the platoon sergeant's position at the rear of the platoon. I was in command again and felt no further illness the rest of the day.

The first mission we were assigned that day was

patrolling the area due south of Con Thien. The terrain at first restricted our movement formation so that we had to employ platoons-in-column, with Don's platoon on the point and mine number two in the formation. We were moving down a narrow trail less than two thousand meters south of our positions when Don's platoon came under light automatic weapons and small-arms fire from what seemed like close range. Gunny Gonzalez, from Weapons Platoon, was just in front of us when the firing began and I heard him yell to his 60 mortarmen, "Get down, dammit! And *get* spread out!"

Don's men were returning fire when Jim Getchell called on the radio to have me move my men up. Pumping my arm with a clenched fist overhead to signal movement at the double, I ran up the narrow trail toward Don's platoon. As I passed I exchanged smiles with Gunny Gonzalez, as if to say "business as usual." When I got up to the CO, he ordered me to have my platoon secure an LZ, which we promptly did. Don's five casualties were quickly carried down from the knoll where they had been hit. When the chopper came in I ordered my squad leaders to keep their heads up in case we had to use suppressing fires to keep the landing zone clear.

The medevac chopper had no sooner lifted out than Jim Getchell shouted a compass heading to me and told me to "move it out as fast as you can." Feeling an apprehension that was not fear, I repeated the azimuth to Desclos, the squad leader nearest to me, and gave him the same instructions the Skipper had just given me. With Corporal D's point man in the lead, Desclos and myself, followed by the rest of our platoon, began running southeast nearly as fast as we could. After about a thousand meters at that pace I felt it was inevitable that we would be ambushed.

As we skirted a hill my radio operator, Meyer, shouted breathlessly to me that the CO said for me to look out for tanks. "Friendly or enemy?" I yelled back over my shoulder. "Friendly," Meyer gasped back a few seconds later. A tank platoon and its infantry platoon cover I soon learned had been ambushed two thousand meters southeast of us. With my platoon on the point the entire way, we reached the besieged units in faster time than I believe we could normally run such a distance in training.

The tank platoon, supported by one undermanned infantry platoon commanded by a young sergeant, had been hit twice on its way to Con Thien. The second attack was a well-planned ambush, with one tank knocked out beyond immediate repair, another temporarily damaged, and many of the supporting infantrymen wounded or killed.

To say the least, the unit we relieved was glad to see our people galloping down the grassy slope toward them. I hustled my platoon into place to secure another LZ right away. My men were winded when they arrived, but as always seemed more than ready to fight. One tank was still aflame, the other had blown at least one track, and casualties were lying or sitting all around the sunlit field as we approached. Our reliable corpsmen set about patching the wounded right away. We received some small-arms and automatic weapons fire in the LZ shortly before the medevac choppers came in, but 3d Platoon laid out excellent suppressing fire and the enemy was forced to withdraw before the helos touched down.

The tank on fire, before long, had its flames extinguished, and within an hour or so the other had had its tracks repaired. With the burned-out tank under tow and the others moving along with our company as security, we escorted the tank platoon back to Con Thien. Before starting out, I cautioned my squad leaders to keep their men at least twenty-five meters away from the tanks since if another mortar attack did come in, shrapnel ricocheting off the hulls would prove deadly at a closer range. We had no contacts on the way back, but at least one tank threw a tread and we had to stop for what seemed a long time as the crews repaired it. Before long Captain Getchell received a much-deserved Silver Star for maneuvering our company to carry out the rescue mission, and for his handling of our successful return with the armor to Con Thien.

On the thirteenth our company did not go on patrol but provided security for the battalion area while companies F and G went out. My light platoon was responsible for covering the entire F Company frontage. Around 6

P.M.—1800 military time—a Huey helicopter gunship that had been flying security for Company F was hit by NVA automatic weapons fire while making a rocket pass in front of our lines. The helo caught fire and careered madly over the CP we occupied on the F Company sector of our lines before falling to earth. With the help of several men from 3d Platoon, the crew got out and the fire was rapidly extinguished. Not one of our men was seriously injured in the incident, although one lieutenant may have been slightly burned. Less than five minutes later, as another gunship flew over the same area, it was also hit. That time I felt sure I had a fix on where the fire had come from and requested an artillery strike on the area. The artillery's fire-for-effect was on target.

We had no enemy contact that night, but just after dark the ARVN forces on the finger of ground on our platoon's left flank evidently became excited and shot off their final protective fires. In the excitement one tank also opened up on our positions, which resulted in one Marine killed from George Burgett's company and one man from my platoon wounded in the legs. The wounded man was a recent replacement whose name I had not even had time to learn.

In a letter to my family on the thirteenth, I noted that we then had thirty-three men, so the casualty reduced our platoon rolls to thirty-two men on the morning of the fourteenth—not a large figure to tackle the mission we soon did. The platoon commanders were summoned early that morning for an attack order. The men were hastily given heli-team assignments for a heliborne assault that lifted out of our company area at 0900. Marv's and Don's platoons along with the company headquarters went in on the assault wave. To my disappointment, 3d Platoon flew out shortly thereafter as the company reserve. Despite the speed with which we had to move out, there was no sense of panic or confusion among any platoon in the company.

The plan was for Company G to fly into a blocking position southwest of us. Hotel Company was to land just north of an abandoned village, Phuong Xuan, where a reconnaissance flight had reported seeing at least a reinforced NVA platoon. As I briefed my squad leaders, I pointed to the area on the map, rehearsed the radio frequencies we would be using, and drew both the frequencies and the landing site coordinates, 124 738, on the plastic battery bag I used for a map cover.

CH-46s flew in to lift 3d Platoon out. The CH-46 helicopter lacked the maneuverability of the UH-34D and may not have withstood damage as well as the 34, but it carried more men and equipment and was therefore better at getting larger units in quickly. The choppers for our wave settled down with an awful roar of wind and splashing water. After we were all buckled into low canvas seats, the 46s took off, tugging slightly a few times under the strain of their battle load and the heavy atmospheric conditions. In a moment we were airborne and droning rapidly northward. Through the circular portholes behind me I could see the assault-wave helos dipping toward the LZ.

Suddenly, we, too, were whipping low over lumpy countryside pockmarked as far as I could see by muddy shell craters. Then our helos swung up again so a flight of jet planes could roar in on a decoy strafing run over an area south of the landing zone. A clever ploy, I thought, one that would perhaps keep the NVA unsuspecting, quite unlike they were when we landed on the first day of the operation. As the choppers from our wave settled into the LZ and I waited for the ramp to go down, I felt that sense of anticipation that was not fear. The truth is, although I hated war—the death, the suffering, and the destruction that it brought—I loved fighting. The excitement, the competition with such high stakes, the sense of camaraderie and the keen awareness that it brings, all served to make combat very compelling to me. I wish I could say otherwise.

Within fifty meters of the LZ one of our assault-wave platoons came upon three thousand rounds of linked machine gun ammunition, so we knew right away that the enemy was nearby. Several correspondents at the battalion CP when the attack order was given flew along with the assault wave into the LZ. One was a stubbily built, middle-age cameraman who I believe worked for one of the three major American networks at the time.

For some inexplicable reason he wore a pink iridescent baseball cap. Gunny Husak and I both watched as the cameraman trundled up the ramp aboard the chopper with Don's platoon. The Gunny and I exchanged eloquent glances, each of us rolling our eyes.

As our chopper wave pulled out of the LZ, the cameraman, his very visible cap still on, was already sprawled motionlessly facedown in the mud. Our unit diary reports that he was wounded at 0945.

When 3d Platoon landed, the other two companies began moving rapidly southward (our LZ was less than one thousand meters below the DMZ). My platoon remained in reserve with Chris's platoon on the east and Don's on the west. The stutter of automatic weapons fire rent the air from the rise of ground just above us. As I sat down to await our orders, the vegetation all around my platoon jumped and twitched from the incoming small-arms fire, but we had no casualties. It was a hot, muggy day, and I squatted down like a baseball catcher to rest and listen to the cracking and buzzing of the overhead fire and the machine gun bullets zipping into the mud above us.

Perhaps because we had so successfully handled many similar engagements before, perhaps also because of the heat of the morning, the situation did not seem serious to me at the time. Slowly but steadily the casualty figures from the attacking platoons rose, so that by the time the CO ordered my platoon forward I believe the Marine casualties on the high ground were two KIA and five WIA. Perhaps it was Captain Getchell's calm voice combined with my feeling of self-confidence, but I did not move my platoon up at first on the double, as I should have, but ambled at the head of my outfit in the direction the fire was coming from. Fortunately perhaps for our company, about thirty-five meters up the slope I encountered Jim Getchell with his sidearm drawn. He looked at me censoriously and asked what was taking us so long—a question that hit its mark. Moved to anger by his just comment, I suddenly got my men cracking in the way that I should have right away.

In seconds our assault line was formed. As I discovered when we moved past him, Marv himself was crouching at the bottom of a huge B-52 bomb crater just ahead of our assault line. He and several others had from this difficult position been fighting off the NVA who were attempting to "finish off" the badly wounded Marines that Marv and a brave handful of volunteers had gone there to protect.

"Squads on line!" I yelled. As soon as the squads were in their places, I designated the men to my left as the base of fire. With the signal, "Commence fire!" I waved our assault force forward, giving Marv and his stalwart men in the crater a big thumbs-up as we sprinted past, our weapons traversing the wood line before us with fire.

Perhaps midway through the assault I must have "snapped out," as they say, since by the time my operator had gotten my attention our assault force had gone much farther south than I had thought. When the word finally got through that we were to hold up, I, my radio operator, and two men from Don's platoon were in a blood-spattered trench line and looking down a hill south of it for additional signs of the enemy that we would have pursued into the South China Sea had we not been called back. On our return we counted NVA bodies and picked up as many weapons and as much equipment as we could carry in order to have it all helilifted out of the LZ.

I received a medal for my actions in the assault, although Chris and his fellow rescuers deserved medals more than I did. They must have snatched their wounded and dead buddies from within ten meters of the NVA soldiers. Whether my citation was deserved I cannot say. What I must say, however, is that upon that field I came to learn for good what I have tried many times to deny, that there lives within me the predatory animal that needs only the necessity to stir it into snarling life.

Casualties for the day's actions were two USMC KIA and five WIA, the cameraman, listed as wounded, eight heat casualties from our tactical movement the four thousand meters south to Con Thien, and one snakebite victim. Enemy casualties were eight KIA confirmed, five probable, seven WIA confirmed, and one WIA captured. Again we had seized several large hills of weapons, ammunition, documents, and other equipment—a haul too large even for us to itemize before we had it lifted out in several helicopter flights to Dong Ha.

The unit diary for October 15 indicates that our company did not go on patrol that day, but we were not inactive. As on the handful of fifty-four other days during Prairie when our company was not on patrol, 3d Platoon had many other duties. All night the men of course were on 50 percent alert. And with our small force of some thirty-three men, we had to cover the entire F Company frontage during the portion of the day that F Company was on patrol.

Since our positions were so close to enemy territory it was imperative that all our men be awake and alert on post at all times. Of all the days and nights I checked posts when we were on Prairie, I remember finding only one man asleep when he was not supposed to be, and that one I found sleeping twice on the same day, one of the handful of days that our platoon was covering the F Company sector. The mist had descended in several heavy layers that day, and that would have made getting "air" in as closely as we liked or needed very difficult. I was always especially concerned about security on days when visibility was poor because bringing in supporting arms in such weather—not to mention medevac choppers—was usually more difficult.

The first time I found the Marine in our platoon asleep on post I dressed him down vituperatively. Even before I left, though, I felt I had not shaken him sufficiently so, after I checked the other posts, I returned to his position. The positions on either side of him were barely visible through the mist, yet he was asleep again. I hauled him roughly out of the foxhole and as I did slammed him hard enough with my forearm that he knew I meant it when I told him he had better stay awake. He glared at me in a surly fashion for a few seconds as I chewed him out, but I soon stared him down. That time when I left the position I felt there would be no more sleeping on post by this man. We checked him scrupulously thereafter that day and found him always awake and alert. I believe the young man fell asleep twice on post that same day because he was just exhausted.

Around the thirteenth our platoon began receiving

one or two replacements a day, among them a senior staff sergeant, Burns, who, until he was wounded, replaced Sergeant Hoole as my platoon sergeant. Hoole for the time being then moved down to be the platoon guide.

Sergeant Burns (who was by November promoted to gunnery sergeant as I recall) was an angular, black-haired and dark-eyed Marine whose home state was Ohio. He was married and as I recall had several children. Roughly thirty-five years old, about six-feet-one, and with a five o'clock shadow just after he shaved, Burns had a deep voice with a country twang. He also had a prominent Adam's apple that was very active when he spoke.

A good Marine staff NCO supplemented a young officer's shortcomings with his own fund of experience and did that in an unobtrusive manner. In areas where they were more knowledgeable than I was, both Rockdale and Burns helped this lieutenant by referring to the solutions to problems as if I already knew what they were. When he joined us, Gunny Burns was not especially adept with a map and compass, but by moving with us in the field he quickly remedied those deficiencies. From the time he came to 3d Platoon he had a sound knowledge of basic aspects of handling a rifle platoon and, like myself, was strong at "rope work" and stream-crossing techniques—expertise that proved immediately useful on our patrols.

Gunny Burns's knowledge of field fortifications and of ways to reinforce defensive positions was far superior to mine. Like Rockdale, Burns's demeanor was on most occasions tactful; and the silences of both staff NCOs were beyond praise.

Burns, I believe now, saw as soon as he reported to 3d Platoon our need to fortify positions much better than they were, and after the first few days with us began putting the men to work to improve our defenses. Since the entire platoon patrolled an average of eight hours a day seven days a week (not to mention many night ambushes), and since after dark we were always on at least 50 percent alert, the only time we could improve our lines was during the few hours of daylight after we returned from our daytime patrols and before darkness.

Platoon Commander James J. Kirschke (far right) with shrapnel-scarred helmet. In the immediate background, members of his platoon, 3d Platoon, Hotel Company, 2d Battalion, Fifth Marines, First Marine Division, are mounting up to move out. Behind them is the much fought over tributary of the Song Thu Bon. Phu Lac (6), 1967. (Larry Burrows Estate)

Capt. Jerry Doherty leads Capt. James A. Graham and two radio operators across the then shallow Song Ba Ren during a dry season firefight outside An Hoa, 1967. (Author's collection)

Marines of Hotel Company, 2d Battalion, Fifth Marines, at a prayer service led by the battalion chaplain, Father Ed Kane. Shortly after the service, they embarked on a company-size nighttime patrol into the DMZ to try to recover a downed American aircraft and its crew. October 1966. (Larry Burrows Estate)

81 Millimeter Mortar Platoon, uncovered H&S Company, 3d Battalion, Fifth Marines, First Marine Division. Camp Schwab, Okinawa, March 1966. (Keystone Portrait Studio)

James Kirschke standing beside 3d Platoon, H Company, 2/5, headquarters, Con Thien, just south of the DMZ. October 1966. (Author's collection)

1st Lts. Terry Ebbert, Echo Company commander, 2/5; Marvin "Chris" Christians, 1st Platoon commander, Hotel Company, 2/5; and Sam Williams, platoon commander, India Company, 3/5, at An Hoa combat base, January 1967. All these officers were wounded in action more than once on this tour of duty in Vietnam. Captain Ebbert eventually lost a lung from a .50-caliber machine-gun bullet wound in his last battle. (Author's collection)

1st Lt. Donald Vogelgesang, weapons platoon commander, L Company, 3/5; rifle platoon commander, H Company, 2/5; and then S-2 (intelligence officer), 2/5; squatting as he holds a disarmed Russian mine. An Hoa, December 1966. (Author's collection)

1st Lt. Michael Litwin. Mike at first acted as executive officer for H Company, 2/5, and then took over as commander of one of our company's three maneuver platoons. During 1966–67, H Company, 2/5, never had the manpower to have a weapons platoon commander, and the company had an executive officer only for several weeks during this militarily arduous period. An Hoa combat base, 1967. (Author's collection)

Capts. James A. Graham and Jerry Doherty outside An Hoa, 1967. Captain Doherty was an outstanding company commander of Hotel Company. Jim Graham, who later earned the Medal of Honor while commanding F Company, 2/5, spent two months with H Company to "learn the lines." (Author's collection)

2d Lt. O. K. Batte, Jr., world class artillery forward observer with Hotel Company, 2/5, near An Hoa, 1967. (Author's collection)

Capts. Jim Graham and Jerry Doherty. Southwest of An Hoa, 1967. (Author's collection)

Hotel Company, 2/5, headquarters position, Con Thien. North Vietnam is visible in the background. An M-41 Walker Bulldog tank sits in front of the position in support. November 1966. (Author's collection)

Except for the rare dirt road, this terrain is fairly typical of the An Hoa basin H Company regularly patrolled from late November 1966 through 1967. (Author's collection)

Eastern segment of the An Hoa region, including Phu Lac (6), as seen from a USMC artillery spotter plane, 1967. (Author's collection)

O. K. Batte adjusting close in final protective fires outside An Hoa, 1967. (Author's collection)

Platoon Sergeant Ronald Hoole, 3d Platoon, H Company, with the rest of the platoon just before the author's last patrol. Phu Lac (6), 1967. (Larry Burrows Estate)

The author receiving a medal from a Marine brigadier general at the U.S. Naval Hospital in Philadelphia in the spring of 1967, four months after being wounded and well after he had begun to regain weight and recover. His mother, Margaret, is to the right. (Author's collection)

Gunny Burns used these hours wisely. "Lieutenant," often followed by a long pause in which he uncovered and stared into his helmet or passed his hand over his five o'clock shadow, "ah figgered ya maht want ta move thet left flank gun up a skosh ta cover thet dead space front a Third Squad a bit better. Shell ah have 'em move it up a bit this evenin'?" And another day he would suggest the placement of claymores (directional mines) in front of each of our listening posts as soon as they were set in. Or, "Scuse me, Sir, but I been thinkin'. If we wuz ta dig *two* alternate positions for each primary one, then we'd be twaace as hard ta pin down. Shall ah have the men hop-to on the extra ones?"

Virtually all of Burns's defensive schemes were good ones. At least partially because of them, the enemy was never able to attack us effectively once we were set in. But these working details also took a toll of fatigue in their execution.

I cannot emphasize too much how hard the men in the infantry worked in Vietnam. As I indicated before, rifle platoons almost always operated at less than half the manpower they were supposed to. The number of men in the field with us fluctuated between twenty-one and thirty-seven, yet the TO (table of organization) strength of a reinforced rifle platoon in combat was supposedly sixty-three.

We always trusted more in courage and discipline than in sheer numbers and we always had the necessary confidence to succeed in whatever ground contacts we had with the enemy. Yet the Vietnam War was one that for the Marine infantryman had no front lines with secure areas behind them and very little "slack." With the exception of one five-day R&R, the men were usually in potentially dangerous situations for their full thirteen months (the Marines' standard tour of duty was thirteen months, but in our company we had a policy that the enlisted men did not have to go on patrol during their last month, but rather could stay at the company CP and help with administrative details), so that while we were not always directly engaged with the enemy, we were always at least potentially so. We were at all times therefore heavily committed. Day and night patrols, at least 50 percent alert every night, listening posts, observations posts, innumerable work parties, and informal classes when time permitted all made for a very tired, understrength platoon that was expected to do—and always successfully did—at least as much as fully manned rifle platoons were supposed to do.

Among the replacements we received around mid-October were PFC Charlie Spain and a corporal named Lewis. Spain had just been released from the brig. His home-town was Pontiac, Michigan, and he was about twenty-five or twenty-six when he joined us at Con Thien. It was ru-mored, and I later learned the rumors were correct, that Spain had for some time had family problems that I believe would have driven a far less aggressive person into difficul-ties. As long as I was 3d Platoon commander, however, Spain was nothing but a first-rate Marine. Before many days with our unit he began volunteering to take the point on pa-trols, and thereby had a hand in starting the only quarrels we ever had among our squad leaders, since each squad wanted to take the point on patrols. I stopped the disagreements promptly by establishing a fairly inflexible rotation system as soon as Corporal Lewis had gotten well "snapped in."

Lewis was about twenty-four years of age when he joined 3d Platoon. About the same size as myself, he had a deep voice, dark hair, and a large, dark, bushy mus-tache. When he joined us around October 20, he was a very senior corporal—with more time in grade than ei-ther Desclos or Villanueva, as I recall—so I felt con-strained to make him a squad leader (finally by then, we had enough men to make three light maneuver squads).

Our immediate problem, however, was that Corporal Lewis had virtually no infantry experience beyond Infantry Training Regiment, which he had attended just af-ter boot camp. He had been "shipped" to us from the air wing, which had transferred him ("sent me to Siberia," as he deadpanned to me not long after he reported) presum-ably because he had been a disciplinary problem. Since he evidently had a Page 11 of some length, Top Peabody did what I requested and sent the corporal to 3d Platoon.

When I ascertained how little Corporal Lewis knew about the infantry, I instinctively rolled up my sleeves and

said to myself, "Now here is a challenge that we welcome."
Enlisting the assistance of Sergeants Burns, Hoole, and
Honeycutt as well as Corporals Villanueva, Desclos, and
Jackson, we set out immediately to give Lewis a crash course
in his spare time that was a cram version of NCO school.

We began at the beginning. First we made sure he knew
the basic types of patrols. Then we rehearsed our hand and
arm signals, radio, and other communications procedures
with him. We also conducted a brief "school" in terrain appreciation, map reading, and direction finding. In order to
help assure that Lewis would be able to understand terrain
that he had studied from the map only, we had him examine a two-thousand-meter grid section from the map that
we were using and then build a three-foot-by-three-foot
terrain model of the area, which showed in detail the valleys, draws, rivers, streams, ridges, and hilltops as well as
some indication of the types of visibility one might expect
to have in each area. The advantage of performing that
type of exercise several times was that after each terrain
mock-up Lewis did, he was able to traverse on foot the land
the map represented since we always arranged to have him
do mock-ups of areas that we would soon patrol.

Next we went over ambush techniques and formations
of movement. Sergeant Hoole and I worked hard to
teach Lewis how to orient himself on the ground, both
day and night, how to employ offset navigational techniques, shoot compass resections, and use map and compass to move his squad to predesignated positions.

After these subjects were assimilated, we passed along
tips about calling in supporting arms. With his cool sense
of humor, solid disposition, and understandable motiva-
tions, Corporal Lewis absorbed all these lessons with incredible rapidity. He was a natural leader to begin with,
and by the end of October I considered him altogether
"snapped in" and as capable a squad leader as I have seen.

I believe it was on the sixteenth of October that our
company went on patrol right up to the DMZ, and the
following incidents—perhaps understandably not
recorded in our unit diaries—took place. We were moving northeastward on either side of a secondary road

that extended into the DMZ. My platoon was on the point with the company CP group not far behind us. My two lead squads had moved up just south of the DMZ without having made contact.

It was a bright, clear afternoon. I was moving just to the right of the road and could see a new, black Marine fireteam (FT) leader in Desclos's squad, but because of the thickness of the undergrowth he was moving in I could not see Desclos himself. The latter was moving along with Gunny Burns and his other two team leaders through dense vine and thorn scrub. The Gunny had his radio operator with him, but I wanted to maintain radio silence as much as possible, and did not use the radio to tell Desclos to hold it up but signaled his new FT leader to do so. I also indicated by hand and arm signal to the new man that he should pass my signal along to his left flank man, who would have been within sight of Desclos. We learned some fifteen minutes later that the signal had not been passed: the new FT leader thought I was just waving "Hi!"

I had held up with the two squads I had on my side of the road and the part of Desclos's fire team that I could see on the other. About half the men with us seemed to be gulping water from their canteens when several bursts of North Vietnamese semiautomatic weapons fire rent the air at what seemed like half the distance to the Ben Hai (north of which was North Vietnam). Desclos's squad and Sergeant Burns with him had kept going and gotten into a firefight about three-quarters of a mile into the DMZ.

I yelled to the CO what I surmised had happened and called back to my men, "Let's go, third platoon! Move it out!" I had hardly uttered a word when Sergeant Hoole slapped the rifle out of Meyer's hand and sprinted up the road by himself, his weapon at the ready. At one point I passed him, but when I stopped to direct Meyer and several other Marines behind him to chuck grenades into each of the enormous tunnels leading south that we saw along the road (some DMZ!), Hoole zipped past me as though on an accelerating motor scooter. About a quarter of a mile into the DMZ both Hoole and myself began yelling, "Desclos! Sarn't Burns!" as loudly as we could. When we drew abreast of the place where we thought the firing was coming from, Sergeant Hoole began crashing into the thick brush to get to our men. I restrained him in the only way I knew how: "Sarn't Hoole. Get back on that road and act like the platoon guide."

"Aye, aye, Sir," he replied with strong emotion in his voice.

I had gone through the heavy bush for about seventy-five meters, calling as loudly as I could for Corporal Desclos and Sergeant Burns when all of a sudden I heard the heavy crunching sounds of a large force moving in my direction. I still had one frag grenade with me and three clips of forty-five ammunition. Not one of my men was as yet in sight behind me. As I began to assume a firing position, I said a quick prayer and thought, *I will take at least a dozen NVA out with me if I have to go.*

I took aim at the brush where the crunching noise was growing steadily louder, and my heartbeat seemed to grow even louder still. Suddenly a hand reached out and parted the foliage some twenty meters to my front. I saw a pale, nearly yellow face with sores all over it wearing a helmet with a camouflaged cover and weeds and bushes sticking out all over. Corporal Desclos had never looked so good! Gunny Burns's face also soon appeared, and not far behind him, PFC Spain.

I felt like rushing forward to embrace every one of them, but it was not the place for this kind of show of emotion. We moved quickly back to the road by the same route I had taken in. By this time most of 3d Platoon had arrived, and we moved the whole platoon back to safer territory as rapidly as possible while still retaining a tactical formation. When the whole platoon had passed, I left the DMZ myself. I received many looks of appreciation for going into the bush after Desclos and Burns from the men in all three squads as they moved past me southward to rejoin our company.

On the morning of the seventeenth our company "saddled up" early and patrolled all day, covering a large area southeast of Con Thien. We made no contact that day.

That night one of my new men was wounded by a newly arrived Marine in an accidental shooting when they were on post. On the night it happened I was exhausted. I had wrapped myself up in my rubberized poncho and felt in my nostrils the moisture from the elephant grass behind our position. I quickly slipped into a deep sleep. *Blam!* Right away I knew what it was. I was up and running straight toward the position, slapping on my helmet as I ran. The wounded man, shot in the legs, was screaming loudly.

"It was an accident, Sir!" exclaimed the Marine whose weapon had fired.

"That's okay," I said. "Clear and lock your weapon. Put your rifle at port arms and walk back and forth in front of the position. Watch out that way for the enemy." Then I turned to the wounded man and reassured him that he would be all right. Our corpsman soon slid into the position.

The corpsman from Houston got to work in his typically quiet, professional manner, cutting the man's trousers, putting tourniquets on his legs, and getting one bottle of plasma started. I held a flashlight for him with one hand and with the other held the wounded man's hand until his screaming stopped and his breathing relaxed somewhat. Before long Gunny Husack had guided the medevac chopper in by using strobe lights to signal where we were. The helo set down only a short jog behind our positions. Several of us carried the wounded man as carefully as we could back to the chopper. As soon as we placed him aboard, it lifted away; one light inside was all that was visible to us as it disappeared into the black sky.

By that time in my tour I was often nauseated by fatigue when I checked posts, yet I knew that it was an important duty. I used my post-checking rounds as an opportunity to see that the men at each position were awake and alert. I also tried to leave every position knowing that I had encouraged the men there to be ready to respond to an attack if they had to.

Despite the fatigue, I found leadership in combat to be not as difficult as it might seem; I felt buoyed up by a sense of responsibility for my men. This sense of responsibility was for me made the stronger by incidents such as the following.

On a very dark night around the third week of October, I was checking posts at Con Thien. It was raining hard ("bucketing," as the troops used to say) and there was little visibility, so I was able to crawl right up behind the position near the center of our "line" that was occupied by Charlie Spain and a new PFC named Pitts. I believe Pitts was officially on watch (Spain seldom seemed to sleep and was usually awake whenever I checked posts). Shortly after I arrived, Pitts whispered to Spain, "How's this lieutenant?"

"A good man," Spain responded in a whisper.

"What? How d'ya mean?"

"He's got balls."

"How's that?" Pitts asked.

"The other day our squad got lost with Gunny Burns in the DMZ. Got into a firefight. Lieutenant got there *way* before anybody else. When the shit hits the fan, the Lieutenant's gonna *be* there."

I am sure this conversation was not a charade, and that neither man ever knew I overheard the exchange. I left without saying a word. I doubt that any man, crawling through the mud on such a cold, wet night, on such a barren hill, has ever felt so warm inside as I did as I made my way to our next post.

For several nights prior to the nineteenth, B-52 strikes pounded the area just west of us where the southern line of the DMZ swung south of Con Thien. On those nights the first sounds we heard were loud, buzzing noises as the planes approached. On the first night they came, as tired as I was I bolted awake when I first heard them. Then they released their bombs, five-hundred-pounders. Each strike seemed to deliver hundreds of the bombs, so for the duration of each attack the earth shuddered continually beneath us. The din was deafening. When I thought of the devastating effect the strikes could be having on enemy soldiers who might have been attempting to infiltrate, however, after the first night I found both the noise and the ground shaking from these attacks consoling. I believe I slept more soundly on the nights when the 52s thundered in. Except for the night a five-hundred-pounder was dropped by accident less than two hundred meters from our platoon "CP," that is, the short, narrow trench where I slept.

On October 19, I received word from the CO that our

company would be running an ambush along the "elephant trail" that night and that 3d Platoon would be on the point while moving to the ambush site. The Marines in our battalion at the time called the track the elephant trail because Company F had seen evidence that the NVA had sent supply-laden elephants down it. Since one of the other two companies that were with us on Con Thien was going to be patrolling very near the trail that day, I arranged to have our guide, Sergeant Hoole, go along with that company so he could familiarize himself with the terrain during daylight hours.

Sergeant Hoole had an excellent terrain memory, but as always I checked his guidance to the trail periodically with my luminescent compass dial. Several hours after our patrol had left Con Thien that evening we reached the trail. In the growing darkness Hoole signaled for us to hold up and turned quietly to beckon me forward. When I approached, he whispered, "This is the elephant trail, Sir."

"Are you sure?"

Pointing to a huge pile of dung on the deck at our feet, he said, "Yes. Look."

Sensing on some level how he would respond, I said, "How do you know it's elephant dung?" With a note of exasperation in his raspy whisper, he replied, "See how big it is, Lieutenant!"

The terrain along that trail was more desolate than any I hope to see again. The ground was churned up for several hundred meters to our southwest with craters gouged out by the B-52 strikes. The air surrounding the trail was fetid with the smell of rank vegetation, blasted trees, decomposing NVA bodies, and blasted elephant carcasses, their bodies scattered around the rims of the craters. Arms, legs, trunks, hooves, tusks, and other body parts could be seen rotting in the dank jungle on either side of the trail. The mostly intact NVA bodies I was able to see seemed swelled to one-third more than life size. I have always had an exceptionally strong stomach, and yet the smell in that area was almost overwhelming to me and many of the men with us.

We set into our ambush around 10 P.M. Not too long after this a merciful breeze began to blow so that enough of the fetid smell around our positions drifted away to make the air at least bearable. Before long all was silent except for the sound of the wind running through the torn trees.

We made no contact with a living enemy that night. As we were moving around one crater when going back in, however, the ground gave way beneath my feet. To stop myself from sliding in I fell sideways against the inner rim of the crater, where my hand made contact with a slimy object that I could not, perhaps fortunately, make out. The heavy smell of death stayed with me for many hours afterward.

It is difficult to describe the conditions at Con Thien during the monsoon season. As I gazed around our platoon position most mornings I saw shell craters, cartridge boxes, slick trails, greasy sandbags, zigzagging trenches, foxholes, mounds of mud, coils of wire, strands of piano wire and "tanglefoot," flares, booby-trapped hand grenades and directional mines, slit-trench latrines (we had two that were not quite far enough behind our platoon CP), and, when the weather was warm, an abundance of flies and mosquitoes. Our positions were permeated by the reek of lime when the air was still.

Aside from a few water buffaloes the only wildlife I saw at Con Thien were members of the abundant local rat population. On several nights when we were in the field a few pranced across the shallow trench where I slept, scampering on delicate paws up my front and at one time over my face. I found even those small signs of nonhuman life reassuring.

Within a week of the outset of Prairie my utilities developed a sour, stale, saline smell which wafted up to my nostrils whenever my flak jacket opened enough to allow my odors to breathe up at me. We worked hard the entire time on that operation: patrolling incessantly, sleeping little, eating C rations almost exclusively, and working to reinforce our positions during much of our "rest time." We did not receive fresh boots and utilities until about a month into Prairie, and we had no "free time" to wash, and no place to do so the entire time of the operation. We did, however, manage time, almost daily, to shave.

Our infantry companies in the field averaged four nonbattle casualties a day. Snake and scorpion bites, malaria, hepatitis, immersion foot, severe colds, bronchitis, pneumonia, accidental shootings or other wounds sustained by friendly fire, severe falls, and bruises and cuts incurred on patrol were the kinds of nonbattle casualties one could figure to have in a rifle company operating in the field in Vietnam.

On many days most of the men looked like zombies as they filed through the wire to go on patrol (Corporal Desclos looked that way most of the time), yet I do not recall a single man in 3d Platoon coming down with a cold, flu, or respiratory ailment. That was especially remarkable since we spent so much time in the cold dampness, often without adequate protective clothing. Moreover, almost from the first, no man in our platoon consented to evacuation to treat a nonbattle injury unless he had been personally ordered to do so by me, and even then there were refusals. Before long that attitude extended to rather serious battle injuries as well. I believe the imminence of danger caused us to experience an intensity of life. We developed a camaraderie difficult to capture in words, but the essence of which stays with me even today.

My men looked out for one another as though they were brothers. It may be significant that, on more than one occasion since my discharge from my long stay in the hospital, I have had offers of physical assistance from men who I felt sure were Marine veterans of Vietnam (remarks they made in passing often indicated this was so), and these men—black, white, and Hispanic—all used the term "brother" in offering to help.

I have sometimes heard it said that the Marine Corps was "racist." From my experience in the Corps, however, I would say the racial harmony there was far better than I have seen in any civilian institution before or since.

Of the men in the two platoons I commanded in Vietnam, probably 25 percent would be considered nonwhite. Yet on the rare occasions when the color of a man's skin was mentioned, it was always done so either approvingly or in a jocular way. One day, for instance, when 3d Platoon was filing through the wire in front of our positions at Con Thien, the troops were laughing and joking with Meyer, the Doc, and Sergeant Hoole, all of whom were white. Several of the black troops (we had seven at that time) made jokes to Meyer about his being a paleface, and PFC Redeye (a Native American from upstate New York) added a few words for emphasis. These remarks drew laughter from the troops. Then Meyer made another jibe at PFC Isaacs, who was black, then turned with a broad grin and remarked to Sergeant Hoole, "We have damned fine black troops in this platoon. Ya know, Sarn't Hoole?"

"Damned *straight!*" Hoole said as he turned to shuffle toward us. The entire CP group smiled with him by way of response.

About this time Corporal Bell and Isaacs slapped each other's hands ("Give me *ten*, my man") and both ran up to Meyer to slap his upturned hands and embrace him, radio and all, lifting him off the ground the way athletes sometimes do when one of their teammates has made a great play.

In late October or early November, on a platoon-size combat patrol southwest of Con Thien, one of our new men, PFC Jones, sustained a serious ankle sprain. This Jones was a tall, sturdily built, quietly self-effacing, married Marine from Chicago. Since our platoon had a much smaller PFC whose name was also Jones, we called the Chicago one Big Jones.

We had just begun moving up a narrow defile when he stepped into an unseen hole (in that terrain amazingly easy to do), and in trying to regain his balance he very nearly fell into a twenty-foot-deep ravine less than two feet to his right. I saw him fall and moved up quickly to check him out. For Jones, walking the rest of the day would be impossible; he was made dizzy by the severe pain and could hardly stand.

I knew that the ground between where we were and where we had to be by nightfall was rough: uneven terrain covered with high, thick thornbushes. The NVA would not be expecting us to come through that kind of ground cover, but it was the type of terrain they might choose to hide in. For several tactical reasons I believed we should not call in a medevac chopper unless we really had to. So I hefted Jones onto my back and carried him piggyback for a long trek that muggy afternoon. I did that to set an example for subsequent carriers, whether individual Marines or teams of up to four at a time. But my carrying Jones also, I figured right away even then, would likely have some other reinforcing effects, morale-wise, in our platoon, and I surmised correctly.

A well-developed sense of humor probably is a supreme asset in most occupations, but for a Marine infantryman in Vietnam it was especially so. After a night of heavy rainfall everyone's spirits were lifted when they saw our riflemen emerge, dripping muddy water, from their foxholes. Several troops would usually exclaim something like "Good-*morning*, Vietnam! It is great to be *green!*"

Among the men who probably did the most to sustain the platoon's morale were Lance Corporals Bell, Frazell, and Ybarra. Ybarra was a quiet, bearish-looking Marine from New Mexico whose nickname, of course, was Yogi Bear. Kent Frazell, who walked the point with Ybarra when Villanueva's squad had that duty, was a well-muscled, curly-haired Marine from rural Illinois. Those two, working the point together, were a sight to watch: each moved as if he were an extension of the other. They studied the territory ahead and covered each other very effectively.

Corporal Bell was a pleasant, courageous, black Marine from Mississippi who lives in Birmingham, Alabama. He had a high-pitched voice, a young Jackie Robinson face, and was built like a small college noseguard. When our situation was not strictly "tactical," he usually found ways to lift everybody's spirits. It seemed as though the darker the weather and the more tired everyone else, the brighter and more ebullient Bell became. I recall one dismal, rainy morning when we were preparing to go on patrol, watching Bell with Ybarra, Kent Frazell, and the members of Bell's fire team. Bell's thick legs were stamping, his body swaying to a song that he belted out as he swung into his flak jacket, buttoned it, and swept up his M-14 without losing one beat of the rhythm of his bawdy song, the humorous lyrics of which were directed at Yogi and Frazell. The latter started to respond, then just smiled and said, "Bell, you sonofabitch."

As a platoon commander I considered mail call a very important time. As soon as our platoon's mail came in I checked through it, making note of who was receiving letters, cards, and packages, who was not, and who the senders were. I usually then either handed out the mail myself or had Sergeant Hoole do it. Either way I always tried to gauge the men's responses to mail call.

One thing that struck me soon after I had taken command of 3d Platoon was the relative absence of mail. It seemed, too, that some of the men who had the biggest problems received the smallest amount of mail. I set out to change that situation at the first opportunity.

I wrote to several of the most charitable friends I knew from my college years and informed them of the situation. My friends, whom I do not believe I ever adequately thanked, responded warmly. Within a week they had written back to ask me for a platoon roster. As soon as I sent this, they launched what they called Operation Send-a-Card. Within two weeks all of our platoon members began receiving a flood of warm letters and packages of goodies from people—mostly from the Philadelphia area, but many from elsewhere—who wanted to correspond with our men. Thereafter we had no more empty mail calls.

Another factor which I believe had a great deal to do with the high morale in our unit was the close proximity of our chaplain and the frequency with which church services were held, even when we were at Con Thien. At Sunday Mass and at Protestant and Jewish services, one would often see more than one hundred Marines in uncovered silence or reading from prayer books as Father Kane or another chaplain led the ceremonies. And some of the men seemed to go to whatever service was announced.

Although often I have not acted as though it did, religion has meant a great deal to me for most of my life. At Con Thien I went to Mass and Confession nearly as frequently as I could. I sought the comfort of feeling close to God, since I knew that at any moment I might find myself leaving this earth for good.

At the end of each Confession, Father Kane asked me sincerely to say a prayer for him. Perhaps on those rainy evenings when he knelt behind our positions to hear the men's Confessions, he had a prevision of the crisis he would soon face. On October 27, Father Ed Kane was severely wounded by sniper fire while giving the Last Rites to several dying Marines from George Burgett's company. He was paralyzed by his injuries, and their severity would almost certainly have killed a man of lesser strength.

On the same day Father Kane was wounded, his replacement joined us. Father Mechan was a modest Catholic priest, in his late thirties, from the Boston area. He was still with our battalion at the time I was wounded, and till that time had helped the morale and welfare of our men greatly. To the best of my knowledge Father Mechan rotated out of our battalion without having been wounded. His replacement, Father Capadanno, was first wounded and then killed in a battle in early spring. When Father Capadanno was killed, he was performing the same work of mercy for members of Company F that Father Kane had done for the men of that company in late October near the DMZ. Father Capadanno was awarded the Medal of Honor posthumously.

From about the third week in October until we left Con Thien for An Hoa, our normal patrol procedure was for the company to go out, cautiously, perhaps three thousand meters from the battalion position. There we would set up a company patrol base. One platoon would generally set up as security for the company command group and be available as a reaction force, while the other two platoons patrolled independently around the patrol base. That system allowed us to cover a great deal of ground every day, and yet the maneuvering platoons were less likely to encounter a force that was larger than they could handle.

Around 10:45 on 22 October, while conducting a patrol out of our combat base, we made contact with an estimated NVA squad approximately five thousand meters southeast of Con Thien. We took them under fire and saw one enemy fall, but were not able to capture his weapon or retrieve the body. After that 3d Platoon surrounded the hamlet, Phu Phuong in Quang

Tri Province, and Marv Christians's and Don Vogelge-sang's platoons searched it thoroughly but were unable to reestablish contact.

That afternoon, with my platoon on the point, we returned to Con Thien. As always we moved back by a different route from the one we had taken on the way out. Our point, which was moving just off the junction of a trail and a loose-surface road, received two long bursts of automatic weapons fire at close range, and I thought, here goes another ambush as I sprinted forward. Ybarra and Kent Frazell returned fire and assaulted in the direction of the gun, but the NVA had already withdrawn to the southeast. We made no contact on the twenty-third. On the morning following, Don's platoon and mine were running patrols out of a patrol base some five thousand meters southeast of Con Thien. Corporal Desclos's squad was on the point for our platoon and Spain was point man for the squad.

The first signs of trouble were booby-trapped rocket rounds and Chicom (Chinese Communist) hand grenades that we discovered on either side of the trail. As we prepared to blow them, PFC Spain moved ahead, suddenly stopped, and gave the rifle signal that meant he had spotted the enemy straight ahead. The two of us moved up quickly to take a look and saw seven well-equipped NVA moving steadily along, skirting a wood line about one hundred meters away. I signaled two squads into a skirmish line and had them lay down a heavy fire.

The NVA took off, hunched over at the double, our fire spitting up the paddy water behind them. I raced up to the left flank squad and snatched the handset from Meyer. Just as I did this I stepped off a steep, grass-concealed drop in the ground and fell backward, pulling Meyer, the handset, and the radio he wore down with me. Within seconds the NVA had disappeared into heavily wooded high ground. We had not hit one of them!

Our machine guns misfired, as did our one and only grenade launcher. The riflemen had without exception failed to run up the battle sights on their M-14s that morning, so all of their rounds were short of their fleeing targets. Under the circumstances I perhaps had the best chance of hitting them, but I was too concerned with reporting our contact right away and neglected to fire. That had to be one of the few days that neither I nor any of my squad leaders inspected the men before we left our positions. And that failure led directly to seven NVA probably escaping who never should have.

I say "probably escaping," since I shortly afterward called in an artillery strike on the wooded area where the enemy disappeared. As always I needed only one adjusting round to get the "arty" (artillery) aimed where I thought it should be. I requested a white-phosphorous adjusting round, since the "Willie Peter" was much easier to spot.

It had been raining steadily all morning, and I knew that the 105 battery firing the mission was the one on Con Thien. Since it was wet and we were almost precisely on the gun–target line, I figured the chances of having a short round land among us were considerable. I called in the mission from a knoll where my field of observation was quite good. After the adjustment mission, I drew the three squads around the platoon CP (where I was) in a 360-degree defense. As we were awaiting the fire-for-effect, I looked around at the dispositions of the squads and noticed that Corporal Lewis's men were bellied out pretty far. Acting on the hunch that we might get a short round that would eliminate a whole squad, I had Lewis draw his men up "just in case."

Just as I said that I heard the first popping noises of the rounds coming out of the 105s at Con Thien. "Aye, aye, Sir," Corporal Lewis responded, and he pulled his men in about fifty meters. I turned back to observe the fire-for-effect.

Eight rounds were fired. First four, then three came chuffing overhead to impact on the designated target in beautifully tight concentrations. The eighth, however, came in with a dreadful *whizz, whistle, whang!*—a short round dropped right where Corporal Lewis's men had been before he moved them. I turned to Lewis but before I could say a word, he stood with the widest smile and stretched a big thumbs-up. I do not believe we exchanged a word; our communication was perfect.

Our company made contact with small NVA units

three more times that day. On one of them, Don's platoon badly wounded an NVA and sent him out on a medevac chopper that we were able to get in despite the apparently socked in weather.

Our unit diary entry for that date shows no USMC KIAs, but I believe it was that same afternoon that a Marine from one of the other two platoons, one of the best-liked men in our company, was shot and killed. While we were awaiting a medevac helo to take him out, both Spain and Sergeant Honeycutt spotted an NVA maneuvering behind a small herd of water buffalo not far from the village where we had taken our KIA.

"Make sure he's not a civilian," I told them, since we were very near one of the few inhabited villages in the area at the time. No sooner had I said these words than both men fired, the M-79 and the M-14 rounds striking the soldier in the head.

One of our favorite tactics was to drop off a fire team on our way back in from patrol since the NVA more often than not attacked Marine units when we were withdrawing. On the evening that action occurred, Lance Corporal Bell's fire team volunteered to provide a stay-behind ambush that would rejoin our platoon within two hours if no contact was made.

On the morning of the twenty-fifth I came down with a bad case of the chills, but after a few hours' rest and some hot beef stew and coffee I was able to make our patrol that day. In a letter I wrote my mother that evening I mentioned that while checking posts the night before, "I fell in a foxhole filled with water and got sopping. The sentinel on post checked a snicker and I emerged spouting water, helmet askew, trying to maintain the posture of an officer." The special dousing may have accounted for the chills the next morning.

During the last week of October we ran many company- and platoon-size night ambush patrols. On our way to one of them, on October 26, we spotted three NVA with semi-automatic weapons running across a trail about fifteen hundred meters south of Con Thien. We fired our 60mm mortars at them, but in the growing darkness found no traces of casualties. On the morning of the twenty-seventh we searched the area south of there and found six NVA killed from the previous days' contacts as well as documents and three tons of bagged rice, but no weapons (they had probably been carried away by the survivors).

Our next contact with the enemy occurred on October 31, when we had firefights in the morning and early afternoon. The immediate result of the last of these was one USMC KIA. We were unable to find any traces of NVA casualties. But in our search we found enemy small-arms ammunition, uniforms, and a canvas carrying bag.

As October drew to a close one of my men passed me a heartrending letter, dated October 25, from PFC Miller's mother. She "had pulled herself together long enough," she said, to inquire if his friend knew anyone who had been with Ronald, her only son, when he was killed. The letter closed thus:

> We loved him so much and hated to give him up but God only knows why he was took. Take care of yourself and if you would care to write me sometime I would answer for anyone that was my son's friend is a friend of mine. Bye Bye.
>   Mrs. Clarence Miller

I am not easily shaken, but her letter moved me deeply. At the time it was passed along I was exhausted in every way. Rather than do a poor job of writing to Mrs. Miller, I discussed the matter with Father Mechan. He wrote Mrs. Miller.

Did her son and his fellow Marines "lose the war"? If we are judged against the aim with which the war was evidently joined, we were not successful. Like every other unit, we are to be judged by what we accomplished, where we were, with what we had at our command. Battalions such as 3/5 and 2/5 that accounted for the high ratio of enemy-to-friendly casualties we inflicted that year cannot strictly be charged with failure. Operating against an enemy who came to the battlefield fresh, on territory with which at least his scouts were almost always familiar, the NVA must be said to have had the advantage in establishing initial contact.

As for weaponry it is true that the NVA did not then employ air cover or heavy artillery (they began using heavy artillery in February 1967) in the areas where we operated. Yet until 1967 they almost certainly had better weaponry on the company level than our troops in the field. Every NVA unit we saw was equipped with the most modern Russian-designed and usually Russian or Chinese-manufactured small arms, machine guns, and handheld rocket launchers. Yet as my narrative perhaps serves to indicate, while our overall military effort in Vietnam was not successful, the units in which I served were not defeated.

As I recall, Jim Getchell was promoted to major toward the end of October, shortly after Jim Cooper. Around early November, Cooper was promoted from S-3 (battalion operations) to battalion executive officer. And when this promotion was carried out, Major Getchell was moved to the battalion S-3, where he continued to do the same outstanding job he had done as a company commander.

Major Getchell's replacement was a young captain named Doherty. Jerry Doherty had commanded Hotel Company when it had formed at Pendleton the previous year and had stayed with the company through its first few months in-country. When I arrived, Jerry was the S-4 (battalion logistics officer).

I would not have thought it possible to have a company commander better than Jim Getchell, but Doherty may have been. Captain Doherty was about six-feet four-inches tall and weighed about 210. He was a year older than me and looked no more than that. He was a quietly good-looking fellow with blue eyes, balanced features, and a generally quiet demeanor. At that time when he spoke he often either omitted or slurred over the middle of words, so that "platoon" was pronounced "pitoon." Jerry had attended Regis College in Denver, and Colorado remains his home state. He has for more than two decades owned Divide Constructors in Berthoud. Without going into details that might embarrass him, Jerry has shown quite as many admirable traits since he has returned from Vietnam as he did

when he served with us. The world would be a better place
were there more Jerry Dohertys in it.

Not long after Major Getchell became S-3, Jerry told
me to report to Major Cooper at the battalion CP tent.
He added that he thought Jim Cooper planned to
offer me the S-2 position (battalion intelligence officer)
to replace Capt. R. L. Hemenez, a wholesomely handsome UCLA graduate who had orders to the States.
When I reported to Major Cooper, he greeted me standing up and asked me to sit next to him on a folding chair
inside the tent.

He said the battalion would be needing an S-2 to replace Captain Hemenez and that Major Getchell had
recommended me highly for the position (the S-2 and S-3
work closely together in a smoothly functioning infantry
battalion). I said a quick prayer and declined. Jim
Cooper raised the flap of the tent and saw me outside.
Don was then offered the position and he accepted.
Surely he did so after much thought. And I believe he
sensed he would do a fine job in the battalion intelligence
position. If he did, he was right.

As a replacement for Don we soon received a first
lieutenant named Michael A. Litwin. Mike was about six
feet tall and weighed at least 230 pounds. When he reported to us he had more body fat than any Marine
of any rank I have ever seen. He also had an
engineer's MOS (military occupational specialty), a pale
complexion, a high-pitched voice, and a superficially af-
fable nature. Whether he had volunteered for the infantry
or not, I do not know.

Around the time he arrived our battalion received five
officers whose MOS was engineering and one who had
been in armor. To my knowledge none of those lieutenants had ever even commanded a Marine infantry
platoon in training.

Even with the six officer replacements our battalion
remained seriously undermanned. Colonel Airheart was
not given to overstatement, yet in our unit diaries for
that period he listed the battalion's "critical shortages"
for the three companies we had with us at the DMZ as

follows: "1 03 Captain (03 is the basic infantry designation), 5 03 Lieutenants, 6 03 Sergeants, 17 03 Corporals, and 4 03 Lance Corporals." In addition, "critical shortages" included 23 Marines of MOSs other than infantry.

Mike Litwin had come to Vietnam for the first time several months before he joined our battalion in November. As an engineering officer at work on his first project in Vietnam (repairing a bridge) he had been hit in the upper arm by a .50-caliber bullet and evacuated to a hospital in the Far East. He had been in-country less than forty-eight hours at the time he was wounded, and he was a huge man—otherwise he would have lost his arm. Even months afterward the wound was one of the nastiest-looking I had seen before I became a hospital patient myself.

Litwin was from upstate Pennsylvania and had gone to Penn State. As a leader he was "a slow starter," but he was intense despite his tranquil-seeming nature. Once he learned the ropes he became as reliable a platoon commander as I have seen, and his men were understandably grateful to serve under that gentleman.

Since Captain Doherty seemed disposed to have an executive officer who acted in that capacity alone, not as a combination exec and platoon commander, I arranged, sotto voce, that Mike was not to tell the Skipper that I was senior to him. This way, for the first few weeks he was with the company, Litwin was able to get snapped in and learn the company's operating procedures before he had to assume duties as a platoon commander. That way, too, I was able to stay with 3d Platoon.

The arrangement worked out well. By the time the loss of a senior sergeant dictated that Mike take command of 1st Platoon, he had come to learn our SOPs (standard operating procedures) and was able to take charge in good order. Jerry Doherty did not learn that Mike was junior to me until he had been to visit me two or three times at the Philadelphia Naval Hospital.

When Jerry learned that Mike had had no previous infantry experience, he seemed to regard that as a challenge comparable to the one I had felt when we welcomed

Corporal Lewis aboard with 3d Platoon, and the Skipper evidently went about teaching Mike in much the same spirit.

But training Lieutenant Litwin on the job was not Captain Doherty's only personnel challenge in his early days with the company. There was the stocky and volatile gunnery sergeant, named Gonzalez, who was in charge of the 60 mortars and the demolitions section in our company. As soon as Captain Doherty arrived he insisted that the 60s and the demo people go on all of our patrols (under the previous skippers they went with us only when we were fairly sure we would not be traveling far). Gunny Gonzalez protested Jerry's decision vehemently. Captain Doherty silenced the Gunny in much the same way I had Gunny Rockdale in our face-off on Hastings in July, and that I would have to do before long with Sergeant Burns on Mississippi. Even in combat the young officer does not automatically command the respect of his men just because he possesses a commission. In my experience such confrontations are to be expected and even planned for. For the unit to run effectively the senior man must come out on top. In the instance with Gonzalez, the Gunny soon became one of the CO's strongest followers.

Shortly after Jerry assumed command of Hotel Company, the colonel went around to inspect all the defensive positions at Con Thien. As I already mentioned, 3d Platoon occupied the company's left flank, and to our left a finger of ground was the commanding terrain on the entire outpost. For the first five weeks or so that we were at Con Thien an ARVN platoon had held that ground. After the colonel's tour, Jerry came up to me and said that the high ground to 3d Platoon's left was the key terrain on the whole battalion position. At that time an ARVN platoon was still up there (they were soon withdrawn and not replaced) and they had supposedly mined the slope in front of them. After they pulled out, we discovered that they had not done so. Jerry also indicated that we could not expect them to hold out long against a heavy ground attack.

If the NVA could penetrate up that finger against anything less than heavy resistance, Jerry said, they could get to the 105s, the 81s, and the battalion CP easily. And if they came with enough troops they would play hell with every company on our position.

If they tried to come onto that high ground, we had to get at least one squad up there to refuse them the flank. "We'll need whatever time you can give us to reinforce you. If they come, we'll be depending on you, Jim." Right away I assembled our squad leaders and briefed them about what we had to do.

I began by sprinting to the top of the ridge while Sergeant Hoole timed me with a watch. Also during the daylight we moved our left flank squad, with at least one machine gun, up on the double while the other two squads practiced moving and covering to the left at the same time we were sprinting uphill. After several more daylight rehearsals I gave another pep talk. After darkness set in we performed the same maneuver several times on as many evenings thereafter as we could. Before long we were able to make the movement with no sense of panic in what I considered an incredibly rapid time. We practiced refusing the flank at that position so often in the dark that I felt the men could get into position in good order even if they were still half asleep when they moved.

In early November we patrolled north of Con Thien almost every day. And throughout November we ran many night patrols and ambushes. For the remainder of the time we were at Con Thien, however, we made only light contact and had very few battle casualties.

Under Jerry Doherty's leadership especially, our company covered incredible mileage every day on patrol so that before long we came to be known throughout the battalion as "Humping Hotel," a term our troops grew very proud of. Jerry made excellent use of all our supporting arms. Before we went on patrol he always checked to see if we had air on-station, and that our artillery concentrations were cleared and ready to fire in case we should need them.

One of his favorite tactics was to use 60mm mortar fire to "prep" danger areas before we moved across them. That procedure was uncomplicated up north since there were very few civilians around and almost all the villages had been completely evacuated, but was much more difficult after we moved down to An Hoa.

At first our 60s ammo was very old—some of it from as far back as 1953—and we had many short rounds in early November. The short rounds wheezed out of the muzzles, a noise the men were soon able to identify. Everyone around the gun would "hit the deck" and hope for the best. On one occasion, one round wheezed out of the tube and plopped into the mud just twenty feet in front of the gun and several feet to the left of Meyer, myself, and Sergeant Hoole. A dud, thank God. Before the end of November, newer 60s ammo that was much more reliable began to come in.

Sometimes Jerry's use of supporting arms to cover our movement made things difficult for us in other ways. One day, when Meyer must have been ill, I had PFC Jiminez as my radio operator. It was a morning nearly opaque with mist and we were moving along a dirt road to rejoin 3d Platoon after we had reconnoitered a trail-crossing site some three hundred meters north of the rest of the company. From out of nowhere it seemed, a pair of jets swooped parallel to us at less than fifty meters, dropping two-hundred-pound bombs as they came. Jiminez and I went spread-eagled and hugged the road as closely as we could. The ground heaved under us, heavy chunks of shrapnel thumped into the dirt all around, and the air clouded with sand and smoke. Miraculously, neither of us was hit.

November 10 was the Marine Corps's birthday. For the occasion we were given two cans of beer apiece and delicious charcoaled steak. I do not recall seeing a cake but there may have been one. Colonel Airheart held a brief formation at which he read the commandant's birthday message and gave a characteristically crisp, no-nonsense speech. There were perhaps several dozen men assembled in our formation outside the battalion CP tent. As I recall, each of the three maneuver companies was represented by a token force of one officer (I was the Hotel Company representative) and about a half-dozen troops. The colonel was wisely concerned not to present the enemy gunners with a good target and dismissed the formation quickly.

On November 11, a clear and beautiful Friday morning, one of our jet pilots went down in the vicinity of Thon Cam Son, just south of the Ben Hai and well north in the DMZ. I saw him go down and marked the position—it was about forty-five-hundred meters north of us. As the jet headed groundward I saw the pilot floating gently down in his chute. Before long another jet appeared over the area as a "cap," circling overhead to call for a rescue helicopter. From where I was the chopper seemed to go down from antiaircraft fire (later I learned that was what had happened) and it did not come back up.

As I watched the action, so near to us yet so far away, I imagined what at least one of our pilots was probably going through at that very moment and felt almost physically ill.

I ran to the company CP, and asked Jerry if I could take a small snatch-team into the DMZ to get at least the one pilot out. Doherty's answer was prompt: absolutely not. That night, however, the entire company went into the DMZ to try to effect the rescue.

Before we left, Jerry ordered me to do a careful reconnaissance of the approaches to the DMZ. I got well camouflaged for the solitary patrol, the second of my four trips into the DMZ. Upon my return I hastily briefed Jerry, and our chaplain held a quick prayer service, photographed by Larry Burrows, before we left our positions at Con Thien. For the brief, informal service I stood on a large rock or small boulder, so I appeared to be taller than the rest of the men in our unit—but I was not.

Because of the thick vegetation, it was necessary to maneuver the platoons in column. We reached the southern boundary of the DMZ just as darkness fell. Chris's platoon had been on the point till we reached the DMZ, then Mike Litwin's platoon assumed the lead.

For obvious reasons we had to keep radio silence as long as we were north of the DMZ, which might have proved unfortunate since Mike's platoon moved out at what I considered a recklessly fast pace at night in such territory. Since my platoon was last in our company column, my men had to move at a dead run the whole way in order to keep up. Under such conditions our security was haphazard at best. Plus, there was little question of our being able to reconnoiter adequately for the pilots. My men, heavily laden with extra ammunition and other equipment we might need to make the rescue, were hard-pressed to keep up. But we could not use the tac net to request that the pace be slowed. Thus, if any of my squads couldn't maintain contact with the unit in front, we might need a snatch-party to come out after us the following night. When the pace was at its swiftest I was running up and down our column to try to help the men maintain contact. In the eerie gray light, the eyes of some of the more badly winded men had looks of near panic such as I have not seen before or since.

Had each of those Marines not been taught discipline from at least boot camp on, we could not have stayed closed up and our patrol could have ended even less well than it did. I am sorry to say we saw no signs of either the downed crewmen or their aircraft. What we did see in abundance, however, were numerous tunnels, larger even than the ones we saw on our previous incursion into the DMZ. Half a dozen of these were large enough to drive a car through with room to spare.

Not many days after that unsuccessful patrol we were covering an area many thousands of meters from Con Thien when Jerry had the 60s fire into heavy woods to the right of the trail we were moving next to. While the rounds were on the way he gave me a compass heading to move on, and said, "Hit it, Jim."

With the almond smells of the just-exploded mortar shells still heavy in the forest air, my platoon moved through the trees and climbed a steep hill. At the top Corporal Villanueva pushed open a heavy door on either side of which were solid walls. We encountered a hushed grotto that dropped steeply away from the high ground where we stood. As we moved around inside it I felt as though the eyes of an unseen presence were on us. It was darker there, with the low-hanging trees, and very silent, as if the earth had ceased to spin and we had entered a world we had known once before. We moved carefully around that beautiful place, then rejoined the rest of the platoon. No member of Villanueva's squad said a word about it afterward, but the looks on the men's faces indicated that our visit had the same entrancing effect on each of them that it had on me.

Throughout the first three weeks of November we patrolled day and night, and it rained for most of the time. During the week of November 21, for instance, we saw the sun only once, and that was briefly. Around Con Thien were rolling hills but the terrain inland was much thicker at this time in the war. At the very border of the DMZ where we so often moved were isolated patches of jungle where rattans and other thorns flourished, and the point had to hack his way through with a bush knife. After patrols in those areas, most men in the platoon found that their utilities as well as their hands, faces, and arms had been lacerated by the thorns. Many of the lacerations became septic in the damp climate and under the conditions in which we lived and worked, yet not one complaint did I ever hear from the men about those problems.

In November we also patrolled almost daily in the tropical rain forest at the northwest portion of our tactical area of responsibility (TAOR). At the time the rain forest was aswarm with leeches. If bloused, one's trousers were fairly effective against mosquitoes and ticks but failed to keep out leeches, which were a constant nuisance. Throughout the rain forest was an abundance of tenacious, low-covering hydnocarpus trees, the fruits of which provide chaulmoogra oil, at one time used to help treat leprosy. Large areas of forest were also covered by lianas and herbaceous climbers which formed nearly impenetrable tangled thickets that likewise had to be cut through with the bush knife and then wrestled apart.

Sergeant Burns was as adept as I was in using lines to put up one- and two-rope bridges. Whenever we went on patrol he and I carried one line apiece. Between us and several other first-class swimmers, we were always able to get the platoon safely across any kind of terrain whatsoever, including the fiercely swollen rivers we often encountered during the height of the monsoon.

I recall one patrol on a very socked-in day when it rained as though it had never rained before. We were in the midst of the tropical rain forest and as far from any friendly units as we ever normally moved. This is the weather, I thought, when the enemy least expects us, so we stalked through the forest like the hunters we were, hour after hour, but found no trace of the enemy. By midday the noise of the rain beating on the leaves and drumming on the water all around us was frightful.

Several men in the platoon were either nonswimmers or did very poorly in the water. I admired their courage on our many "aquatic patrols" on those days when it bucketed! On one day of very heavy rain, I crossed the largest stream myself first. In order to be heard above the noise of the rushing river, I had to yell back across to Gunny Burns to give him instructions about the kind of bridge we were to put up. On that occasion at least one of our nonswimmers "took a dip" after falling off the rope bridge. Villanueva went in after at least one of his men. Corporal Lewis dived for one of his squad members, too. All the men who fell in were retrieved, as well as their weapons. The intrepidity of our squad leaders as swimmers must have done much to bolster the confidence of all the men in the platoon.

After one such day of arduous patrolling I watched Gunny Burns as he unzipped his flak vest before evening chow at Con Thien. When he released the zipper, great billows of steam emanated from his upper torso. He noticed me watching and we exchanged grins as if to say, "It's not such a bad life."

When I took platoon-size patrols out, I followed Jerry Doherty's example and planned our prep fires carefully in advance, then had them cleared so we would be able to use them right away if we needed them. Additionally, I ascertained ahead of time when air would be on-station. Partially, I think, because we did use prep fires whenever possible in the danger areas before we crossed them, the platoons I commanded were never taken by so much surprise that we were not able to react effectively.

It was of the greatest importance to remain mentally alert while on patrol. As we moved I continually adjusted my estimate of possible courses of action as the terrain and tactical situation changed. A platoon commander in

Vietnam had to have presence of mind at all times and know how to react to each bend in the trail, each new vista, each sign of enemy activity.

Problems of security occupied most of my waking hours in Vietnam. On patrol I had to be sure that the platoon was not surprised by an enemy force and at the same time do my utmost to take the enemy by surprise. The main concerns I usually ran through on those patrols included adjusting our formations to make best use of the terrain, keeping track of our exact location, considering the possible supporting arms that would be most effective at each juncture, and taking stock of the personnel, ammunition, food, and water we had with us.

I recall several evenings when we were moving back into Con Thien across large, undulating fields. I signaled nearly continually with my hands and arms to have the squad leaders spread their men out even farther in case of enemy attack and to vary their formations: echelon left, echelon right, V formation, and "one up, two back." By making these adjustments in our formation, by moving whenever possible to discourage an enemy attack, by assuring that the troops were dispersed so they could respond effectively should contact occur—by those means the platoon commander was most often able to help his unit be successful in Vietnam.

Defensively, one had to supervise the laying of wire, when it was available, and the reinforcing of positions. One also had to cover avenues of approach by fire, obstacles, and explosive devices, to adjust and register supporting fires, and to dispatch ambushes and security patrols.

These aspects of leadership in the field were especially important in Vietnam, since we were not fighting for terrain features as such nor were we fighting against an enemy whose identity was usually certain before he opened fire on us. Thus, the most successful platoon commanders probably were the ones who managed to patrol most thoroughly over the largest areas, and who sustained the fewest casualties while doing so.

On the one sunny day that month, we did not patrol but reregistered the close-in fires around our positions and test-fired most of our weapons. The registration fires were brought in so close that we had to withdraw from our lines while the rounds came in. Needless to say, the shrapnel sang loudly most of that time.

In contrast to the M-14s, which I never recall misfiring, the M-60 machine guns were a continual problem to maintain. More than half the time we needed them, it seemed, the guns would malfunction (often due to a broken firing pin) and would more often than not only fire single shots. Moreover, when they were in good working order the guns tended to overheat rapidly, even when the crews "talked" their weapons in steady fashion.

The LAWs we had never misfired when I was in Vietnam. The LAW was a tube-shaped rocket launcher with a pullout barrel and flip-up sight, and which looked no less like a toy than the plastic mortar I had Zlatunich bomb my 81 platoon with at Pendleton. The LAW was generally carried bandillero-style by the members of the rocket squad, and each man in the squad had two or three. The LAW was strong enough to take out most tanks with one shot, was lightweight, and had a sharp back-blast. In many ways it was the ultimate modern infantry weapon.

The 3.5-inch rocket was also primarily an antitank weapon. As with the LAW, however, we often employed it in attacking bunkers and other fortified positions. If anything, as I was later painfully to learn, the 3.5 round packed a bigger wallop than the LAW. And it fired a white-phosphorous round that could be used for marking targets and screening movements as well as for antipersonnel attacks.

Like the LAW, the 3.5 was shoulder-fired and weighed about twenty-two pounds when the round was in the tube. The 3.5 also had a back-blast, but was not disposable. In good hands it was accurate at ranges up to 250 meters.

The 40mm grenade launcher, or M-79, was likewise single-shot and looked like an outsize popgun. It broke in the middle, where the stubby round was loaded by hand like an oversize shotgun shell. The M-79 weighed about six-and-one-half pounds when loaded and had a dull, heavy aluminum, possibly brass, barrel. The recoil was not much heavier than that of the old-fashioned .45-caliber Thompson submachine gun. The M-79 was almost as accurate as the M-14 up to about 350 meters. Since the projectile was large and traveled rather slowly, if one had keen eyes one could follow the round on its deadly path.

On the day we test-fired I shot three rounds with this weapon. I aimed at three branches of a dying tree some three hundred meters in front of our positions. Before every round, like everyone else, I called the branch I was aiming at: nine o'clock, eleven o'clock, three o'clock. Each round was a hit, and the third felled the three o'clock branch. As I handed the weapon to the next man and scrambled out of the trench I fired from, Corporal Jackson laughed and smiled irrepressibly at the new men.

During the rest of the afternoon Jackson had his men lay an M-60 out on a clean poncho and then reassemble the gun blindfolded to simulate what they would have to do if their gun malfunctioned after dark. He timed his men's sessions and recorded each of their times in the squad leader's notebook he always kept with him and up to date. Before and after those sessions, Corporal Jackson huddled his men around him briefly to give them a few twanging words of advice and encouragement. The gunners generally looked after their weapons better than most racers do their automobiles.

L. Cpl. Robert J. Meyer was my radio operator for all but about three weeks of the time I was with Hotel Company. We went through a lot together and I came to know him well. He was from Sidney, Ohio, a Dayton suburb, and had just turned twenty-two years of age the June before he died. Like myself and Sergeant Hoole, Bob Meyer was becoming "a short-timer" (I believe his tour was to have ended in early spring).

Among the plans Meyer had made was to get season tickets to the Browns games for himself and his wife, and to have as many good meals at his parents' home and his own as he could. Meyer, Hoole, and I also spent many mouthwatering moments recounting the home-cooked meals we liked best. And Meyer at one time showed me pictures of his wife, a stunning blonde in her early twenties. When I remarked upon her attractiveness, his face lit up with a proud smile.

Of the celebrities I've seen, former Denver quarterback

John Elway reminds me the most of Bob Meyer. Meyer had dark blond hair, clear blue eyes, and sharp features which came alive whenever we talked about home or made one of our jokes. During the monsoon, for instance, we often said we would "move between the drops" on our patrols.

"Amen, Sir!" he replied with his full-blooded laugh and wide-beaming smile.

It seems impossible to believe that someone so full of life as Meyer has ceased to exist. To me, the knowledge of the man's death is doubly sorrowing, since an error of judgment on my part caused the injuries that caused him to die. He died of wounds in the hospital in Japan on January 14, 1967, five days after we were wounded.

Bob had been overdue for R&R by then and had become flummoxed by his wife's having several times "put off" meeting him in Honolulu. I have learned only fairly recently that she had withheld from him the information that she had become pregnant just before his departure. On January 11, however, she had planned to arrive to meet him with a new surprise: their first child, a no doubt stunningly beautiful baby girl. Although Bob failed to show at the expected gate, Mrs. Meyer remained, sleeping there with her infant, night after night, until at last, beyond the date he was to have returned to Vietnam, she flew home with their daughter. Their neighbors had been alerted, and not long after she returned the somber casualty affairs officers came to call.

Not long after I turned down the S-2 offer, a notice came through that all officers below a certain age would be eligible to return to the States to take a test for flight school at Pensacola, Florida. I cannot say that I was not tempted. I had little interest in becoming a pilot, but the prospects of going to Florida for a physical were indeed attractive. I had less than one hundred days remaining on my Vietnam tour and was scheduled to be discharged in less than six months. Were I to return to Florida and either fail the flight physical or flunk out of flight school, I would have no additional military obligations and would be discharged soon thereafter, since it would have been impracticable to send me back to Vietnam once I had returned to the States.

I received the flight school notice late one afternoon after we had just returned from a long, arduous day of monsoon-weather patrolling. Most of the men in the platoon sat down to their evening meal, which they ate at their positions on Con Thien. From the platoon CP I could see almost all of them. And there I made my decision.

Moments of choice come to each of us, and on our choices the direction of our journey through life often largely depends. As I ate, I watched the men, whose unselfish spirits were high, who relied on each other very much, and who had seemingly come to rely on me also. In the lowering light of evening I recollected the things we had been through and anticipated what we might go through in the future. I could not leave them. I tore the sheet with the notice on it into small pieces and burned the pieces with the heat tabs I used to heat my coffee. The decision is one I have not regretted.

Shortly after this, before 3d Platoon was headed out on an independent combat patrol, a burly second lieutenant approached me where I squatted, finishing a can of C rats coffee, bent over, extended a large hand, and said, "Howda. Ahm O. K. Batte, FO. Ah just got in heah. Y'all maand if Ah come 'long on patrol?"

"Not at all," I responded, sizing him up carefully as I did all second lieutenants I encountered for the first time in Vietnam. He was about my height but at least twenty pounds heavier and seemingly all muscle. The sleeves of his jungle utility blouse were rolled up to his biceps, exposing a pair of hairy forearms as large as an average man's calves. While we waited for the platoon to saddle up, he produced from his flak jacket a thick, pint bottle of honey. He offered me a slug, then gulped hungrily from it himself.

O. K. Batte's hometown was Jackson, Mississippi. We never talked much—we never felt the need to—yet we became good friends. When I was wounded he was one of the first three men to come to my aid.

On our patrol that day I asked Batte to call artillery on a danger area that I knew we would be coming to. "Ya mean in the break in those trees?" (he pronounced the word "treees"). As the rounds were on the way, I prepared to dive into the nearest ditch since I felt that any new lieutenant might be as prone to egregious errors as I had been when I was one. His adjusting round was precisely on target. I knew right away that the calm lieutenant was a winner: so he was then, and so he remains today.

On Operation Tuscaloosa, shortly after I was wounded, our company overran a VC Main Force regimental headquarters. In that action, O. K. Batte earned a Bronze Star with V (for valor). Had he performed the same actions in any previous military conflict in our nation's history, he would almost certainly have received a Navy Cross at least, the next-highest award for valor after the Medal of Honor.

On the last few days of Prairie we went on platoon- and company-size ambushes virtually every night. We killed no NVA on any of the patrols although if wishing could have made the enemy cross our path, the NVA would have.

One of those late ambushes was laid along a stream running south-southwest from the DMZ. The position was difficult to gain access to because of the heavy foliage that surrounded it so I reasoned that the stream itself would make a good avenue of infiltration for the NVA; there would be no visible footprints so long as they waded in the stream, which ran far south of Con Thien.

In our movement to the ambush site, knee-high scaly vines and anaconda-thick branches made our attempts at stealthy infiltration slow and difficult. The noise of the rain beating on the leaves overhead helped somewhat to keep us from being detected. As we began descending toward the streambed, the darkness seemed to descend with us, dropping like a veil from the overhanging trees.

Since the going was so difficult I moved on the point myself. When we reached the clearing at the final open space before the stream I thought I saw several figures gliding steadily south, just below us. I signaled to our lead squad to follow me and we gave chase. Before that patrol we had made special plans for capturing prisoners. In keeping with my instructions we did not open fire but attempted to seize what I thought were three NVA without having to fire on them. About a dozen of us galloped down the moss-covered slope and splashed into the swiftly moving stream but found no one.

After the noise of our splashing had subsided, we moved upstream a bit and all three squads settled into the ambush. Soon the beating of the leaves and gurgling of the stream was accompanied by the noise of every species of cicada, grasshopper, and tree frog in the province—joined in a melody of clicking, piping, drilling, and crying that suffused the rain forest all around us. On that night, as so often, we were attacked incessantly by armies of mosquitoes and sand flies. The latter did not buzz but did bite.

From October to December 1966, altogether ten Marine infantry battalions participated in Operation Prairie. On October 1 the commanding general of the 3d Marine Amphibious Brigade (MAB) sent the following message to all Marine units. Until many years afterward the message was classified top secret. "VC/NVA threat to economically vital An Hoa/Nong Son industrial complex may be expected during monsoon season. Continuous recon of western approaches to this vital area imperative to ensure early detection and counter action."

General Lewis W. Walt, the senior Marine in Vietnam at that time, considered the security of the An Hoa area the first priority for the Marines in-country. General William C. Westmoreland, overall commander of Allied ground forces in Vietnam at the time, as well as most other senior Marine generals there then, felt similarly. By the end of the month, it was decided that on the first possible opportunity a seasoned battalion should be moved from the DMZ to An Hoa to replace 3d Battalion, 9th Marines, the unit that had been operating there. Our battalion, 2d Battalion, 5th Marines, was the one chosen for this mission.

FIVE

2d Battalion, 5th Marines: An Hoa

Shortly before Thanksgiving, the three companies that were with us at the DMZ, along with the battalion command group, were moved by air from the DMZ to the Da Nang airport. At the same time Lt. Terry J. Ebbert's E Company, which had been left behind when we left Chu Lai in early October, was also moved to the Da Nang airport. From Da Nang all four companies and the battalion CP group were flown by helicopter to An Hoa. In less than twelve hours from the time we began displacement, all four companies and the battalion CP were in place at An Hoa and ready to do their job.

An Hoa was an important area for several reasons. Most remotely, perhaps, it was not very far from Da Nang. The town of Da Nang was on the map sheet northeast of the one we mainly used when we were at An Hoa. The town of Da Nang ran approximately three miles along the left bank of the Cam Le River (Song Cam Le) close to where it entered the Da Nang harbor. In all of Vietnam, that harbor, formerly known as the Baie de Tourane, was second only to Saigon's in its ability to accommodate deep draft ships. Moreover, one of the two best Marine airstrips in Vietnam was also located at Da Nang. The I Corps headquarters, responsible for all Marine operations in the northernmost quarter of South Vietnam at the time, was located in Da Nang. And perhaps 95 percent of the Marine Corps's fighting units operated in that northernmost sector of South Vietnam.

The military, cultural, social, and financial gulf separating Da Nang from An Hoa at the time was immense. An Hoa was approximately eighteen kilometers southwest of Da Nang, yet very distant from it in all the cultural and material qualities one associates with civilization. The An Hoa base consisted mostly of a dirt landing strip for aircraft, a series of hardback tents for the battalion staff and certain standby units, and a combat operations center (COC).

The latter was a long, narrow room in a heavily sandbagged bunker perhaps six feet underground. The COC was the operational nerve center for our battalion when we were deployed around An Hoa. In the COC were usually found the S-3 (Major Getchell) or his assistant, the S-2 (Don), several radio operators with radios, message men with pads, maps, many colored pencils, and empty ammo cases that served as desks.

The area inland from Da Nang had for many centuries been very poor and culturally backward. At the time we were there the VC did their best to keep things that way. In March 1965 the North Vietnamese had cut the railway just south of Da Nang. The railway had at one time passed within a thousand meters of the base and connected with the central line to Saigon, which once joined the An Hoa railroad less than two kilometers northeast of the base. For nearly two years both lines had been completely severed, most of the tracks torn up and removed; all of the bridges leading into the An Hoa area had been blown.

"Liberty Road," which had been cleared part of the way along the abandoned An Hoa railroad right of way, was intended to reopen An Hoa to transportation from Da Nang, but during the period when we were there the monsoon rains and the Communist forces made travel along that road from Da Nang to An Hoa virtually impossible. For all but two weeks when we were in An Hoa the base was accessible only by air, and that had been the situation for the better part of the previous two years. "Lines of Communication" difficulties notwithstanding, just before we were sent there, General Walt had determined to make An Hoa the model for pacification in all of Vietnam, and apparently induced General Westmoreland to agree with him.

For South Vietnam the An Hoa area was comparatively rich in natural resources. Carefully laid out rice fields covered much of the immediate area. In the rainy season (when we were there), only the narrow dikes between the fields stood higher than the water in which the rice plants grew. And rice cultivation in that area was almost continuous.

Even more important in the eyes of the Allied higher command was An Hoa's potential for development as an industrial site. To my knowledge the only coal mine in all of South Vietnam was in the An Hoa region. Combined with the confluence of rivers in the area, that mine made An Hoa seem an ideal place to build a hydroelectric dam, which it was hoped would eventually provide power for all of South Vietnam. As far as I know very little coal was mined at the site and I do not believe the hydro-electric dam ever got beyond the blueprint stage, if it reached that.*

Our battalion officially relieved 3d Battalion, 9th Marines on December 27 but we moved into An Hoa and began operating on November 22. When we arrived the only friendly units other than 3/9 in the area were a lightly manned PF (South Vietnamese Popular Forces) platoon and one company of the ARVN 51st Regiment supported by a pair of 105mm howitzers. The PFs and ARVNs occupied two or three outposts on small hills less than two thousand meters south of An Hoa.

On one of the first days after we arrived at An Hoa, Don briefed the four maneuver company commanders on the intelligence situation in the area. Since Don was a good friend I asked him for a separate briefing. It was memorable.

Under a drizzly sky we walked outside the COC to an open area from which, even in the overcast air, we could see the high ground to east and west. Squatting on our haunches over the map that Don had spread out on the deck, he oriented me to the terrain. Looking at me sadly, he said, "Bad news, Jim." After a pause he pointed to the high ground to our east and west, which he told me was in the complete control of the NVA and Main Force VC. Much of the rest of

---

* The reader interested in learning more about plans for the development of An Hoa during these years is referred to Jack Shulimson, *U.S. Marines in Vietnam, 1966: An Expanding War* (History and Museums Division, Headquarters, U.S. Marine Corps, 1982).

the immediate area around An Hoa, he explained, also was controlled by the Communist R-20 (Doc Lap) Battalion.

Two supposedly unfordable rivers, which our Marines crossed four times during the next month, ran through our area of responsibility. The Thu Bon ran through our tactical area of responsibility (TAOR) north of An Hoa. Another heavily reinforced Communist battalion was on the other side of it. The region north of the Thu Bon, and the Ba Ren River which flowed into the Thu Bon, had for a very long time been considered "militarily inaccessible." The heavily populated area immediately around An Hoa had moreover for a long time been the most politically difficult section in the upper quarter of South Vietnam.

The province of Quang Nam, which we were in, was just south of Thua Thien. Captured documents I have since seen indicate that Thua Thien was then considered by the NVA to be their primary corridor for infiltration. Once the NVA had entered the south by way of Thua Thien by staying in the hills to our west, they had a not difficult access to the An Hoa region. In short, the two most often used avenues of infiltration ran right around our positions.

For two years previous to our arrival, under coercion or not, nearly 50 percent of the population was supposedly paying taxes to the Communists rather than to the government in Saigon. As Don related that drizzly morning, perhaps 80 percent of the countryside we were to operate in was considered under Communist control.

Our battalion moved into the An Hoa TAOR shortly before Thanksgiving, which came on November 24 that year. We assumed full operational control in the area around November 27. From our arrival on November 22 until the twenty-seventh, our companies were briefed and snapped in in good fashion by 3/9.

Our primary mission at An Hoa was to patrol our large tactical area of responsibility. In the process of doing that, we were to provide security for the hoped-for industrial site and the Nong Son coal mine, which were separated by a distance of over five thousand meters. In addition, we were to attempt to keep Liberty Road open and usable. And we were supposed to provide security from the enemy for the large number of civilians in the area who looked to us, primarily, for their protection. While 80 percent of the countryside in our TAOR was Communist-controlled, very many internally displaced refugees surrounded our outposts and sought out our Marines and corpsmen to protect them.

Needless to say, those duties were made more difficult because the battalion's TAOR was bisected by the Thu Bon and Tink Yen rivers and contained numerous flooded streams, marshes, and swamps in all quarters. Around An Hoa the monsoon winds were at their strongest from mid-November through January—the period when we served in the region. In Colonel Airheart's unit diary summary for December he remarked that the entire TAOR was "infested" with organized units of well-trained, well-disciplined, and well-armed Communist forces. Neither Don nor the colonel was wrong.

Shortly after Captain Doherty was briefed, he met with his platoon commanders. Jerry's instruction wisely, I thought, included specific orders as to how we were to conduct ourselves in dealing with the civilians in the area. In his remarks he emphasized that we should be courteous to them at all times, and that platoon commanders should be strict about seeing to it that the troops do no "hobnobbing" with the civilians. After our briefing we moved out on foot to our outposts.

As the crow flies, Hotel Company's positions were from six to eight thousand meters northwest of An Hoa. The company's headquarters was set up on Phu Lac (6), a muddy hill where the virtually unusable Liberty Road crossed the Song Thu Bon. Shortly after we arrived at Phu Lac (6), the CO dispatched 3d Platoon to another outpost, My Loc (2), about two thousand meters to the southwest. At that position we relieved a platoon from either M or K Company, 3d Battalion, 9th Marines.

The units in which I served were genuinely interested in helping the South Vietnamese civilians, but we were not always able to do as much as we would have liked. In some ways, I believe, the situation we faced at My Loc (2) reflected the general difficulties the Allied forces seemed to encounter throughout the war. At My Loc (2) we occupied an outpost outside a small village comprising at first perhaps twenty-five closely set huts and at least as many families. From that position we patrolled heavily and sent out ambushes nearly continually day and night. We also had to provide security for the road sweeps that went through whenever they could from An Hoa to Phu Lac (6).

In addition, we did our best to provide security for the village just outside our wire. But to do that with the size of the platoon we had was virtually impossible. On average we had from twenty-five to thirty-five Marines actually with us on the outpost. That meant that our numbers were insufficient for us to set positions around both the village and hill. Moreover, since we were not raised in a system like the one we were combating, we were not naturally disposed to wiring, mining, and booby-trapping around the whole ville.

If we covered the village only we would have to give up the tactically important high ground, and if the enemy made a coordinated attack against the village from there, it would be nearly impossible to defend. In addition, not long after I arrived at My Loc (2), the naive-seeming lieutenant who commanded the 3/9 platoon we relieved casually showed me their ammo bunker. Inexplicably, the bunker had enough ammunition and weapons in it to keep an NVA regiment in business for at least a year. For that reason alone it was imperative that we keep the villagers outside our defensive wires and that we not be overrun.

My attempts to find out why so many weapons and so much ammo were to be found at a position so small and difficult to defend were as futile as our subsequent plans to have them removed. During the monsoon virtually no land transportation could reach us and the helicopters were needed for more urgent missions. Unfortunately, there was so much hardware in the bunker, it would have been impractical for us to blow it all up, even if we had had sufficient demolitions on hand to do so.

Many of the surrounding fields were under cultivation so it was with considerable reluctance that I even registered close-in fires around My Loc (2). Moreover, before we did the registration, we had to temporarily evacuate—no easy chore—all of the village against the possibility that either a short round from the 81s section that was with us or a long shot by the artillery at An Hoa would land in the ville.

Speculation on the might-have-beens does not take us far. Perhaps our whole enterprise in South Vietnam was miscalculated from the beginning. It may well be that by the time we entered the war with American infantry battalions, the South Vietnamese leadership had already been too severely decimated by the terrorism of the previous eight years to recover enough strength to fight off the NVA—especially when world opinion more or less constrained the South Vietnamese and their Allies to remain on the strategic defensive. From the standpoint of the American forces in-country, the numbers in the field alone were inadequate.

The commander of the 3/9 platoon we relieved was a medium-size, pale-faced, blond lieutenant with a crew cut and an indeterminate speaking voice. He was perhaps twenty-four but looked younger. He had situated his CP in a huge, white teepee near the military crest of the hill. It was the most inviting-looking target I saw the entire time I was at An Hoa. That he had not already been hit in this landmark, where he seemed to spend most of his time, is inexplicable. Shortly after we arrived he invited me to sit with him in his teepee CP. It was the only time I did so; I entered with trepidation and left as soon as I could.

We had hardly sat down when he pulled his loaded .45 from its holster, thrust it toward me, grip forward, and said, "See this? I got this for being Honor Man at Basic School. Where did you graduate in your Basic School class?"

This lieutenant's youthful platoon sergeant and Sergeant Hoole were both standing at the teepee entrance when this inquiry was delivered. I glanced at Hoole. So as not to seem impertinent, the latter paced briskly away to swallow his response.

For the next several days we patrolled alongside the men of 3/9. They struck my men and me as being timid in the extreme. On at least one of those days, for instance, the whole of the lieutenant's company was for some reason on our small outpost. In the morning one of the three platoons went on patrol due north of My Loc (2). Perhaps one thousand meters out they were hit hard by an NVA ambush. The *tap-tap-tap* and high shriek of the NVA automatic weapons made clear to all at our position who was taking the beating. A relief platoon from the same company was ordered out right away but the reaction force took incredibly long to move. During this panic-stricken time for the 3/9 relief force, the men from 3d Platoon stared in disbelief at the fumbling and confusion. When the platoon finally departed, many of our men exchanged looks of amazement mingled with amusement. To me, another indication of the poor morale in 3/9 was the way its members spoke in hushed tones of the dates of their previous battles—"9 October," "10 September," and so forth—like characters in a Hemingway novel.

The companies in our battalion did a more aggressive and enthusiastic job than the 3/9 outfit we relieved. We patrolled a much larger territory and with far fewer men. We probably suffered more casualties but we also probably provided better security for the civilians and we performed more wide-ranging duties, such as distributing food and supplies to the local noncombatants.

Around An Hoa the men in 3d Platoon proved as big-hearted as were the men in my 81 platoon in 3/5. All the Marines I served with in Vietnam continually shared whatever food and other supplies they had with the local villagers. Around My Loc (2) some of the men were so charitable I had to caution my squad leaders on several occasions because men were giving so much of their food away, they seemed to be damaging their own health. And I had to give special orders to some of the squad leaders to prevent that from becoming a major problem.

About the time we got to An Hoa our company was joined by Capt. James A. Graham. As I understood it, Jim would travel with us for the next month or so primarily as an observer. As soon as he became familiar with our operating procedures he would take command of one of the maneuver companies in the battalion. When Capt. George Burgett was seriously wounded and evacuated during Tuscaloosa, Jerry Doherty had Jim take command of Company F.

I already knew Graham fairly well. We had served together in 3/6 on the East Coast, had been under some small-arms fire together in the Dominican Republic, and had gone through the same class at Mountain Climbing School during the summer of 1965. Against rugged competition Jim graduated number one from that arduous course.

He was born in Wilkinsburg, a small town in Allegheny County, Pennsylvania. He attended Frostburg State College in Maryland and graduated with a B.S. in 1963. By then Jim had already accumulated substantial time in military service (by way of the Reserves and the National Guard as I recall). In some ways his military skills were outstanding. Like all of us, however, Jim had his flaws and failures. The fall after graduation he received his Marine commission. Jim had light brown hair, large gray-blue eyes, heavy eyebrows, somewhat large ears, and a prominent nose—a combination of features that gave him a cheerfully regal appearance.

By the time he had even joined 3/6, Jim had already graduated from flight school in Pensacola. Somewhat a mathematical genius, he had also been accepted into the astronauts program before coming to us in Hotel 2/5. Before he went into the conventional space program, however, he felt he should use his already extensive and valuable infantry experience in Vietnam. Jim seemed to be a very deep-believing Christian and showed positive evidence of his beliefs in many ways. When I was wounded he was among the first to come to my assistance. When he went to Vietnam he was already married and had two beautiful children, whose pictures he proudly showed me one day shortly after he arrived. I still remember the way his eyes shined when he spoke to me about his family. It cannot be that someone who was so much alive can ever sink into oblivion.

When Jim Graham died, his children had hardly had a chance to get to know him. If they read his Medal of Honor citation, they must realize that their father was not just a gentleman on the day he came to my assistance. On June 2, 1967, Jim was killed while commanding Company

F on Operation Union II near Quang Tin. His posthumous citation reads in part as follows:

> During Operation UNION II, the First Battalion, Fifth Marines, consisting of Companies A and D, with Captain Graham's company attached, launched an attack against an enemy occupied position, with two Companies assaulting and one in reserve. Company F, a leading Company, was proceeding across a clear paddy area one thousand meters wide, attacking toward the assigned objective, when it came under fire from mortars and small arms which immediately inflicted a large number of casualties. Hardest hit by the enemy fire was the 2d Platoon of Company F, which was pinned down in the open paddy area by intense fire from two concealed machineguns. Forming an assault unit from members of his small company headquarters, Captain Graham boldly led a fierce assault through the second platoon's position, forcing the enemy to abandon the first machinegun position, thereby relieving some of the pressure on his second platoon, and enabling evacuation of the wounded to a more secure area. Resolute to silence the second machinegun, which continued its devastating fire, Captain Graham's small force stood steadfast in its hard won enclave. Subsequently, during the afternoon's fierce fighting, he suffered two minor wounds while personally accounting for an estimated fifteen enemy killed. With the enemy position remaining invincible upon each attempt to withdraw to friendly lines, and although knowing that he had no chance of survival, he chose to remain with one man who could not be moved due to the seriousness of his wounds. The last radio transmission from Captain Graham reported that he was being assaulted by a force of twenty-five enemy; he died while protecting himself and the wounded man he chose not to abandon.

Soon after we arrived at An Hoa, Captain Doherty went on R&R. For the days Jerry was away, Jim Graham assumed temporary command of our company. That period included Thanksgiving, which came on November 24 of that year. At that date I had 3d Platoon on independent service at My Loc (2) and Jim had 1st and 2d

Platoons along with the Hotel Company forward head-quarters group at Phu Lac (6).

A warm meal was flown into our position as dusk was almost upon us. On the cover of the menu is a pair of Eagle, Globe, and Anchor seals with *Semper Fidelis* above the head of the eagle on both emblems. Between the emblems are a helmet and a rifle. And below them is a peaceful New England country village scene pictured in color behind a wooden rail fence. On the page inside the cover is the commanding general's Thanksgiving message. It reads as follows:

> On this truly American Holiday we pause to offer our profound thanks to our Creator for the innumerable blessings inherent in our way of life. We may look to those precepts of individual rights and liberties laid down by the founders of our government and find that they apply equally to present times. Today, it has never been more apparent that these precepts would be forcibly denied the peoples of smaller nations were it not for the combined efforts of freedom loving nations. We of the 3d Marine Division are presently a part of such efforts in the Republic of Vietnam. Therefore, on this Thanksgiving Day let us give thanks for our many opportunities and freedom, and fervently pray that someday they will extend to all mankind. A Happy Thanksgiving to you and to your loved ones.

The menu lists twenty-nine items, all of which we had in superabundance. After the meal I had the squad leaders tell the men we would beat off any attacks that evening by hurling turkey bones, fruitcake, and hard candy. Among the most delicious items were: shrimp cocktail, chilled fruit cup, roast turkey, baked ham, raisin sauce, cornbread dressing, mixed vegetables, salad, assorted fresh fruits, olives, several kinds of bread, butter, already melted ice cream, pumpkin pie, and warm coffee. The fact that our outfit was not in the 3d Marine Division but the 1st did not matter to us a bit. We were very grateful for the non–C rats chow.

Below the Thanksgiving prayer on the back of the menu

I had written hastily to my mother that we were off Prairie and now were at An Hoa. "We are supposed to start Mississippi in two days. Thanksgiving meal was great. Love, Jim."

Operation Mississippi was to begin on November 25 but heavy rains and an exceptionally low weather ceiling necessitated its daily postponement till November 29. During the period from the twenty-fifth through the twenty-ninth we were joined by one platoon from Company K, 3/9, which was to form 3d Platoon's relief at My Loc (2) while we went on Mississippi. During the four days' delay time, 3d Platoon patrolled vigorously around our positions; the K, 3/9 platoon remained on My Loc (2) as security for the position itself. During that period, 3d Platoon made several brief enemy contacts and picked up over a dozen mines and booby traps around our position. We sustained no casualties.

Hiep Duc Valley, where Operation Mississippi would be run, was also known at the time as Antenna Valley because of the number of Marine radio operators killed there in recent months. During the few days after the warning order had gone out and before we went into the valley ourselves, I sought to allay Meyer's evident concern by suggesting that we run between the bullets and move like a pair of hyperactive rabbits. He was in agreement.

As I reread it today, I see that the preoperation intelligence report written by Don reflected that officer's good sense and knowledge of the enemy situation. He remarked that "enemy strength in the area of operation, the Que Son valley, was carried . . . to include the 3d NVA Regiment and elements of the 1st VC Main Force Regiment" (each regiment was over three times the size of a full-strength Marine battalion). He said that we could expect to contact "from 1 to 14 men . . . in small unit sniper fire, and ambushes of the rear elements of march columns."

From the landing zone to our objective, "the trail West was characterized by mountainous terrain with fighting holes about every twenty meters." As we saw when we moved through, the L-shaped holes appeared to have been recently cut into the side of the mountain. We would also have numerous rivers and streams to cross, and only five of these had bridges spanning them. Most of the hamlets we passed through were, as Don had written, "characterized by fighting holes and trench lines with tunnels throughout. The mountains surrounding the valley are very steep and covered with extremely thick foliage. All of the trails and especially the main trail [the one we would generally have to use during the early operation] are excellent ambush sites."

"Viet Cong influence has prevailed in this area since November 1964. Large numbers of the populace," Don wrote, would be "willing to help the Marines with information." In conjunction with 3d Battalion, 7th Marines, our mission was to conduct a "coordinated reconnaissance in force, search and destroy in Quan Son, Quan Duc Duc . . . and to locate and capture or destroy enemy forces, supplies, equipment, and documents."

For the only time I was in Vietnam, on that operation I felt that our air support let us down. We were scheduled to lift off at first light, but the helos did not begin picking men up until 1015. The flight itself was only fifteen minutes' duration, yet the lift was not terminated until 1500, or 3 P.M. civilian time. Moreover, we had additional air support problems later. Those flaws and deficiencies in execution cost us lives right away.

The order of landing was Company F (reinforced), the battalion command group, Company H (reinforced), and Company G. 3d Platoon was the last one in for our company. We embarked aboard large, green CH-46s to make the rapid flight over the ridgeline separating An Hoa from the Que Son region. We embarked at 1315. By that time the sky was clear and shooting visibility much better than it would have been seven hours earlier, our originally scheduled time to fly in.

As our helo shuddered into its descent, several holes, each one slightly larger than the diameter of a finger, appeared in the bulkhead above the Marine sitting across from me. Ground fire. Judging from the size of the holes it was probably from at least one .50-caliber machine gun. The rounds passed so close to where I sat, strapped into a low canvas seat, that I felt a tingling sensation over my forehead and a prickly heat down my back. I prayed that the fire would not hit either me or my men.

When we landed and the ramp went down I led my men out the tail of the chopper and circled around in the direction we had been briefed to move. As I passed the other chopper on the deck next to ours I saw two of our Marines drag another down the ramp. Gunny Husak took a quick look at this man and waved the men back inside the helo with him. The wounded man's chin hung down on his chest and his feet bumped along behind him. He had been shot in the spine by the same ground fire our chopper had just received. He died of wounds the following day.

Our company landed several hundred meters north of Thon Hai (1). As we were flying the wounded man out, Captain Doherty sent me to recon the river crossing some three hundred meters northwest of us. In moving to the river I took caution. When I got there I crawled around carefully to observe prominent terrain features surrounding the only likely crossing point. I did not like what I saw.

I returned in about a half hour with my report: we could get men across without having to throw up our own bridge, but there were enormous boulders to either side of the area and the foliage around them offered excellent concealment. If the enemy were to open up with fifties from either side while we were crossing, we would be in serious trouble. I asked if we had air on-station. We did.

Jerry sent O. K. Batte across with me and Meyer. The CO also told me to move across as carefully as I thought I had to.

Before we began crossing, I had O. K. call artillery on what I saw to be the two worst danger areas. As the rounds whistled cheerfully in, I had him request that those targets be marked for concentrations, which he did. Even then, however, we moved across the wide expanse with no small amount of trepidation. After that river crossing, Foxtrot Company moved past us along Route 536. About two thousand meters farther, Hotel Company again resumed the point for the battalion, and 3d Platoon again was in the lead.

As Don's pre-op intelligence report had indicated, the terrain throughout the day's movement was ideal for an enemy ambush. We had, moreover, four additional river crossings that day. Because of our extreme vulnerability to ambush, I remained on the point myself the entire operation but maintained visual contact with my closest squad leader and at least one of his men. I did not generally think it best for the platoon commander to be on the point, but in that terrain I had to be. At every turn in the road I assessed our situation carefully, calculated the most likely ambush positions, and considered how we would counter them should the firing begin. Needless to say, I also watched every step of the way for trip wires and probed with my field knife wherever I thought there might be a mine dug in the road. We had no mine detectors.

In the hours before nightfall I encountered a silence throughout the landscape that seemed almost palpable. The air was, for the most part, very clear. Huge boulders loomed on either side of the road. Behind them steep cliffs seemed to stare down upon us. Toward dusk a violent storm kicked up suddenly over the cliffs and rain poured quickly down. The terrain at that time was so bleak that I might have been scared had I been there alone, even if it were not enemy territory. But, because I had my platoon to lead, I felt only a sense of anticipation and a consciousness that I had to get through the day with the fewest casualties I could.

We moved slowly but steadily throughout the afternoon; by evening we had covered nearly eight thousand meters— a good crack under the conditions. About the time our company had reached a village known as Bon (1), a long peal of small-arms and the heavy *tat-tat-tat* of .50-caliber machine gun fire reverberated up the valley toward us.

The last platoon of Golf Company, the last in our battalion to cross the first river I had reconnoitered so carefully earlier, had been hit by an effective ambush. The attack came from the same coordinates I had told O. K. to register concentrations on. I am quite certain the platoon from G Company was commanded by one of the high numbers of noninfantry officer replacements we received when we were on Prairie. I would not be surprised to learn that its lieutenant had by then grown slack and dropped his guard.

Since he seemingly had not made the necessary mental

preparations in advance, the artillery fire brought in was late and largely ineffective. The ambush began at 4:15 P.M. civilian time and the enemy did not break contact until 6 P.M. This was an exceptionally long time to be under fire without effectively silencing the enemy.

Here, too, our air support had let that platoon down. Although air had been on-station when our platoon was going across, it was not available when that last platoon needed it. Fixed-wing support took more than an hour to come up over target. And when two aircraft finally came on-station, they reported that they had another mission and left our area to run what we later learned was a lower-priority strike ten miles south of us. As darkness began to set in, support aircraft finally arrived and stayed on target to enable the G Company platoon to maneuver and evacuate its casualties. By that time, the men had all been wounded nearly two hours: two were already dead and four others seriously wounded. Why the other platoons were not able to move back and help out effectively remains a mystery to me.

As darkness began to fall, our company moved back one thousand meters along the trail and prepared to spend the night on either side of a bridge spanned by steel runway matting supported by railroad rails. The river was about one hundred meters across and eight hundred meters southeast of Ap Bon (1).

The spray and roar of the river several hundred feet beneath us and the bone-wearying fatigue of the day's vigilant patrolling came to me at the same time I realized I would not have to check posts that night. Jammed in as we were on either side of the bridge, and with two companies on the high ground around us for security, we did not even set up a watch for the night. Shortly after dark, with the sound of water roaring beneath us, I leaned backwards against a boulder and lurched into a night of dreamless sleep. When I awoke it was after dawn. The big Marine on the rock above me was still soundly sleeping, his large, jungle-booted feet resting squarely on my shoulders. When I looked up out of curiosity to see who he was, he startled awake, rubbed his eyes, and said with some alarm, "Excuse me, Sir!"

"No problem."

At 0700 Company F remained in position on the ninety-meter hill above us while our company, Company G, and the battalion command group advanced westward. By eleven that morning our company had moved to the vicinity of a village known as Tu Tan (1) in Hiep Duc, where a man who claimed to be a VC agent approached us and asked to turn himself in. He also volunteered to provide us with whatever information he could if we would evacuate him and his family (wife and four children). He told us he had been an ARVN soldier for seven years. When he left the service in 1963 he was captured by the Communists and taken into the hills where he received political indoctrination for one month. Thereafter he had been forced to grow rice for and give information to the Communists.

Shortly after we had the man and his family flown back to the Duc Duc district headquarters, an astonishing thing happened. Several other families soon materialized, approached our interpreter, and said that the people in the three hamlets closest to us likewise desired to be evacuated. They said in essence that the North Vietnamese had controlled the valley for two years and that the people could take no more of it. Stories of subjugation and destruction poured forth so voluminously that our interpreter soon just shrugged his shoulders; he was unable to translate the volume of hardships those people related. Within hours we were besieged by hundreds of families, all of whom pleaded with us to take them out of the area. Many of the people asked to be put to death by us if we were not able to get them out of their present situation.

Men, women, and children from the families swarmed around us. Nearly all were carrying shoulder poles, hastily put together to carry the essentials they hoped to bring with them. We were able to evacuate roughly twenty-three hundred of them, but with more helicopters available we could have lifted out at least twice that number. Most of those we were unable to lift out—the healthiest-looking—we provided such infantry security as we could afford to march back with them to An Hoa, where they were either resettled within the An Hoa compound itself, just outside it, or around My Loc (2).

There is no evidence from the movement of refugees in Indochina that a majority of people in North Vietnamese–occupied areas had welcomed the sort of government it brought with it. True, many refugees probably fled the fighting zones as much because they were afraid of the government's counterattack as because of what the Communists did when they arrived. Nevertheless, they always seemed to move away from the North Vietnamese.

During the next several days we patrolled incessantly day and night. On these days I was struck once again by the beauty of parts of Vietnam. We operated mostly in the mountains on those days. I recollect the way the cool breath of the morning rose up to meet us as we moved out early in the day. Next to the II Corps seashore area we had operated near on Deckhouse I, I found the Hiep Duc Valley to be the most beautiful part of Vietnam that I had seen. It must have been an especially painful move for those refugees who left that peaceful-seeming valley they had once called home.

One afternoon we suddenly came upon a waterfall that we were able to hear for some time but did not see until we were almost under it. Some twenty-five meters across, the falls emanated from a rock ledge about one hundred meters above us. The jungle ran almost right up to its edge, but there was heather on either bank of the stream that tumbled past us. The water was fast-flowing, clear, and cold. For several minutes I paused to watch our men standing shin-deep in the rushing water and dipping their canteens in the stream, a few plopping in iodine tablets for good measure.

Later that day we forded a larger stream, a swirling, brownish-gray flood about thirty-five meters across that was over chest-deep for our shortest men. As they waded in, weapons held high, I thought how important it was to have unit integrity. It must have taken great discipline, especially for our nonswimmers, to move across streams like that in tactical situations.

On December 1, perhaps about the same time the Selection Board in D.C. was deciding on my promotion to captain, I almost made the promotion superfluous.

Around noon my platoon drew automatic weapons fire from a squad of NVA that was dug in about three hundred meters east of Ap Hai (3). When the first burst came I was moving out of a tree line on the edge of a clearing. The bullets chopped back the leaves and branches and sizzled into the paddy water in front of me.

Without a word from me, Corporals Desclos and Lewis yelled, "They're shooting at Lieutenant!" Both squads moved up on the double, formed a skirmish line in front of me, and, firing from the hip, moved smartly after the enemy. As they advanced the only sound was the assault fire they laid down ahead of them as they squelched through the mud. In the meantime I deployed our third squad in reserve, called an 81s mission behind the enemy positions, and joined the charge myself. The enemy broke contact and fled.

Before we had a chance to search the area, one of my squad leaders spotted three stones piled on top of one another on the outskirts of Ap Hai (3). He gestured to me cautiously to come take a look. Several meters away we uncovered a heavy steel, clamp-like bear or tiger trap near the entrance to a deserted hootch that we might have considered as a CP for the night. Before we moved on to surround the now deserted ville, we triggered the trap by using the hook and line we carried with us to set off booby traps. When we hauled the line to, the trap clanged shut with a sickening metallic bite. That device would have amputated an elephant's leg.

In the course of Mississippi we encountered four other traps of the same kind; each one slammed shut on our hook with the same vicious sound. Thanks to the alertness of our men we did not suffer any casualties from them. Nor did our platoon, which often had the point, have a single mine or booby-trap casualty on that operation. On the night we found our first tiger trap, however, I again became an unreported nonbattle casualty in a strange way.

We set in for the night around Ap Hai (3). It was a dark, still night with a light rain falling. About midnight we had a probe near one of our gun positions.

As I began moving to the area of the probe, I called to my men that I was coming; it was so dark I could not see a thing. I took several steps when the ground suddenly disappeared beneath me—I had fallen into a well over twelve feet deep. As I found out the next morning, the mouth of the well was nearly covered by grass and barely visible from above even in daylight. The well expanded as it dropped, so that in order to keep my head above water I had to press both my hands and feet against the slick sides. I remained in this position, about six feet below the opening, for a very long time.

I later learned that my troops at first had no idea what had happened to me. When the sky turned from black to dark gray they were finally able to trace my voice to where I was (they told me afterward that they could hear me calling for help, but that I sounded very far away and they could not figure out where my voice was coming from). At first I called out softly but after a few minutes I began bellowing as loudly as possible. Never have I been so thankful to have been born with strong arms, legs, and lungs.

By the time my men reached me, I was exhausted and waterlogged. Three men, including Sergeant Hoole, attempted to haul me out but lost their grip as I was almost out and I slid back down. I then removed the weight of my helmet, flak jacket, and pistol belt, which did the trick. When they finally got me all the way out, Sergeant Hoole whispered, "Jesus Christ, Lieutenant!" and stepped back to catch his breath.

At the CP hootch I found I had itchy, fat, purple leeches all over my stomach, back, crotch, and both legs. If leeches are pulled off, their teeth stay in and fester, so they had to be removed by touching them with either a lit cigarette butt or the flame from a match. In order to effect this procedure, our platoon corpsman, Jerry Holub, huddled with me under a poncho.

Surveying one part of my body at a time with a flashlight, he carefully removed each leech by touching it with the butt of a lit cigarette. First I stripped from the waist down. Then I removed my flak jacket and blouse while he went over my upper body, chest, and back. This was complicated a bit, however, when midway through the procedure his tiny flashlight was apparently spotted by

Communist gunners. Thereafter we were under steadily cracking and whizzing small-arms fire for the rest of the de-leeching process. When he was finished burning, the youthful-looking, nineteen-year-old corpsman carefully washed the clotted blood off each site with water he poured calmly from his canteen. When he finished, he smiled and said with a broad, northern Illinois accent, "That's it, Lieutenant," as if he had just filled my car's tank with gas.

For the remainder of this operation, whenever any of the troops spotted a well, "the word" was passed in deadpan fashion to their august platoon commander.

During Mississippi, Meyer and I drew fire very often. True to our pre-op vow, we kept hopping and jumping, alertly and continually, so that neither of us was hit, although we had a number of close calls. To my recollection, the only time I wore my bars turned outward when we were in the field in Vietnam was that day the previous summer when I had strolled up and down in front of my 81s to provide a moving target for the Communist gunners. Yet the Communists usually knew who the platoon commanders were, and we were always the prime targets. Next "most wanted" seemed to be the radio operators and corpsmen. The latter were noncombatants, and I never saw one draw his .45 in combat.

On one of the early days on Mississippi I had my first and last run-in with Gunnery Sergeant Burns. After we set up our positions for the evening, we usually arranged to have our squads displace several hundred meters just after dark. Thus, as soon as we moved into a position for the night, I usually sent the CO two pairs of fire plans: one for the positions we would occupy before the move and one for afterward.

In most night defensive plans the emplacement of our machine guns was especially important. On the occasion of our run-in, shortly before nightfall Gunny Burns had moved the platoon's machine guns so that neither position accorded with our night defensive fire plans. This was a serious breach of discipline. I summoned him right away and dressed him down for several minutes. Even then he seemed unrepentant, so I went after him a second time. Thereafter I became somewhat sterner in my dealings with Gunny Burns. Whether or not he came to respect me personally I cannot say, but after this incident he understood who was commanding 3d Platoon.

On that operation, for the first time many of my men became seriously hampered by immersion foot. Fording so many rivers and streams and patrolling through flooded rice paddies continually took its toll in a number of immersion-foot casualties (on December 3 alone, twenty-eight men from our battalion had to be evacuated due to that problem). Our jungle boots tended to dry quickly. And by way of precaution, as often as possible we had the men remove their boots and shoes, wring out their socks, massage their feet, and then powder them. After this, we inspected each man. But on Operation Mississippi we patrolled too extensively in continually wet weather to allow the time to take these preventive measures very often.

During these days, one way that I helped relax our troops was by holding ugly foot contests. When I had time to inspect the men's feet, I sometimes had the squad leaders precede me in the inspection as if it were a formal guard mount. We had each squad leader designate one ugly foot representative. The ugliest feet in each squad then marched front and center, and from them we picked the winner.

In my best hambone fashion I made much of these contests, and the men seemed to love it. Some of the ugliest feet I have ever seen were presented at these inspections. To the winner I usually made some large, ceremonious gesture, such as presenting a delicious can of C rations ham and limas (one of the least favorite of C rats) or a mouth-watering dessert of crackers and cheese.

On the morning of December 4, our company was moving northeast up a trail near Ap Hai (4) when a recon battalion unit spotted a half-dozen NVA by a streambed three hundred meters northeast of us. For reasons unclear to me, Jerry had Marv's platoon reconnoiter first to see if the recon unit's report was correct. Then he ordered 3d Platoon to the assault.

While the 2d Platoon was making its reconnaissance, I

had time to brief my squad leaders and they were able to relay my orders to their squads. The men appeared elated. As we began moving to the river where the enemy had been spotted, I called 60s and 81 mortars on overhead fire missions. The missions had hardly landed when we arrived but the enemy had already vanished almost without a trace, taking their weapons with them and leaving no signs of casualties. The meals they had been cooking, however, were left untouched on small fires.

We continued moving northwest. Around noon, with my platoon still on point for the battalion, we again came under small-arms and automatic weapons fire from across an unmarked stream southeast of us. As we were using fire and maneuver to silence the attack, Captain Doherty had moved 1st and 2d Platoon onto high ground north of us. When these two platoons were in position, he ordered 3d Platoon to break contact and double-time to where he was.

Two of the evacuees we had gotten out a few days before, who had previously been forced by the NVA to carry rice up a steep mountain trail to an NVA rice storage area, flew out to the field with us to direct us to these rice bins. When we arrived at Jerry's position, he sent one of the informants with us and told us to follow the man up a steep trail to the rice.

As I left, Jerry smiled and said, "Go get it, Jim." Leaving Gunny Burns with the base of fire, I took at least one squad with me in trace of the sprinting Vietnamese. We swung rapidly into the draw from the left at a dead run and ascended a steep, overgrown jungle trail.

On the way up our scout stopped several times to point to the deck: *"By no. Coo rup. High"* ("Booby trap. Explosives. Two."), where 60mm mortar rounds had been rigged to trip wires at several places on either side of the trail. We blew most of these with our four-pronged hook and line. On one occasion we used a well-placed frag grenade.

At first we found three bins, then two more—five in all. Each was made of heavy wood and the size of an average seashore vacation cottage. In a letter home I estimated at the time that we had taken thirty-five tons of rice, but I later learned the figure was nearly fifty-one tons.

Before we could bag the rice to ship it back to the refugees at An Hoa we had to clear several LZs in the jungle canopy, no mean feat, as those who have tried it will say. All day long, from the fourth through the seventh, our men bagged the rice and hauled it onto the choppers.

Every night I retired to our platoon CP on a cliffside at the summit of the trail that led up to the rice. From there I could make out a whitewater river swirling through a steep gorge some two hundred meters below. Around mid-morning each day I clambered up to the platoon CP to have breakfast. From there Bob Meyer and I talked occasionally of home while we watched foaming swells cascade over the polished rocks below. A mist wafted over us the whole time.

Operation Mississippi ended for our bone-weary men around 1700 (5 P.M.) on December 7. Our helicopter extraction was in the area where our platoon's assault had begun on the third. The lift-out was smooth, rapid, and well executed—the kind of support we normally had in Vietnam. On that operation we had denied the enemy nearly fifty-one tons of his staple food and evacuated thousands of refugees. Our battalion had had two men killed, one who died of wounds, six WIA, and forty-nine nonbattle casualties, mostly due to immersion foot. On that operation, for medevacs the average time from request to completion was approximately thirty-five minutes—longer than usual.

In addition to the rice we captured enormous caches of enemy clothing and equipment as well as several weapons. Of enemy casualties we had only one KIA, three probable, one WIA, and about two dozen prisoners. Of those, eleven rallied to our side and began operating with ARVN units. In his postoperation summary, Colonel Airheart remarked that "Operation MISSISSIPPI was undertaken with approximately 50 percent of equipment and personnel on hand to support two Battalion-size units." In the two battalions (less Company E from our battalion) combined, there were less than one thousand Marines when we began the operation—this was somewhat less than 50 percent of TO strength.

We had no direct enemy contact from December 7 to 14, but continued working hard on patrols of all kinds around My Loc (2) and Phu Lac (6). In the fifty days from the time we moved into the An Hoa area on November 22 until the day I was wounded, our platoon ran approximately 72 combat and reconnaissance patrols and laid in 31 ambushes. We had had, moreover, at least as much activity when we were up north on Prairie. During those 110 days alone, I planned and briefed my squad leaders for more than 150 combat and recon patrols and 65 ambushes. When we were not patrolling, we were often conducting civic action missions. About both of those I shall have more to say later.

After Operation Mississippi, all the villagers we had evacuated from Antenna Valley were resettled in the An Hoa region. As a seeming reward, most of the refugees were resettled outside My Loc (2) where my platoon often served on independent duty. Thus, to the twenty-five or so families who had been living just outside our barbed wire before Mississippi we now added more than a thousand South Vietnamese. I cannot speak for the other men in my platoon, but I can say this: after the new villagers arrived and we helped them get set up, whenever we returned from a patrol through their area, regardless of the time or the weather, the new villagers all mustered out to greet me and my men as we came back in. The South Vietnamese did this always in the same fashion; they made a lengthy human avenue for us by lining up in absolute silence as we passed by into our positions on My Loc (2). I recall, for instance, returning on a cold, rainy night from a several hours' patrol at roughly 0345, and yet still having this silent human lane formed for us roughly the last two hundred meters out from our wire. Somehow the adults even managed to have the children remain silent as we passed through, an earnest gesture of respect the memory of which remains with me even today. At An Hoa I wrote my mother, "I think I will like it [the An Hoa area]. It has been raining a great deal. As long as we keep busy, the time goes by fast." The first statement was intended to cheer my family but was not strictly accurate; the last two were.

As I peruse my letters home, I see continually such

expressions as, "I don't care to leave these men now [to go on R&R] since all of them are so great and they seem to depend on me." I believe my men thought I was somewhat of a "warmonger," as I put it in one of my letters. I also seemed to enjoy myself a great deal in the field, and those emanations may have made the men somewhat more aggressive and enthusiastic than they might have been under a platoon commander who was more morose.

It is difficult to convey the high spirits and morale we had in 3d Platoon. And I have reason to believe the same kind of spirit existed in many other units in the Corps at that time. Statistics are the driest form of evidence but they sometimes serve to indicate significant aspects of experience. Till that time in the war, over 9,000 Marines had been wounded in action in Vietnam. Of them, more than 80 percent returned to duty. Of that 80 percent a remarkably high percentage returned to duty in Vietnam. In 1967, the year I was wounded, 13,089 Marines were wounded severely enough to require hospitalization. Of that number, too, many returned to duty in some capacity.

Among them were many of the men in the platoons I commanded in Vietnam. One was an unheroic-looking Marine corporal named Kennick, whose hometown was Pittsburgh. He joined us after an extended period in a hospital in Guam where he had been recuperating from wounds that included a shattered right hip. Unassumingly he mentioned this to me one day before we went out on patrol. He added, almost as an afterthought, that his injuries had left his right leg without feeling. My first impulse when he told me this was to give him a large bear hug but I restrained myself.

After Mississippi we were also joined at My Loc (2) by PFCs Sinke and Richards. Both men were draftees and, like all the ones we had in 3d Platoon, they proved the infelicity of the adage "one volunteer is better than three pressed men." Both were somewhat older than most of the other Marines in the platoon: Richards I believe was twenty-three and Sinke twenty-two. Both were machine gunners.

Richards had rejoined us from the hospital where he had been recuperating from a hernia he had sustained while carrying some of our wounded into an LZ on Prairie. He was black, of medium height and build, and had a B.S. degree in botany from Chicago State University.

Sinke was a former football player and a large man. In his hands the machine gun looked like a child's metal toy. Shortly after he joined us, he extended two years in the Corps. As the reader may recall, Sinke had received serious leg wounds on Prairie, injuries which should have been his ticket home. When his orders to the States came in, however, he protested vehemently. As was related to us by unimpeachable sources, the doctors told him, "No, you are going. Your legs can't take another wound."

Not so, Sinke responded. The doctors insisted. Sinke requested Mast (a meeting) to see the general. General Ryan was still commanding general of the 9th MAB, the quiet officer I had met on that overcast day when we left NTA. He had responsibility for all Marine Corps personnel in the Western Pacific, exclusive of Vietnam. When PFC Sinke went to General Ryan, he asked to be returned to Vietnam and to rejoin 3d Platoon. General Ryan read Sinke's medical report and said no. At that, Sinke did several series of deep knee bends and squat thrusts in front of the general's desk. About the time Sinke began running in place, General Ryan reportedly shook his head and told Sinke, "Well if you want to go back there that badly . . ." The general stamped the orders himself.

When Sinke rejoined us at My Loc (2) he was smiling as though he had just discovered gold. The men in the platoon went over to shake his hand, put their arms around him, and welcome him back. Need I say we were glad to have him?

Within several weeks of his having rejoined 3d Platoon, PFC Richards was badly wounded by an enemy explosive device. I was moving near the point at the time. I turned to grab the handset from Meyer to report that we had discovered another mine and would be taking a few minutes to blow it before we moved on. As I turned back to Meyer, Richards, some seventy meters behind us, tripped the device, flew six feet through the air, and landed on his stomach. As always, our corpsman, Doc Holub, got to the

wounded man in a hurry. As we were waiting for the medevac chopper, I told Richards, "You'll be all right."

"I'm not going, Sir."

"What do you mean? You can't stay out here in the
boonies with wounds like those."

"I'm not going, Sir. I'm going to stay with this platoon and man my gun," he said weakly but steadily. "Nobody can handle this gun like I can, and I'm not going."

After much unsuccessful coaxing by me and Gunny
Burns, Captain Graham finally persuaded Richards to assent to go out on the medevac chopper. It was nearly settled into the LZ by the time we finally persuaded him to
leave. Tears were streaming across his forehead as we carried him, head hanging back over the torn shelter half, to
the chopper. He looked up and waved good-bye as the
chopper lifted him up and away.

As he left I thought to myself, when the only discipline
problems one has are squad leaders who quarrel as to which
squad will take the point and wounded men who refuse
evacuation, one may have what is known as good morale.

Every once in a while I went on squad-size patrols, usually as an ammo carrier for the machine gunners. On one of
those days as I jogged forward, PFC Spain made an audible
crack about "the best paid ammo humper in the Corps." On
the rare occasions when we had hot chow flown out to us on
our outpost, I usually joined the three-man serving line, and
the troops seemed to appreciate the gesture.

The infantry platoon commander must know how to
lead his men, and when to leave them alone. But he must
also know how to care for them. I found daylight post-
checking to be a particularly good time to do that. At night
I was forced to whisper, but in the daylight we could speak in
conversational tones.

On these tours of the lines I was able to see if the men
were alert and if their morale was high. I was also able to
see if the area around each position was well policed and
if the men were in good health. Under the conditions,
left to themselves, a large enough number of the men
might have littered the area sufficiently to cause a health

hazard. By continual inspections we were able to help head off many health problems before they developed.

On my tours of our positions I was continually impressed by the way the men were able to make themselves comfortable in the most difficult circumstances. Their ingenuity in rigging waterproof shelters and concocting "special treats" for themselves seemed to increase in proportion to the hardships presented by their environment.

I looked after my Marines as best I could, but they looked after me also. I cannot recall, for instance, how many mornings Gunny Burns, Sergeant Hoole, Meyer, or someone else from the platoon CP would bring me a good, freshly heated cup of coffee as soon as I got up in the morning. Often, too, men from the squads placed small packages of "goodies," such as a canned ham or a cake from home, outside the flap of my tent in the morning so the items would be there before I could know who had left them.

On the rare days when no patrols were imminent, the platoon sometimes cooked up "stews" in a large can we had. The concoctions were usually made from C rations that most of the men did not like, such as "Beefsteak and Potatoes," "Pork Steak," "Beef, Spiced," and "Ham and Limas." To those were often added handpicked wild onions, hot sauce, catsup, and whatever other spices or condiments we had on hand. Amazingly, the mixtures often produced tasty meals.

At that time I had a great appetite for chocolates, a liking Sergeant Hoole had remarked upon. One day when we were at My Loc (2) we were anticipating an incoming load of fresh ammunition, C rations, and mail, but by a logistical foul-up we received two enormous, transparent plastic bags full of Hershey Bars. Sergeant Hoole and a working party had been standing by the LZ, awaiting the drop-off of the expected supplies. When he saw what actually came in, he hauled both enormous bags over to the platoon CP and said in his best manner, grinning broadly, "Here you go, Lieutenant! We got enough of these here Hershey's to last you on patrol all day today. This bag is plain. And this here bag is Hershey's with nuts!"

When we were at My Loc (2), a pair of replacements flew in to join us one dreary, rainy evening. After talking to the men briefly, Hoole called over to me: "Lieutenant! We have two new ones. They both say they like Ham and Limas. And one doesn't even like Hershey Bars."

"We'll take them!" I responded enthusiastically. Nearly everyone within earshot laughed vigorously, except the bewildered replacements.

On early-morning patrols around My Loc (2) the scent of the long, dewy grass drifted up to us as we filed through the wire to leave our positions. Many of the men carried mosquito repellent or a can of rifle oil under the black rubber camouflage band on their helmets. On daytime patrols they generally also had large bushes of camouflage protruding above their helmet covers. When we were not on patrols, one could often read on the sides of a man's helmet cover his nickname, possibly his girlfriend's name, and often his hometown.

On the tenth of December when we left our position, the air was still opaque with mist. We moved southwest about fifteen hundred meters, where we began a search-and-destroy mission through a pair of small villages, Phu Nuan (8) and Phu Nuan (2). As we wove through, we had the difficult task of searching every house to look for signs of the enemy.

In one of the centrally located houses in Phu Nuan (2), Meyer and I encountered a husband and wife who carried themselves with more dignity than almost any people I have met. I later ascertained he was the *xa quan* or village mandarin, a man looked up to in the village because of his learning and the degree of political influence he had on the local chief. When we entered, Bob and I endeavored to convey our apologies for having to conduct our search. We were doubly embarrassed since we had entered as they were just preparing to have breakfast.

Both husband and wife acted far more understanding than I could have, had I found myself in similar circumstances. On that occasion, Meyer and I could not resist being somewhat more friendly than we generally were when on an S&D mission. Our overtures presumably cost this old couple dearly.

"Chow" (Hello).

"Chow," they replied, nodding graciously toward us as we entered.

"Um mon yoy come?" (How are you?) I asked with a smile.

"Toy mon you" (I'm fine) the old man replied as both smiled and stood up, nodding toward us again.

They were perhaps in their late sixties, slender, and graceful in white gowns. In that small household there existed a sense of peace such as I have seldom felt.

The husband said something to his wife that I did not understand, then both gestured to Meyer and me to sit down with them and have breakfast. They offered us tea, a nearly unpalatable biscuit, and vegetable soup. The soup was flavored with *nuoc mam,* a fermented sauce made of fish and salt that gave the soup a strong odor and made it hard for me to take. The tea was weak, made with lukewarm water and not at all tasty. The generosity and grace with which everything was served, however, induced Meyer and me to eat everything we were offered and to refrain from using iodine tabs for purification, since we felt that might offend our host and hostess.

"Come un um" (Thank you) we both said sincerely.

"Um noy tyen Ahn come?" (Do you speak English?).

"Sin loy um, toy come hew" (Excuse me, I don't understand) he replied with an apologetic smile. She whispered to him and both shook their heads, *"Yah kum"* (No).

Meyer and I sat there with them for a few additional moments. Scarcely a word was spoken, but with smiling faces we may have communicated the goodwill we felt toward them. Before we left we rummaged through our packs for all the C rations we had with us and placed them on their dining table. With a thoughtfulness most typical of him, Meyer removed a can opener from his dog-tag chains, showed them how to use it to open the cans, and left that with them, too. He also left several packs of matches. For those small gestures both husband and wife seemed very appreciative.

"Come un um" (Thank you), we said as we stood up to leave.

"Kum Kaw chee" (You're welcome). *"Come un um!"*

they repeated with more emphasis as we began to walk away. *"Choop (um) my man!"* (Good luck!), they called out as they waved good-bye. They stood together on their narrow veranda and waved quietly to us.

"Choop (um) my man!" we called back to them.

About three days afterward we moved through the ville again. The small house had been firebombed, its apertures scorched all around, and the narrow veranda torn up board by board. The beautiful old couple were nowhere inside. Behind the house one of our fire teams found the boards on the edge of the encroaching elephant grass. The putrefaction led us into the brush where we discovered them: their slender bodies clung together even in death.

Meyer and I looked from them to each other and back again in silence. Neither of us ever said a word to each other about it, but by the look on Meyer's face, I could tell that he felt the same sense of devastation I did.

By mid-December the other companies in our battalion had already made a great deal of enemy contact in the An Hoa TAOR. 3d Platoon's first firefight in the area, however, did not take place until the fourteenth. The contact was light but memorable for me. At least two of our platoons and the company command group were patrolling five thousand meters southeast of Phu Lac (6). Just after noon, 3d Platoon, which was bringing up the rear, drew rifle fire from several enemy gunners who were across a small stream not marked on our map. Captain Doherty told me to go get them, and added, "We'll put 60s on them while you're going across."

We moved with one or two squads across the stream and had the rest lay down a base of fire to provide direct coverage as we crossed. The first volleys of 60 mortar fire landed in the heavy brush atop a high bank on the other side of the stream, at just the place where the enemy fire seemed to be coming from. Soon after that, the enemy small-arms fire appeared to cease, but the 60s rounds continued getting closer and closer. I grabbed the handset and told the CP that the mortar rounds were coming very close. Two more whistled within six feet of us, plunking geysers of water out of the stream and spraying Meyer and myself.

The blasts nearly knocked my helmet off and sent shrapnel singing all around us. Right after these volleys Gunny Gonzalez came up on the company tac net: "We stopped firing our 60s several minutes ago." With a stifled laugh he released his handset as he said, "Over."

"Move it out in a hurry! These 60s are not ours!" The squad ahead of us moved across the rest of the way as though the men were waterborne. When we searched the area across the stream, we found tracks to indicate that two or three men had been there. We also discovered blood on the ground and drag marks that led into heavy brush, but we did not pursue them.

I believe it was on the fifteenth that Captain Doherty told me to fly into Da Nang to get our company's pay records squared away. That morning a helicopter came to lift me back to An Hoa, where I met Sergeant Smith from company headquarters. The two of us picked up a helicopter to take us into Da Nang. The pay roster was badly scrambled: we had sustained many casualties on Prairie and many of our killed and wounded were still being carried on our roster at Disbursing. With Sergeant Smith's assistance, in hours we straightened out in person an amount of administrative confusion that would have taken reams of written messages.

Even at that time in the war Da Nang was more a small city than a town. It already held many thousands of refugees from the countryside, and far more people— Marines and civilians—than I ever expected to see in one place in Vietnam. I could not help but think that at least some of the support personnel there might have been better employed out in the field where the war was really being fought. My limited contact with the Marine officers in Da Nang, however, soon led me to believe that virtually all of them were quite happy where they were. I met only two there—Lt. Dave Harbor and one other—who seemed to me to really care very much about the war.

On my return to My Loc (2), our whole company was flown back into An Hoa, where, for several days, we served as battalion reserve in our TAOR. For that mission, 3d Platoon was designated sparrow-hawk platoon. The sparrow-hawk unit was on around-the-clock standby with full weapons, ammunition, and equipment. We slept with our uniforms on and the squads stayed together at all times.

The actions described below I am nearly certain took place on December 17, but our unit diaries attribute the mission to a platoon from George Burgett's Company F, and most of the details of our day's activities are incompletely recorded.

At the An Hoa base our troops were billeted in squad tents over wooden decks, and the company officers and NCOs were in wood-frame huts with screens in lieu of bulkheads, with wooden decks such as the troops had. At the time of our sparrow-hawk landing, my platoon had twenty-nine men, including myself. All the men were billeted in three squad tents not far from where I slept. Around 1100 a messenger ran huffing into our quarters to tell me that the CO wanted me to alert my men and come as quickly as possible to the battalion combat operations center. I ran to the 3d Platoon's squad tents and gave Gunny Burns a warning order to have the platoon drawn up near the runway. Each of us already had three C ration meals, enough ammunition for at least a day's fighting, and two canteens of water apiece so there was no scrambling to issue supplies. I told the Gunny I would join the platoon as soon as I could.

As I jogged down the muddy street I swung into my flak jacket and snicked a fresh clip of ammunition into the butt of my .45. In covering the one hundred or so meters to the COC, I felt the way I always did before field day meets in training and before other competitions I was well prepared for: I had an empty feeling in the pit of my stomach and felt steadily disposed to yawn.

When I reached the COC, Captain Doherty was standing outside looking more worried than I had ever seen him. He briefed me quickly on the situation: an aerial observer had reportedly spotted one hundred NVA moving through a ville at coordinates 962 532, eleven thousand meters northeast of us. The colonel then appeared and took Jerry below to brief him. Captain Doherty earnestly tried to talk Colonel Airheart into allowing us to land our whole company right away. I believe I assured Jerry, if only tacitly, that 3d Platoon could handle the job well by itself. And that was the course the colonel had apparently already decided upon. With a somewhat doleful look Jerry climbed out of the narrow, sandbagged COC bunker to relay the landing order to me.

I ran almost as fast as I could to the runway, where my platoon was drawn up and waiting with the patient coolness I had come to expect. By that time I was so excited I could hardly breathe, but when I saw the way my men were assembled, I calmed down quite a bit. "Squad leaders, up!" I briefed the squad leaders as fully as I could but before I did, I said something like: "We have them where we want them now."

I told the squad leaders the size of the enemy force, and said that as soon as possible we would be landing north of the village Le Bac (2), where the NVA were seen. I related the supporting arms information and told them our mission was "to search for and kill the enemy." I gave our order of movement into the LZ and the place where we were to land.

As always, I double-checked to make sure the men had sufficient ammo, rations, water, and equipment. I indicated how we would handle casualties and prisoners, were any taken. Our hand and arm signals remained the same, and I mentioned the color of the smoke grenades we would use for various purposes. I related our radio call signs and frequencies for unit transmissions, including supporting arms and medevacs. I reminded the NCOs of our chain of command, that is, who would replace whom if we had casualties, and I told Gunny Burns where to look for me after he landed.

As always, I paused at the end of my five-paragraph order and asked if there were any questions. There followed a silence as eloquent as it was brief, a moment in which Gunny Burns, Sergeant Hoole, and each of our squad leaders exchanged looks filled with depths sufficient for a lifetime. With my confidence in that unit greater than ever, I concluded, "The time is . . . 11:30."

As an afterthought I said, with perhaps too much theatricality, "Gunny, make sure the men are locked and loaded—and have them fix bayonets."

"Aye, aye, Sir."

Just after that a Marine helo flew in that carried a general from division along with his small staff. Thinking I might be able to persuade the chopper pilot to take at least some of us in right away, I ran across the runway, waving my arms to have the pilot hold his aircraft down. I climbed onto the side of the chopper and showed him the place on the map where I wanted him to take us, but he shook his head "no" and indicated that he had other missions.

As I returned to the platoon most of the men seemed to be trying to suppress smiles at my antics. By the time I rejoined the platoon, the Gunny had prudently countermanded my order about the bayonets. There would presumably be time enough to fix them, if needed, after we got off the choppers; having exposed bayonets aboard the choppers would complicate egress, as the Gunny correctly explained. In my mind I already knew that, but my emotional side had taken over. Soon the first wave of helicopters shuddered down to the runway to lift us out.

Just before noon I came in on the assault wave with my second squad. Our helicopter bounced once and skidded a few yards before it stopped and the ramp went down. I led the men out the tail of the chopper and circled around behind a hedgerow to wait for the rest of the platoon to land. I believe my senses were keener then than they have ever been before or since—the instincts of the hunter reappeared again in the clearest fashion. I saw nobody moving in the compound; the only sounds were those of wounded animals. The hut closest to me was on fire and the pungent smell of burnt cordite was heavy in the air.

Gunny Burns came in with the rest of the platoon in a helicopter which arrived a few minutes after ours. When the Gunny signaled that all were present, I gave the order to advance and we began to move through the village. I approached the rear of the first house still standing. It was a small place with orange mud walls dotted across with cannon holes from the attack aircraft that had just preceded us. In the yard a water buffalo lay on its side pawing the air slowly, and a few ragged chickens scurried back and forth. I sprinted across the yard and kicked open the back door of the house, where I found them. I did not stay there long, but what I saw then I would not soon forget.

As I stepped out to the flashing sun, the world pivoted, hard and crystalline. Every detail of the stained scene registered; the mother with the infant's body across her lap; the grandfather rocking back and forward, smitten to silence on the shell-blasted veranda; the scattered pots on the crimson earth; the fine plume of smoke drifting from the compound; the cicadas drumming in the shade, denying the monsoon had come. I stood still for a few moments. I knew my mind must follow the arrow and trace its path, from the hunted to the hunter and back again. That in one vital, private respect, I had almost done with war.

Just inside the next few houses were other bodies already laid out on pallets and covered by straw mats, their edges thickly clustered with flies. "Four more KIA," I muttered, almost as though I were talking to myself. "And three more," I said again, only half aloud, as we came to the next building.

"They want to know if they're VC, Sir." Meyer's voice broke through to me. "Sir, the CO wants to know if they're VC. Lieutenant? Sir?"

"They're VC," I mumbled, remembering on the edge of my consciousness the comment I had overheard the pilots make at Cubi Point.

"Sir?"

"Tell them they're VC!" I responded testily, gazing at the pink slabs of jelly on the fetid pallets resting on a sturdy wooden table that must have recently served meals for this family.

When I stepped outside of the third or fourth hut we went through, I encountered a half-dozen or more women, and perhaps as many children, swaying back and forth, clutching each other, shaking their handkerchiefs at Bob and me, wailing and screaming more piercingly than I ever hope to hear again.

Meyer said nothing more, but looked at me with a sense of disappointment and grief.

"Tell them we can't really tell if they are VC or not."

"Aye, aye, Sir," he promptly responded, his confidence somewhat restored. ". . . that's affirm. Over."

"Tell them we just found a few more, Meyer."

"Aye, aye, Sir," he replied dolefully.

We had probably moved halfway through the ville when we received a transmission ordering us to join F Company, not far west of our position and moving in our general direction. To effect that liaison I moved toward the point of our lead squad. As so often happened when we were moving away from an area in Vietnam, the enemy opened fire on our tail unit. Moderate rifle fire directed at our trailing squad snapped me out of my dark mood. I had come to detest war, yet I still believed we were trying to do the right thing, and as long as I was in the field I would take care of my men.

We expended nearly all the 60s rounds we had with us in countering the enemy squad that was firing at us. In addition I called in artillery that seemed effective. The adjusting round, however, came very close to Meyer and me, raising a fountain of brown paddy water some few thirty-five meters away. The two of us emerged dripping mud after diving headlong to duck the round.

Shortly before we made contact with Foxtrot Company, Gunny Burns was wounded. When I inquired as to how serious the wound was, PFC Rommans—presumably at the Gunny's command—replied, "Minor. Over."

"Where is he hit? Over."

"Wait one. . . . In the head. Over."

"In the head—a minor wound? Wait out."

I sprinted to the tail of our unit and found Gunny Burns standing, one foot on a rock, supervising our return fire with the dignity of Washington crossing the Delaware.

"Where are you hit, Gunny?"

"Down here, Sir," he replied, pointing to his crotch while gazing into the brush where the rifle fire was coming from. A small hole was visible in his utilities.

"Unbutton and let me take a look."

"No, Sir," he responded firmly, a touch of annoyance in his voice. "I ain't gone ta unbutton an' I ain't gone ta leave this platoon."

In the middle of what seemed increasingly heavy small-arms fire, we had a brief discussion as to whether the Gunny would consent to leave. Throughout, I felt the impulse to lie down as flat as I could, but feared that from below I would not be able to induce him to leave. Still, the Gunny did not relent.

I had Meyer call for a medevac chopper anyway. I figured we would somehow or other get the ornery s.o.b. aboard. After finding that Burns could walk all right, I ran back to the head of the platoon and led the troops several hundred meters until we established contact with the leading elements of Company F.

Capt. George Burgett was still commanding that company; he was seriously wounded and evacuated on operation Tuscaloosa the next month. George was a solidly built captain with long, powerful arms, a perpetual five o'clock shadow, square jaw, and casual demeanor.

Before we resumed our tactical movement to An Hoa, George gave a five-paragraph order spelling out for the five platoon commanders present everything we might need to know about the tactics of our movement. I was surprised when George said, "Lieutenant Kirschke, if something happens to me and I can't maintain command, you will take command of F Company and your own platoon." I looked around and noticed there was not one other lieutenant in George's company at this time. And at least one of the maneuver platoons was commanded by an E-5 sergeant who appeared to be younger than any of my squad leaders. Before long that NCO showed evidence of an inability to read map and terrain.

About the time the movement order was completed, the evacuation helo was on-station. Finally, the Company F gunnery sergeant, Gunny Brian Jones, an older man than Gunny Burns, was able to hustle the latter onto the helicopter. I recognized the deliberateness of the F Company gunny's gesture as he grasped Burns's arm and "escorted" him along—it was the same one that Captain Getchell used when he had spirited Don to the last evacuation chopper after the "Clausewitz ambush" in October.

Within less than a thousand meters of where we

joined Foxtrot we came to a large, open area—a sizable field affording little cover—about three hundred meters from the Cay Khe Vinh Trinh River. All of F Company had crossed the field without a shot being fired. The area was overlooked by high ground to the south. From there the enemy had excellent fields of fire. And they used them. About the time I got across with our leading squad, a reinforced squad opened up on our trailing two.

My trailing squads were at the edge of the clearing when the fire began. The enemy appeared to be shooting from semiautomatic weapons positions that had apertures just above the deck. Our troops not yet across went to ground right away. I directed the squad I was with where to fire, although I was not absolutely sure where the fire was coming from, and became less so when I moved onto the open field myself.

Seeing that my trailing squads were stalled, the F Company Gunny, Brian Jones, with the idea of keeping our men moving across, hustled from his position toward the center of the field. Instinctively I was up and running. With a jerk of my thumb I told him to go back to his own company.

There was a dip in the ground on the side of the trail where I positioned myself. By having the men run past me they could take advantage of whatever cover the lower ground afforded for that part of their crossing. On my command, both squads moved across in fire-team rushes. I moved the men along in much the same way a football coach might encourage his men in pregame drills, except I kept sprinting back and forth myself over about a twenty-five-meter area so as not to provide a very stable target. It seemed I was running among the spatting, whizzing, and cracking bullets a very long time, but it probably was not more than several minutes. That none of our men were hit in that action seemed just short of miraculous and brought me no small sense of satisfaction.

After F Company crossed the Cay Khe Vinh Trinh, 3d Platoon moved to the point—our position the rest of the way back. That evening we covered the eleven thousand grueling meters back to An Hoa and had no additional casualties.

By the time we returned to An Hoa it was after midnight,

yet the battalion mess sergeant had prepared a hot meal for all our troops. As I watched the men filing through the wires my impulse was to hug every one of them.

When I returned to our quarters my adrenaline was still flowing strongly and I paced back and forth over the boards. Jerry Doherty said something like, "Lie down and get some sleep, Jim. You may need it tomorrow." I followed his advice and drifted off as if someone had clubbed me asleep.

Jerry, alas, was right. I was shaken awake by him less than four hours later. For some reason we had to move back right away to My Loc (2).

After a day like the one we just had, I felt I needed about twelve hours' sleep and a good meal. I had had less than four hours' sack time and had not eaten since breakfast the previous day. Before 5 A.M. we were on the muddy road, standing in the rain while waiting for a movement order from the Skipper. Feeling nauseated and dizzy from hunger and fatigue, we waited for what seemed a very long time for our point fire team to clear the first hundred meters or so out of the camp. Before dawn the rain grew heavy, trickling down my helmet and into my flak jacket and producing goose bumps over my shivering frame. Physically, I believe that was the low point of my tour. At first light, however, we were on the move and slowly I began to warm up from the mental and physical activity of supervising the platoon's maneuvers into My Loc (2).

Our next enemy contact was on the nineteenth. I took a security patrol two thousand meters or so south of My Loc (2). Around 6 P.M. we received about eighty rounds of small-arms fire from an estimated ten VC. We had one WIA, whose name I do not recall (that man at first also refused evacuation). We returned fire and gave pursuit, but the enemy fled west and left no signs of casualties.

On the night of the twentieth we conducted an ambush on the swampy edge of a village called Phu Lac (5), about one thousand meters west of My Loc (2). We went out with two reinforced squads. Aside from a few rounds of small-arms fire just before we set in, we made no contact on that long, dark night of pouring rain.

After dark, keeping the men awake and alert on post was a major concern but it was especially so during the monsoon season. Every evening the squad leaders, platoon sergeant (now Sergeant Hoole again), the platoon guide, and myself would arrange a post-checking schedule to ensure that the men were not sleeping on post.

Several times Sergeant Hoole and I found PFC Holdberg asleep on post. On these occasions we had his post-mates Jackson, Lance Corporal O'Connor, and the young Marine from Long Beach remove their flak jackets, blouses, and skivvie shirts and lie in the prone position in the mud until we got back to their post forty minutes later. By the time we returned we found all three shivering in the wind and rain. The looks on the faces of Jackson and O'Connor indicated that they would do their best to assure Holdberg would not make that mistake again.

We had, of course, many nighttime probes at An Hoa. As our intelligence briefings correctly observed, the enemy swarmed around our TAOR; it was the remarkable night that had no contacts after dark. What the enemy seemed to do was probe our various units' lines. Where they found a weak spot they tried to pour in as many men as possible. Thanks mainly to the vigilance of our NCOs, our platoon remained invulnerable to such probes.

We got to know the terrain we were operating in quickly, and the men on post rapidly became familiar with what belonged in front of them and what did not. Around My Loc (2) and other populated areas, however, guarding a post after dark was difficult partially because there was often more activity in the villes at night than we would have liked. We could not very well stop people from going outside after dark to relieve themselves (needless to say, there was no indoor plumbing where we operated), children often made much noise, and of course, the farm animals moved around in their pens. To me, the landscapes around My Loc (2) and the other areas we operated in near An Hoa sometimes assumed a sinister aspect after dark. Our platoon's alertness and fire discipline under those circumstances I found especially admirable.

When checking posts after a probe, I always tried to exude a sense of cheerful aggressiveness as if to say, "How many of these bastards are we going to get to kill tonight?" After a week or so with my platoon, I found that after contact was made after dark, in particular, the men appeared to look forward to having me slide into their positions on the double. I believe the men thought I was more of a warmonger than I was, and if anything, my "visits" helped us present a strong, well-knit front.

On the morning of the twenty-second, our company participated in a "County Fair"—a joint operation with ARVN and Popular Force units in our TAOR. The operation was scheduled to get under way officially at about 0800, but, in order to do that our company and elements of H&S had to meet both the ARVN 3/51st and at least two platoons of South Vietnamese Popular Forces from Company 369 at different locations prior to first light.

The operation therefore involved an extended night movement before the commencement of the County Fair itself. In order to reduce the chances of confusion, Captain Doherty ordered me to take a small security force to reconnoiter the approaches to the 3/51 ARVN company and the PF outposts and do whatever I could once I got to each position to aid our liaison early the next morning.

About three hours before nightfall we moved out. Meyer looked especially tired that evening and, since I thought we could do without the radio for the brief mission, I decided to have him stay behind and get some sleep. That was very nearly a grave mistake, for reasons I shall not go into here.

During the County Fair we made several light contacts. The PFs apprehended two VC and four VC suspects. Our company and the ARVN provided security, and the PFs and H&S Company distributed clothing and food, and administered much medical treatment to the civilians in Phu Nuan (2) and Phu Nuan (3).

About the operation itself the only specifics I recall are that we encountered another of those infernal bear/tiger traps, which we spotted before it did us harm; also, when we surrounded Phu Nuan (2) my men found a wild pig, which they asked permission to kill and roast. I gave permission, but, for civic action reasons that was probably wrong. For the next half hour or so a chase ensued, with "here piggy-piggy" being heard here and "here piggy-piggy" there at different places in the brush. Before long the squealing started. Then there was the smell of roasting pork. And then PFC Spain, with a wordless smile, brought me a flattened C ration carton covered with the greasiest, tastiest roast pork I have ever eaten.

The forty-eight hours after the conclusion of the County Fair were busier than usual. The existence of Communist-held territory across the Song Thu Bon and the Song Ba Ren within our TAOR was the cause of no small amount of confusion on my part. When I was informed of the situation by Don our first week at An Hoa, on the one hand I thought, why should this situation be allowed to continue? Why not send our units across and wipe them out? On the other hand, I thought of the large number of casualties we would likely sustain if we did, and I concluded that the effort might not be worth making. With air strikes and artillery we could perhaps have eliminated most of the population within twenty-four hours. But that did not seem a very moral or honorable way of proceeding. There would be many innocent people—both non-Communists and uncommitted, old people unable to leave if they wanted to, and many children and their mothers. Within forty-eight hours of the beginning of the County Fair, with the monsoon in full force, we went across with our Marines.

Not long after the County Fair had officially ended, Captain Doherty summoned me to his CP and told me to reconnoiter possible fording sites on the Song Ba Ren. If I could get across I was to do so clandestinely and report on its fordability as soon as I got back. Lieutenant Ebbert's company would attempt a crossing the next morning.

I did not ask why I had been chosen for the mission but presumed it was a feather; it was unusual for a lieutenant from one company to do a reconnaissance for another. I have always been a strong swimmer and Jerry may have known that. Moreover, I have always had an ability to concentrate all my powers on the job at hand, what one of my university professors once referred to as my "passion for thoroughness." Both traits were needed in doing a river reconnaissance. But by then I may have been the only 0302 (officially qualified) lieutenant platoon commander in our battalion.

Sergeant Hoole had Desclos's entire squad join me as security. In the gathering darkness I briefed Corporal Desclos, who in turn had a short time to brief his men before we moved out.

The night was black when we moved out, the rain drumming loudly enough to obscure most of the noise we made in moving. It was the best weather for patrolling, I thought, since we did not need to fear detection too much, and even the roaches were likely to be in their beds. Not far north of My Loc (2) we came across a large bomb crater. Rather than risk having any of the men fall in, I turned and whispered, "Pass the word. Bomb crater to the left." By the time "the word" got to the end of the column, one of the last men thought it was "move to the left" and fell into the crater, where he splashed around in nearly shoulder-deep water.

We could not find a ford at the main river, but found one at the Quan Dien Ban that was in many ways better since it gave attacking troops better access to the enemy positions. I instructed Corporal Desclos to deploy his men along the near bank. I also told Corporal Desclos to come across only if I called for him. I had Meyer, also a strong swimmer, accompany me, but I told him to turn off his radio and keep it off unless I explicitly told him to switch it on while we were doing our recon.

We moved slowly across the Quan Dien Ban just below Thanh My and Bao An Tay. There was something almost palpably sinister in the air. The river was moving more slowly than I had feared it might, and the water was surprisingly warm despite the heavy rain. All the villages on the other side were considered "militarily inaccessible." While we were on the way across, from the northern—enemy—bank, perhaps a dozen rounds of rifle fire cracked fairly high overhead. I believed it was random harassing and interdicting fire, released after dark. To my knowledge Meyer and I were the first Marines to cross to that side after dark in many months. After pausing briefly to catch my breath, I slid back feet-first, lizard-like, into the warm, rustling stream and did not stand up fully until I had to. Meyer followed my lead.

The next morning Company E crossed at the fording site we had found. Before morning Lieutenant Ebbert wisely prepped the northern bank heavily with artillery. Unfortunately it had continued raining from the time of our reconnaissance until 0800 when Company E began moving across, and the river then had a heavier flow than Bob and I had experienced. The company had no small difficulty getting across. At least one of their men was swept downstream by the current and drowned. They also drew heavy fire in making their crossing. We have no record of how many casualties they sustained while going across, but I have reason to believe they had many. For them that was just the beginning.

On the morning of the twenty-third my platoon was on patrol when we shot and killed one gunner on the "friendly side" of our TAOR. He was wearing a slick mauve cape and a round straw hat with a string tied under his chin. He fired at our point, who returned fire right away.

Within the hour we captured a Communist suspect hiding in the weeds near a riverbank we were patrolling. The VC suspect, a skinny teenager who was scantily clad and shivering when we found him, was presumably the one who had just fired several bursts at nearly point-blank range at Corporal Lewis's squad. Our flank security brought him in.

The dead man and his young partner together had twenty-eight thousand piasters (Vietnamese paper money, about the size of Italian lira notes), documents, syringes, and other materials with which to administer shots. Before we moved back to Phu Lac (6), where we planned to have the VC suspect flown out for questioning, I asked him, *"Done vee kwa um oh dow?"* (Where is your unit?).

He smiled in a gesture of incomprehension, shook his head, shrugged his shoulders, and extended his palms upward next to his body. After this I moved to the point briefly, but when I turned to look at him I saw a goodly number of our troops bunched around him, laughing quietly, joking around, giving him cigarettes, candy, and so forth. He was obviously having a good time.

I charged to where the congregation was, ordered the men to spread out, and reminded them that this little s.o.b. had been shooting at them several minutes before. I made it clear I did not want them to "thump" him, but I wanted him handled firmly. To this end Corporal Desclos put PFC Spain in charge of the man. In my experiences this incident was more typical than not. If anything, the men in the two platoons I commanded were characteristically very generous.

On Christmas Eve morning, a medevac helo attempting to evacuate casualties from Captain Gruner's Golf Company was shot up and made an emergency landing near Liberty Road, three thousand meters west of Phu Lac (6). By 1100 our company had moved to that position and relieved Company G as security for the helicopter. During the previous hour both of our companies had been in brief firefights, the details of which I do not recall. As we took over the guarding of the downed chopper, Golf Company moved to join Company E north of the Song Thu Bon. Both units soon became engaged in a sizable battle.

By 3 P.M. the helicopter was extracted. At just about this time Companies E and G began their assault on Phu Tai (1), north of the river. At 1511 (3:11 P.M. civilian time), Golf Company and elements of Company E were moving forward when they received several thousand rounds of small-arms, automatic weapons, RPG (rocket-propelled grenades), 57mm rifle, and 82mm mortar fire. The contact took place just north of the Song Ba Ren, not far from where Meyer and I had crossed. When G and E Companies were hit, Hotel Company was south of the river but less than five hundred meters from the enemy's farthest positions, and much closer to the closest ones. We were therefore in a good position to provide support by fire.

By then the river was too swollen at any point to reford and far too wide to bridge with the lines we had. Had the Song Ba Ren been narrower there or had it rained somewhat less during the previous forty-eight hours, I do not believe I would be alive to write this book, since the assault platoon on the fording mission would probably have been 3d Platoon.

Although we were not able to get across, we were able to keep the enemy battalion's left flank pinned down. On Jerry's order I hustled 3d Platoon on line along the streambed. From our positions there we had excellent fields of fire, but so did the NVA. I went out to a small sand spit, where I would have the best visibility. I had Corporal O'Connor fire a 3.5-inch white phosphorous rocket round at the approximate position I thought to be the forward line of battle for the NVA battalion. After about two such rounds, adjusted by either Lieutenant Ebbert or Captain Gruner, but I believe the latter, we were able to define the zones into which we could pour our fires without fear of hitting friendly forces. After the marking rounds were "talked in," we opened up.

The squad leaders repeated my fire commands, the rockets banged away, and our tracers streaked through the air. Amidst the smell of gunpowder I alternately stood and lay down to observe, to avoid the heavy volume of fire I sensed was being directed at me. I was in my glory, especially since our fires were evidently helping to ease the pressure on our other companies.

It got dark early that rainy evening, so that by 6:30 we had to begin to withdraw; to attempt to support our companies by fire after dark might inflict more casualties on our two companies across the river than on our enemy.

To my recollection, except for mine, our platoons received little incoming fire while we were adjusting and firing into the enemy's positions. As soon as 3d Platoon began its withdrawal up the steep, slippery banks, however, we received moderate small-arms and automatic weapons fire from across the river. Most was a bit high or low, but at least a half-dozen rounds zipped into the mud near me as I clambered up the bank. With seemingly none of the panic then felt by their commander, 3d Platoon withdrew in an orderly and quiet way to a defiladed position, which they reached after nightfall. They were so quiet that I stumbled over them in the darkness where they had quickly assembled to await orders. Before long we returned to Phu Lac (6), 1st and 2d Platoons alternating on the point, and did not get back to this desolate outpost until 2200 (or 10 P.M.)—cold, wet, and tired. Some Christmas Eve!

On Christmas morning our platoon moved from Phu Lac (6) back to My Loc (2). When we moved out we found Communist propaganda pamphlets and leaflets—some in English and some in Vietnamese, which we later had translated—all over the ground. As I wrote to my family that evening, "The men were so miserable they just muttered quiet curses pretty much to themselves when they read this trash. . . . If anything, propaganda like this makes us fight harder."

In the opening paragraphs of the same letter I wrote:

> We just had hot chow flown in to us by helicopter—hot turkey, spinach, potatoes, gravy, coffee, pumpkin pie, peanuts —it was great. Seconds on everything, too! The troops were filled for the first time in quite a while. It was a good feeling.
>
> My Platoon is outposted up here on this hill by ourselves—the kind of assignment I like—a little dangerous. I have 55 men, 2 81 mortars and 2 ONTOS [mechanized weapons carriers that mounted six 106 recoilless rifles]. It's a pretty easy area to defend . . .

The last statement, of course, was intended for my mother's peace of mind.

Of the dangers in the An Hoa TAOR at that time, perhaps foremost were mines and booby traps. The ground was alive with them. Until December 26, 3d Platoon had done a remarkable job of spotting and disarming the devices. For the next three weeks, however, we were not so successful.

It occurs to me now that the sharp increase of mining after Christmas probably represented the enemy's attempt to paralyze our aggressive battalion into inaction. They were not able by more conventional tactics to stop us from moving into their territory and patrolling day and night, so it appeared they would try to stop us by mining more extensively and cleverly. They did not stop us by those means, but they did channel and slow our movement somewhat. As the statistics indicate they also inflicted many casualties. Most of these were gruesome leg and body injuries that anger me even today to recall. Some of our men died of such wounds.

In order to present a full account of our tour in Vietnam, I feel it necessary to discuss in some detail this aspect of the war. When we were around An Hoa we never saw a journalist or reporter. They occasionally traveled with us—mostly for very short periods—when we were at the DMZ. My presumption was that they stayed away from An Hoa partly because it was too "hot" with enemy units, but mostly because of the abundance of mines. Surely there was no absence of stories to cover or action to capture; our manifestly incomplete unit diaries for those months contain entry after entry describing, in fragmentary fashion, our intense contacts with the enemy.

Throughout the war there was an insufficiency of reliable reports concerning land mine warfare, a situation no doubt brought about mostly because of the paucity of in-depth personal accounts of the subject. Throughout the years of armed conflict, the Marine Corps's Historical Section gathered hundreds of taped interviews with Marines who had served in Vietnam. And some of those interviewees were Marines who had had recent firsthand experience of land mine warfare. In preparing this book I reviewed dozens of those interviews and almost none yielded much of value. A large exception, however, is the interview conducted at the San Diego Recruit Depot on March 10, 1967, by Sgt. A. E. Frost with my company commander, Capt. J. J. Doherty. That ninety-minute interview contains an abundance of historically valuable material for the student concerning the tactics of that phase of the war (that is, from early April 1966 through February 1967). Captain Doherty's remarks on the land mine warfare in the areas we operated in during that period are especially illuminating. Nevertheless, as potentially helpful and valuable as that interview is, I know of no one—military or civilian—who had listened to this tape before I began to write this book.

Because there were never any reporters in the field around the mined areas in which we operated, because the

Marines I served with encountered so many mines and other hidden explosive devices, and because there is such a paucity of reliable information on the subjects, either in published form or in taped, historical interviews, it may therefore be especially important to write about one of the main aspects of the warfare in the areas where we patrolled—the one which, no doubt, served to keep the members of the news media away, and which too often served to silence, permanently or temporarily, the individuals whose experiences might have served their Marine comrades to advantage.

First of all, on a number of occasions we had mines and booby traps pointed out to us by friendly South Vietnamese; when people helped us, they were, at least potentially, "voting with their lives." On two occasions South Vietnamese peasants—one an adult woman and the other a boy in his early teens—alerted us to the presence of enemy mines and booby traps. The woman pointed out the place in a nearby trail where an enemy mine had recently been planted. The teenage boy on another day approached me as I was leading one of our patrols into a ville. He smiled and held up four fingers: *"Coo-rup, Bone. Coo-rup, Bone,"* he repeated while yanking my sleeve and pointing to a bend in the trail where, cautiously, we uncovered a booby trap that would have destroyed King Kong had he detonated it.

During the 1966 election for the South Vietnamese Constituent Assembly, held when we were at My Loc (2), one of the enemy's favorite tactics was mining the paths leading to polling places. Despite that, in the I Corps region, where the Marines operated almost exclusively, 80 percent of the registered voters showed up at the polls.

For detection devices, the units I served with had only the most primitive instruments. To my recollection, mine detectors were never used on any cross-country patrol I was on. At the time we were in Vietnam the Navy had a metallic mine detector known as the MK-15 (or M-15), but to my knowledge it never got to any of the units we operated with in the field. The mine detectors used by the engineers on their road sweeps were World War II models and not very practical. They often failed to discriminate large objects, such as rocks, from explosives of any kind, and hindered movement to slower than a crawl.

On one such "routine" patrol in 1966 a platoon from Hotel Company, 2/5, entered an entrenched village in the middle of a large rice paddy after nightfall on a combat patrol. Working on hands and knees in nearly total darkness and probing continually with bayonets, this platoon uncovered and either disarmed or detonated more than twenty-five types of mines and booby traps without incurring a single casualty. Among the devices uncovered at the time were numerous rigged M-26 grenades, rigged Chinese Communist grenades, standard pressure-type mines, pressure-release mines, a forty-pound shaped charge with a 3.5-inch white phosphorous rocket booby-trapped beneath it, and so forth and so on. Moreover, all the gates to the village were booby-trapped before the platoon's entry. And as almost always in Vietnam, every one of these cunningly planted mines, explosive devices, and mantraps was uncovered and disarmed or detonated while the platoon had to remain alert for ambushes. That work was done without benefit of mine detectors on a nighttime patrol in almost complete darkness. Although the interview with Captain Doherty does not specify the outfit involved, it was 3d Platoon.

In addition, at least a few Marines, including one platoon commander I know of, on occasion encountered and disarmed pressure-release mines buried cleverly underneath punji stakes on which Marines were impaled. Moreover, during the period of our narrative at least one lieutenant platoon commander I know of had the teeth-chattering experience of discovering and disarming a rigged, 250-pound bomb—a device so potent that, before it could be safely cleared, the entire village nearby had to be evacuated hundreds of meters away. These explosive devices, successfully handled by the 3d Platoon of Company H, 2/5, probably were among the largest explosive devices uncovered and detonated without injury to friendly forces through the year 1967 in the Vietnam War.

As far as detection went, our biggest daily asset was an alert point. We always carried at least one grappling hook that was secured to a line. We used the hooks to yank open from a distance any gates we had to pass through, since they were often booby-trapped. Moreover, if the point absolutely had to move through a gap in a hedgerow, he was instructed to hurl the hook through ahead of him to try to "clear" the avenue in advance. The point man also often carried a light-weight bamboo probe or other small stick to test the ground ahead of him for concealed punji stakes or explosive devices.

The punji traps were generally holes in the ground covered by reeds and a light covering of dirt. If not detected, a soldier could fall into a small pit from which sharpened sticks protruded, thus usually receiving lacerations in his lower extremities. In my experience the punji stakes themselves seldom did much damage. But in about 25 percent of the circumstances, the enemy had buried beneath them pressure-release explosive devices that would detonate if a man pulled his leg off the stakes right away. Thus, when a man fell onto the stakes, he had to remain as motionless as possible until the corpsman and senior man on patrol could reach him. Clearly the enemy's objective in using the pressure-release mine in conjunction with the punji pit was to have the wounded soldier's comrades come to his aid so that the mine could injure more.

Generally, the senior man on patrol would probe carefully around the pit with his K-bar (knife) or bayonet while the corpsman stood at a safe distance ready to assist. The probe process was more difficult to do in a careful way than one might imagine since the Marine in the pit was often in some pain and occasionally calling out for help. On such occasions our corpsmen almost always did fine work in talking to the wounded man to calm him down and reassure him as the senior man did the probing. Finally, the senior man present got into the trap himself and checked underneath the stakes to make sure there was no device under it. If all was clear, the man finally lifted his leg and stepped off. Once the pit and its environs were cleared, the corpsman moved closer, prepared to help the man out of the pit and treat his injuries.

Particularly around My Loc (2) and Phu Lac (6) we often encountered booby-trapped M-26 fragmentation grenades and the standard pressure-type mines. As it was primed by the enemy in our areas, the booby-trapped M-26 was especially deadly. In every instance where we had casualties from a primed grenade, the VC had removed the delay fuses so that the explosion occurred as soon as the spoon flew rather than four to six seconds afterward. Thus, the man who tripped the device had no time to move to cover. In our experiences, the devices were usually rigged by running monofilament wire through the ring to the grenade's safety pin, and then securing the running end to something solid such as a tree limb or a ground stake. If one tripped the wire, pin and spoon flew, followed, almost always right away, by the explosion. The fishing line was usually green or brown—the former if the device were rigged above grass and brown if above mud—and was difficult to spot, particularly since the point also had to keep his eye out for the enemy and natural obstacles.

We sought to hold down casualties in several ways. First of all, we tried to hold the men accountable for the grenades they took on patrol with them. In truth, we were not nearly so diligent about that as we should have been. Also, we always smashed our discarded metal containers when we were on patrol. In that way we hoped to deny the enemy as much as possible the materials for putting together homemade explosive devices. Also, we found it safest to stay off trails and paddy dikes whenever possible. But the nature of the terrain in the monsoon season made that tactic not so easy as one might think.

Generally, we figured it a good sign if there were many villagers moving around in the areas we patrolled, but usually there were not. If we came upon a rice paddy and saw adults scurrying and youngsters switching their water buffaloes away, a knot of fear grew inside me, and perhaps in my men also.

In moving through an area we believed mined or booby-trapped, we generally had two men work the point: one probed for devices and scanned the area for signs of them, and the other provided security for the man doing the probing and searching. In those instances, unless we were under fire at some other place in our formation, I generally moved very close to the point so I could clear the explosive devices, encourage our point, sometimes direct them where to move next, and perhaps support them a bit just by being nearby. My experience was usually more extensive than that of the men who worked our point, so I was sometimes able to spot signs in the landscape such as recently cut vegetation, newly dug ground, or markings—such as specially piled stones—that served to give away the presence of the devices.

As physical protection against mines and booby traps, the platoons I commanded had little. Our helmets occasionally but not often provided stoppage. Almost always we wore flak jackets, sleeveless and zipped up the center. They were somewhat cumbersome and weighed about eight pounds. They were made of fiberglass panels approximately four by six inches each, held together by green cloth about twice as strong as that of our jungle utilities. Against frag grenades and mortar rounds exploding at distances of more than fifteen meters, the jacket was excellent protection for one's trunk. At closer ranges, however, shrapnel was known to penetrate. Thus, we stressed repeatedly that the men were not "to bunch up," a tendency I noticed too often in Vietnam—both in the platoons I commanded and in other units in-country. Of tactical errors I saw in the war, I believe bunching up cost us more casualties than any other.

Of the men we lost to mines and booby traps in our TAOR, one of the first incidents had a humorous sidelight. In the early morning hours of the twenty-sixth our men overheard extensive digging at the low ground across Liberty Road from My Loc (2). My first concern was that the enemy was tunneling under our position to try to reach our mammoth ammo bunker. After some thought I concluded that such a scheme would be impracticable. Then I feared they might be setting up mortars, which at that close range would have proved devastating. At the same time I presumed they would have booby-trapped the approaches to their digging, since they had to be aware that we could hear them. Moreover, I presumed that they had ambushes set to intercept patrols sent from our positions. Thus, I ordered our Ontos to open up with its 106s on the area where the digging was taking place. With several ear-shattering roars, it did so. The digging immediately ceased.

Several hours later, however—about 0400—the noises recommenced but stopped before we could take further action.

After breakfast that morning I had one of our squads send a fire team to the platoon CP where I ordered them on a security patrol around the wire to look for signs of digging or any other kind of infiltration, as well as for casualties from our Ontos fires. The fire team leader was an eager and alert-looking lance corporal named Parkson.

I remarked on the security precautions they were to take and emphasized that they keep their flak jackets zipped and maintain at least twenty meters' interval between men. I allowed the team leader plenty of time for his briefing. I considered inspecting them before they left but did not, because I was averse to becoming involved in the direct supervision of units at so low a level in my command. In principle that was sound; in practice, in this instance, evidently it was a mistake.

Within an hour of the time the patrol left our wire we heard a loud explosion. A booby trap. When the explosion occurred, our nineteen-year-old corpsman, Jerry Holub, an Illinois native, was standing barefoot in his skivvies and washing up outside the CP bunker. Without a moment's hesitation he sprinted downhill, swooped up his medical kit without losing stride, and glided over our concertina wire with the same ease as a world champion athlete clearing a high hurdle. Across Liberty Road at a dead run, he scrambled up the muddy incline on the other side of it and disappeared into the gully beyond.

Along with several other men from that squad, I arrived shortly afterward. At my first glimpse of the Doc, he was lifting the wounded men gently off one another. How it happened I still do not know, but the blast knocked three of the four men on top of each other. PFC D. H. Howell (known as Little Howell) was bleeding heavily from the legs. PFC D. D. Howell (Big Howell) appeared to have a fractured leg as well as multiple fragmentation wounds. Lance Corporal Parkson was wounded in the trunk and arms, which the corpsman soon bandaged.

When he saw me come up, Parkson remarked, "At

least we all landed in a neat pile, Sir!" D. H. Howell said, with mock sadness, "I knew I'd go home before I made lance corporal. I'll *always* be a boot." Between spasms of pain he joked off and on thus for a few minutes. While our corpsman worked on D. H. Howell's wounds, I sent the healthy men with us to set up security around the only LZ nearby, then turned to grasp Howell's hand as the Doc worked on the wounded man's injuries.

D. D. Howell asked PFC Rice, the only uninjured patrol member, when he planned to move out. I also jokingly said the same. Rice took us seriously, placed his weapon at the ready, and began stalking along again by himself until we called him back. While that was happening, our young corpsman, Holub, dressed all three men's wounds and got intravenous plasma running from bottles held aloft either by himself or one of the unwounded men.

Our corpsmen always pasted a strip of white tape on the forehead of each man for every bottle of plasma the man had received. As I was told, this was done as a precaution since a person supposedly could not take more than three bottles of plasma in a twenty-four-hour period.

In calling for the medevac chopper, I asked specifically for a UH-34D, if possible, since the LZ was not large. The 34 had a single, large rotor and more maneuverability than the tandem-rotor choppers. Moreover, it needed comparatively little space in which to land and take off. Also, the pilots and crew chiefs I had spoken to when we were on Special Landing Force duty had told me the 34 could sustain moderate battle damage and continue to fly, which was not generally true of the other model helicopters in Vietnam at the time. Since I knew the enemy would more than likely be expecting our chopper to come in where it did, I wanted one that would be able to get our casualties out in good order. On that occasion, too, I requested a "duster"—an escort helicopter that would fire around the perimeter of the LZ—to provide additional protection.

With the *thwacka-thwacka* noises of the incoming helo growing louder every minute, PFC Charlie Spain acted on one of the inspirations that made our platoon such an effective unit. He figured that since the enemy more than likely knew where we would bring our medevac chopper in, they also had probably thought to mine our LZ. Acting without orders from anyone, he began probing with his bayonet gingerly in the center of the LZ. After less than a minute he called calmly: he had "found one."

Using an E-tool, he dug with controlled fury for perhaps another minute and unearthed an olive-drab box mine that must have weighed at least forty pounds. It was a pressure-type device and could have meant the end for the helicopter, its crew, and our casualties. We blew the mine just before the helicopters came over the treetops.

On the twenty-third and twenty-fifth of December, two helicopters were shot down within three thousand meters of My Loc (2) and, as already mentioned, on Christmas Eve another was shot down not far from Phu Lac (6). I therefore took special care in "talking" this medevac helicopter in and out of the LZ. These large, green "birds" almost always presented favorable targets, but were especially vulnerable when on the ground and just after takeoff.

The average medevac time, from our sending the request until the casualty was inside the field hospital, was approximately twenty-five minutes. When the medevac choppers came in, we had to load our casualties aboard as rapidly as possible since the helicopter's chances of being hit seemed to increase exponentially with every second it remained down. Generally we guided the chopper to our location by throwing a smoke grenade. As soon as its color began to unfurl sufficiently to be seen from the helicopter, we came up on the medevac frequency with, "We popped . . . (whatever color it was)." If the pilot spotted it he would radio back right away, "Roger, I see. . . ." It was most important that one keep in touch with the helicopter pilot since the enemy occasionally had smoke grenades of his own and used them. When our helos began to near the LZ, we popped red; the enemy popped yellow. Had the platoon commander not been in radio contact with the chopper pilot, the enemy might have provided a landing zone greeting of his own design.

In the early morning of December 28, two platoons from our company along with our company CP group went on patrol to the southern edge of the Song Ba Ren. There Captain Doherty had the other platoon spread out as a security force while 3d Platoon attempted another ford. We had not yet found a suitable spot when we received about four hundred rounds of automatic weapons fire from across the river. We returned fire and withdrew with one casualty, whose name I do not recall. Since we had silenced at least one machine gun right away with our covering fire, we may have inflicted some Communist casualties. We also apprehended a wounded woman whom we presumed to be a Communist and flew her back to An Hoa.

Between noon and 3 P.M. we drew enemy fire twice more. On the second contact we were moving next to a road leading into a village called Thon Bon (1), about six thousand meters east of My Loc (2), when we received 150 or so rounds of small-arms fire. The shooting seemed to be coming mainly from several houses inside the village. When the shooting started, half the platoon was moving eastward alongside the road and the other half was moving southward into the ville. The enemy fire came both down the road east of us and from the village to our south.

The first bursts came just as our forward elements had crossed a bridge leading into the village. The forward half of our platoon took cover by diving into a ditch sheltered from the village, and the other half jumped in another ditch that turned so that direct fire down the road was not effective either. Fortunately, the ditches had not been mined. When the first bursts whizzed past, Spain stood calmly in the center of the trail leading into the village, flipped up the sights on his LAW, checked behind him to see that the backblast area was clear, sighted, and fired. A high explosive round flew into the enemy position down the trail. He was about three men in front of me at this time. He discarded this LAW, then bent over and said to someone in his squad, "Hand me another one of those, will you?"

As he was preparing this second shot, I yelled, "After Spain fires this round, everyone from myself forward, on your feet and charge!"

Whamm!

"Let's go!" We sprinted forward yelling like a band of maniacs and firing into the village. When we got there we found two wounded VC, numerous ripple-sole sandal marks, fighting holes, extensive trench works, and one pack of documents. The VC and the documents were sent back on helicopters. The buildings we fired at were burned.

Ordering the burning may have been a mistake on my part. At least two women and perhaps a half-dozen children screamed, wailed, and wept in protest when I ordered Corporal Lewis to put the flame to the houses the enemy had been shooting from. In giving that order I was probably doing something the Communists had wanted; it would not endear us to those people. I do not offer this as an excuse, but at the time I felt the three houses at least would not provide shelter for enemy marksmen hereafter. Thinking like that, I believe now, was influenced to some extent by the fatigue I felt at the time—a tired way of looking at the war that about then, I think, had begun to adversely affect my tactical judgments.

In early January, Colonel Airheart wrote his fitness report appraising my service with the battalion during the period from early October through early January. At the time it was written the report was confidential, and like my other reports I did not see it until I began to write this book and requested my records. As with all the other reports done on me in combat, that one I believe rated me more highly than I deserved. The colonel's concise appraisal of my professional character for that reporting period read: "This Officer consistently performs with a high degree of professional competence and tireless energy. He has proven to be cool and aggressive under fire and completely dependable. He is considered to be qualified to direct a Rifle Company at this time. His potential is considered to be outstanding."

Although I did my best to hide the fact, I was nearly exhausted by the time that report was written. One of the physical signs of this exhaustion was the rash I first reported on the evening of December 28. It showed at first in the form of tiny boils that appeared all over my trunk and arms. First the skin cracked, then water blisters appeared. Inside them clear serum developed which, in a day or two, turned to pus. The sores itched incredibly. Scratching them provided temporary relief but soon the pus dried, gluing my skivvy shirt to my flesh, and that made me even more uncomfortable. When I wore my flak jacket, which had to be most of the time, the pain induced by its rubbing back and forth around my torso was excruciating. When I removed my flak jacket, blouse, and shirt to try to get some sleep in our command bunker, mosquitoes and flies flocked to my torso and arms.

Almost from the day I had taken over as platoon commander, various members of our platoon had suffered from what seemed to be the same problem. Corporal Desclos in particular had had a similar infection for two months, but his covered a larger area. Not until I came down with the rash myself did I come to know the fortitude demonstrated by Desclos and others.

I do not know to whom—if anyone—Corporal D complained about his infection, but I could pour out my misery every evening only to our corpsman; if the troops had heard of my difficulties, not to mention the way I complained about them, that would have had an adverse effect on their morale.

Off and on since we had been at Con Thien, I had had various kinds of dysentery. Two bouts were so long and severe, I am quite sure now they must have been bacillary or amoebic. The dysentery sapped some of my strength, yet not nearly so much as one might imagine. As with most physical ailments, when the spirit is willing, the flesh is usually strong enough. Likewise, I had had several malaria attacks when we were actually on patrol, but I was determined to master each of them and I did. I believe now that by treating both the dysentery and malaria as minor difficulties to be handled in a lighthearted manner, I might have made the problems work for us. Surely the troops were aware of both these ailments; the dysentery I referred to by some joking title, and the malaria as "the shake and quakes." At the least, my comments about them probably provided some comic relief. And I never missed a patrol because of illness.

On My Loc (2), around 1215 on December 30, the men on our perimeter spotted three armed NVA moving north of our wire. We took them under fire and they ran northwest. We searched the area at first light but found no traces of them.

That evening we laid in a platoon-size ambush near Phu Lac (4). As we moved into positions, we received small-arms and 60mm mortar fire. We took no casualties from the fire yet it was so close I suspected it was preregistered. In that instance, as on many other patrols, we found indications that the enemy knew in advance where we were going. The only thing that saved us from casualties there was the smartness with which our Marines returned fire and advanced. Had the men gone to ground right away, surely we would have had many men hit. The enemy withdrew southeast and we were unable to reestablish contact.

At 0415 the next morning, perhaps the same group of enemy shot and wounded a villager on the outskirts of La Thap (1), less than two thousand meters southeast of the enemy force we had contacted the previous evening.

New Year's Eve day we went on an early-morning patrol. We had no enemy contact, but an untended water buffalo charged our point. Corporal Bell killed it with his M-14 on automatic. After it was shot—Bell needed seven rounds to bring it down—it crashed into a ditch on the side of the trail. By the time I got there most of its enormous body had lodged into the slimy ditch and we were already being besieged by several angry villagers. One man in his late twenties was especially vociferous, and I assured him we would do our best to secure payment (solatium payments were made within days), yet I was angered by his attitude. When he started waving his hands toward my face my impulse was to knock his head off, but I restrained myself and tried to appear reasonable and calm. I was concerned that any show of temper on my part might lead to a reaction by my troops that might be more difficult to control.

After our early-morning patrol, New Year's Eve was a day of disciplined insobriety. Our platoon had security at Phu Lac (6). Two cans of beer per man were flown out to us on our outpost. At the time we were surrounded on one side by the flooded Song Thu Bon and on the others by oceans of multicolored mud. While an attack by a determined enemy could of course have been launched, it would have been extremely difficult to sustain.

After the beer had been distributed to the troops, Sergeant Hoole brought four still-cold ones to me—"compliments of some of the men who don't drink," he said. In my weakened condition, after having not had a beer in so long, I could not even finish the fourth can and slept "like a log," as I wrote my family.

Either New Year's night or the one after that, Captain Doherty told me that a colonel from Recon had phoned Colonel Airheart to ask if I could be released from our battalion to take command of a platoon in division reconnaissance. This colonel, whose name I do not recall, explained to our battalion commander that higher command hoped to groom me at 1st Recon Battalion for a position later in 1st Force Reconnaissance—a unit whose mission primarily was doing very long-range recons. The CO said Colonel Airheart's response was prompt: "Absolutely not."

Jerry, however, asked me if I would like to have a spell as S-4 (battalion logistics officer). He said that whether or not I accepted the 4, he had recommended to the colonel that I take command of Hotel Company when Jerry's tour had ended, and that the colonel had agreed. Jerry had other complimentary things to say that evening. And he did his best to talk me out of extending in Vietnam. He said, in essence, that if I kept up the way I had been, he was sure I would get myself killed. Coming from my own company commander, that was at least sufficient to dissuade me from staying overseas at that time; until then I had considered extending my tour in Vietnam three to six months beyond my scheduled return date. Another lieutenant—Christians—accepted the S-4 when it was offered to him. Chris, like Don at the S-2, I feel did a better job in his position than I would have been able to.

Throughout the first week of January, our youthful-looking corpsman gave me penicillin, vitamins, ripe bananas from God knows where, and extra C ration meals. In addition I was getting two-a-day dressing changes. Before each he applied some kind of ointment—bacitracin?—to the boils. In a letter home that was scrawled all around the ad pages in the *Chicago Tribune* (evidently the only spare paper I had available), I also remarked that my men had obtained for me some candles, heat tabs, an air mattress, a cot, and lots of extra food. Where they obtained those items remains a mystery to me.

Through early January heavy rain fell almost continually. Most of that period we remained at Phu Lac (6) with at least one other platoon from our company as well as our company CP group. Less than a grenade's throw from my position at Phu Lac (6), a huge, disabled tank squatted on its haunches in the mud. The tank was quite unable to move and was an excellent target. Almost every evening we were at Phu Lac (6) we were fired at by snipers posted all around our position. I recall almost as though it were yesterday the pinging of the small arms ricocheting hollowly off the tank's dark green hull.

Every evening before nightfall I met in a defiladed position with our squad leaders, platoon sergeant, guide, and corpsman. Under a makeshift corrugated metal awning we made plans for post-checking that night, rehearsed our call signs and passwords, and reviewed night patrol information and supporting-arms plans. Streaming water and stamping our boots to warm up, we greeted each other before the nightly briefings as though we were long-lost friends. Generally, I arranged to have hot coffee or cocoa and some other small treat that we could share for a few minutes before our briefing. It seemed that the darker the weather on those evenings, the more buoyant were the NCOs' spirits.

The men in the two platoons I commanded in Vietnam would give away almost anything to villagers who seemed in need. On the battalion level, too, the same spirit ruled. In the month of December alone, for example, our understaffed medical crew—doctors and corpsmen—treated 2,472 South Vietnamese for illnesses of all kinds and flew fifty civilians back to Da Nang for more extensive treatment. That month the list of food and equipment distributed to the villagers in our TAOR included an average of 20,000 pounds each of bulgar wheat, corn, and cooking oil. In addition we distributed 46 cases of powdered milk, 40 tons of rice, 720 pounds of clothing, hundreds of yards of nylon cloth, hundreds of blankets, truckloads of cans for cooking, and many other items to the people we were trying to assist.

In addition, at no small risk to themselves, our corpsmen provided diphtheria, tetanus, and plague shots to over two hundred people in one village during the month of December.

The day after the New Year, our Med CAP patrols commenced for 1967. Regardless of what our other commitments were, these civil action patrols operated six days a week, four weeks every month, for every month that year. Whatever adjectives might be used to characterize the Navy–Marine effort in Vietnam, it was not mean-spirited.

Nearly every day in the An Hoa TAOR there were casualties from mines and booby traps. Often, however, the devices were uncovered and disposed of by our troops before they could do harm. If we were moving along with another unit and an explosive device was spotted, one would usually hear, "Fire in the hole!" three times (the signal that an *expected* explosion would occur and that those nearby should seek cover) followed by a loud *crump*ing sound and a cloud of powder and smoke. But if one heard a loud explosion only, then there usually followed, "Corpsman up! Corpsman!"

After one of the more ghastly land mine incidents in our company, I remember watching Gunny Husak guide the medevac helicopter in by drawing his straightened palms deliberately down from overhead, like a solemn Indian chieftain performing a ritual to bring rain. He wore an iridescent orange helicopter vest that, even in the storm, must have been visible for miles. I recall thinking what a great target the Gunny often made in hot LZs. As the helo touched down, several groups of four Marines apiece, some accompanied by a corpsman holding a plasma bottle aloft, hustled the wounded men into the chopper hatchway.

The casualties were usually carried in green, rubberized

ponchos. Now and then one of the figures going aboard would be draped completely with a blanket or poncho—sights that anger and sadden me even as I recollect them today.

From October through December our battalion officially sustained over 425 battle casualties—over 67 percent of the actual strength of our four maneuver companies. And that figure represented the reported battle casualties only. Moreover, as the reader may recall, E Company did not go up to the DMZ on Prairie with us and had sustained few casualties in October and November.

On January 5 our battalion began Operation Lincoln. Fortunately for me, the operation lasted through the afternoon of the ninth. Our company was not directly involved in this operation but, because of it, for the next five days two helicopters were moved from Da Nang to An Hoa, which cut valuable minutes' flying time off the flight to the field hospital in Da Nang. As Jerry Doherty related to me several months afterward, because of Lincoln, additional medical personnel had also been moved out to An Hoa. At Jerry's request, several of those people, including a doctor and a corpsman, were sent aboard the chopper that picked us up on the ninth. Had it not been for those extraordinary measures I would not be here today.

The fifth of January was a rainy, dismal day. 3d Platoon patrolled from just after dawn until early evening. Our unit diaries indicate that we made five separate enemy contacts; perhaps because of the degree of fatigue I felt, I have no clear recollection of any of them. Between 0845 and mid-afternoon we exchanged fire with several small enemy units. We sustained no casualties from the small-arms fire nor did we find firm traces of enemy casualties inflicted by us.

At 0900 that day three of our men were wounded by a land mine explosion which took place about five hundred meters south of La Thap (4). On a security patrol the next day, on Hill 31, we ran down and seized a healthy-looking Vietnamese male with a betel-stained mouth, of perhaps thirty-three who had tried to outrun us as soon as we saw him. His ID card had a birthdate on it that would have made him a teenager, and the identifying picture was burned off. We sent him back under guard to An Hoa.

The patrol on January 6 I remember fairly clearly. From the time we left our outpost I sensed something sinister in the moist air. We followed a narrow, undulating path northward beyond La Thap (4), almost to the Song Thu Bon. I was very reluctant to have us move on such a trail, but the terrain around it was such that we could not move across country and make headway. Because of what I sensed to be the danger in such a movement, I walked the point myself and had the rest of the platoon follow—well dispersed, I hoped—at a good distance. The path was brown and made undulating turns continually. With no small apprehension I turned each bend, praying as I placed my foot down each time that it would not be my last touch with slippery earth. When we got through the wire at Phu Lac (6) that evening, I breathed an audible sigh of relief.

On January 7 we again patrolled from early morning till late afternoon. We moved out early from Phu Lac (6) after a cold breakfast before first light. As we moved through the wire the damp breath of the morning rose all around us. We did not make contact with the enemy until we were on our way back to Phu Lac (6) late that afternoon, at the juncture of a road and the same trail we had moved down so warily the afternoon before. Of that light contact, again, I have no clear recollection. We had no battle casualties that day.

After the patrol on the seventh, 3d Platoon moved tactically by squads to My Loc (2) where we set up security for the evening. Our last radio transmission on patrol came from Cu Ban (2) at 1700. Since My Loc (2) was three thousand meters from Cu Ban (2), in order for us to move cross-country to the former position without incurring casualties, our platoon must have made the journey quite stealthily, so we probably got to My Loc (2) quite late.

Thus the letter that follows must have been written by candlelight in our subterranean platoon command bunker late that evening. It was the last letter I wrote home from Vietnam.

7 January 66
My Loc (2), Vietnam

Hi Mom:

Thanks for having those Masses said for me. I'm feeling better now. My sores are all but healed—thanks to the care our Corpsman gave me—constant dressing changes, penicillin, bacitracin treatments, pills and sympathy. Our Corpsmen are just great.

It didn't rain yesterday and it hasn't rained today. A break in the weather really buoys the spirits. It was very crisp this a.m. when we started on patrol—I'd say it was 50 degrees—crisp for this country. I enjoy walks just after daybreak in the States in weather like this and I must say I enjoyed this morning's patrol for that reason.

I understand you were snowed in on Christmas Day. Did you enjoy your white Christmas? It must have been nice to see the graveyard filled up with snow. I wish you would have visited me last year on the holidays or before I went overseas like I had proposed. I'm sure you would have loved revisiting the West Coast.

It seems hard to believe but by the time you receive this letter I'll have less than 75 days to do overseas—four of which will be a Viet New Year Ceasefire and seven of which will be R&R.

I expect to be home by April. By the end of this month I should have my orders and then I'll know even what my flight date will be.

Take care of yourself and stay well.

Love you,
Jim

Early next day we again patrolled around Cu Ban (2), where a likable, soft-spoken, black lance corporal, whose hometown was St. Louis, had a foot sheared off by a booby-trapped M-26. He was moving down a trail just out of sight of me when I heard the explosion and saw the earth fume gray powder and brown smoke.

On the night of January 8 we set in a perimeter defense at Phu Lac (6). It rained very hard all night, yet on post-checking rounds I found all our posts awake and alert. We had no probes that evening.

January 9 was a warm, misty Monday morning. Along with the other platoon commanders in our company, Captain Graham and O. K. Batte, I reported to the company CP to receive our patrol order from Captain Doherty. Our mission that day was to conduct a company-size patrol southeast through La Thap (4) to La Thap (1) to search for and kill the enemy, look for signs of enemy troop movements, and try, if possible, to take prisoners. We would return that evening to Phu Lac (6) by a route that would be designated by a frag order after we moved through La Thap (1).

In the bloodstained pages of my platoon commander's notebook, which I still have, I copied Jerry's order. Under the section devoted to enemy situation, I wrote and underlined, "area around La Thap (4) believed heavily mined."

"Jim, your Pitoon will be on the point on the way out."

When I returned to our platoon CP I called the squad leaders up for their briefing. I am certain I emphasized the danger from mines and booby traps. I more than likely stressed that we were to stay off the trails wherever possible, take our time, and remain alert and steady. I also probably tried to exude a confidence I may not have felt.

When I swung into my flak jacket I was determined that we would lose no men that day to mines. And I recall wincing as I zipped and buttoned my flak vest; despite what I had written home, my trunk sores were still not healed; the pressure of the flak jacket against them assured that they would not heal that day.

Within eight hundred meters of leaving the wire around Phu Lac (6) we encountered three booby-trapped explosive devices. Corporal Lewis had the point squad and he had one man on the point—the tall, sturdy, quiet, black PFC from Chicago whom we called Big Jones, whom I had carried piggy-back on patrol near the DMZ after he sustained a severe ankle sprain. As I recall, Jones and Corporal Lewis, working together, uncovered the first booby trap; Jones himself the next two.

In accordance with our platoon SOP, as each device was

spotted the men in the platoon "froze and passed the word." I would then move up to examine the device, make a radio report, and figure out the best way to either blow or disarm the device. On that morning I felt a special sense of alarm for three reasons: first of all, we had never encountered so many enemy explosive devices so close to our wire; second, no civilians were in the nearby fields; and, most distressing, when we came over the brow of the first small hill southeast of Phu Lac (6), Corporal Lewis and I spotted a half-dozen fighting-age adult males sprinting as though their lives depended on it into La Thap (4).

Corporal Lewis looked sharply back uphill to me and asked if he should take them under fire. My instincts told me it was best to do so, but first I called the CO to ask permission.

"Not if they don't have weapons. Out."

On more than one occasion we had drawn fire from La Thap (4). I was concerned about exposing our entire platoon—possibly the whole company—to flanking fire from that village. I therefore moved very close to the point and directed Jones to move somewhat north of the route he would otherwise have taken. The northern route would take us through more heavily wooded country in which mines and booby traps would be harder to detect, but that would also give us cover and concealment from direct fire across the paddy from La Thap (4), where our "civilians" had just run.

Indeed, when Jerry had been away on R&R some weeks before, a patrol I had taken out from La Thap (4) had drawn so much fire from that village that Jim Graham had radioed me from his CP, then on La Thap (6) or Phu Lac (6), that he could have us put 81 mortars on La Thap (4) if we wanted. As always in combat, the senior man on scene has important judgment decisions. During the week when Graham had been acting CO, I had reasoned that, although the fire we had been receiving had been moderate, it was also very inaccurate and I did not think it was worth destroying the better part of an entire village in order to neutralize it.

Through Corporal Lewis I directed Jones to move into the woods but halted him just as he was about to pass through a tight gap in the hedgerow in front of him. In doing this I probably saved his life: a booby-trapped frag grenade had been rigged less than a step in front of him.

"Don't move, Jones, I'm coming up." Until after we had moved through La Thap (1), I intended to stay on point. Believing as I went that I had covered the same ground he had, I hustled to where he stood. Unfortunately, Meyer followed close behind me. At first I thought to tell him to stay back, then to go back, but my fatigue had taken its toll and I said nothing. Stupidly, also, I did not hold our young corpsman, Jerry Holub, farther than fifteen meters from us. When Bob advanced our corpsman did, too, but he stopped about ten meters away.

After a study of the positioning of the booby trap, I figured out the best and safest way to blow it. After I told Jones what to do, I said something supportive and he got into position. When he was ready, I believe I said "Outstanding" and moved back behind a mound of dirt. I thought that in doing so I was retracing my steps.

By this time it was 1300 (1 P.M.) and we had not moved more than a mile and a quarter from Phu Lac (6), so I thought I should call the Skipper to let him know why we were delayed and inform him of the nature of the ensuing explosion. Meyer was still behind me as I stepped back to grab the handset.

At once I felt like I had been slammed by a train at full career. My body flew backward through the air and Bob flew in the opposite direction. Next to the explosion itself, the pain I experienced when I landed was the greatest I can ever recall.

Meyer had been facing me when I stepped backward and tripped all three devices. He caught most of the shrapnel in his lower body and screamed more loudly than I ever hope to hear anyone scream again. I tried to turn to help him but found I could not move. My left hand, still raised, was split wide open across the top, the bones and tendons exposed. I looked to our corpsman for help but he was slumped some fifteen meters away, sleeping what seemed the deepest sleep of all.

About this time I heard our men yelling, "The lieutenant's hit! Corpsman! Corpsman up!"

I summoned the strength to look down at the lower half of my body. From the waist down my trousers were already awash with blood. My left leg canted outboard at a crazy angle and I saw bones protruding from my utilities on either side.

I did not think I would live much longer, but I thought I had already had a full life, had done most of the things I really hoped to do. I began saying the Act of Contrition.

Suddenly Doc Washington slid to us through the mud, and I thought for the first time that maybe we had a chance. Without regard for his own safety, as was typical of him, that corpsman moved from one of us to the other, then back to work on me. At the same time he gave orders to the other brave individuals who came up to help. As he worked on my tourniquets and plasma he instructed the healthy men how to try to help Meyer and our platoon corpsman.

Sergeant Hoole moved past and looked at me more despondently than I had ever seen him. I wanted to tell him to take charge but my voice sounded thick, my words garbled.

Soon after Washington and Hoole came up I saw Captain Graham and O. K. Batte. When Graham approached he looked at me, smiled, and said, "Hello, Jim." Graham and O. K. helped Doc Washington work on my injuries. I did not know it yet but the mammoth explosions had severed both of my femoral arteries, fractured both legs in many places, ripped a large slice across my lower abdomen, ricocheted metal into my hip, and given me numerous other shrapnel wounds. I was losing blood very quickly, but thanks to Washington's skills I received two whole bottles of plasma before the chopper came in.

I was losing so much blood that it was probably vital that either Jim or O. K. noticed I was also losing blood from a large wound underneath. This they pointed out to Washington, and they lifted me as gently as possible so the Doc could place field dressings on the back wound. By that time we were drawing small-arms fire from our friends in La Thap (4).

As weak as I was, I summoned the strength to ask Jim Graham how the family jewels were. After what seemed an incredibly long investigation, he responded, "Looks just fine, Jim!" (Jerry later told me he was sure I was a goner by then. Needless to say, he thought the investigation superfluous. Fortunately, he was wrong.)

I may have blacked out a bit before the helicopter came in. I was at least semi-awake, however, when I heard the feathery sound of the medevac helo beating toward us.

La Thap (4) looked directly down on the area where we were wounded, and that certainly was the reason why it had been mined. With excellent fields of fire from the village, the Communists' hope was to also hit the recovery teams as well as the rescue helicopter and crew. Enemy fire in the only practicable landing zone in the area rapidly became intense as the helicopter began to settle down (we had only two helos forward at An Hoa for Operation Lincoln and could not afford to use the other one to "dust off" the village). Our Hotel Company direct fire and the overhead fire Jerry had called in silenced some of the shooting from La Thap (4) but by no means all of it, so that as the helicopter first tried to land it evidently took so many rounds that the pilot brought it hastily up and began to streak back to An Hoa. Fortunately, both Jerry and our men recognized that the departure was not a feint, but a real departure.

With typical presence of mind in an emergency, Jerry asked the men to stand, which they all did (some even waved and gestured "Come back in, it's not bad down here!"). Jerry then quickly radioed the pilot: "Whoa! Where're you going? We've got three wounded men down here." These timely and valorous actions saved my life; they encouraged the helo pilot into attempting another dangerous landing.

"Stay down. Please, stay down," I thought as the chopper settled into the paddy. As it did several men from that platoon I loved so much hefted me up, carried me through a hail of bullets, and placed me carefully on the deck of the beating chopper.

As we moved past Gunny Husak, he spun around and said, "These bullets tickle!" (Jerry later told me the Gunny had removed his blouse and flak vest and asked the chopper pilot to "Try and land the helicopter on the guy with his shirt off.") The Gunny wanted to make sure the medevac helo got in and out in good order. When the helicopter was almost on top of him, he skipped out from beneath it, dodging bullets as well when he moved.

A man in utilities who wore a flight helmet with a large red cross painted on the front knelt by the open hatchway next to where I had been placed. As soon as all three casualties were settled in, that fellow and at least one other made quick inspections of the three of us. The red cross individual looked at me and said, "Don't worry, I'm a doctor" as he pointed to his helmet. "You're going to be all right," he added briskly with a wink and a thumbs-up. Then he started working on my lower body and I passed out.

Not long before we landed I awoke to find the red cross man thumping stoutly on my chest—I must have had a cardiac arrest. "Wake up!" he shouted. "Stay with us!" he added, pointing a finger at me as if to say, "and that's an order." It was one I wanted to assent to.

The next thing I recall, the chopper settled onto a runway and many hands were present to jog us into an examining room. Things seemed well organized. A pleasant-looking young doctor worked on me right away while someone else held a plasma bottle overhead. As the doctor worked he talked casually, "What'd you hit?" I believe I said a mortar round. (I learned much later that it was a pressure mine filled with rusty nails rigged to a 3.5-inch rocket round with a fragmentation grenade set beneath it. When the mine detonated, it exploded the frag grenade and the antitank rocket round simultaneously.)

"I guess you'll go back to Pendleton. Lots of pretty nurses there; you can believe that, Lieutenant! Say hello to _____ _____ for me when you get there, will you?" *Nnhh,* I thought to myself, *does she like badly mangled corpses?*

Soon they hustled me on a carrier the short distance to the OR. As I entered, a chaplain leaned over and asked, "What religion are you, Lieutenant?"

"Catholic," I whispered.

"Wait just a second and I'll have a priest here right away."

As my carrier moved again, a large man with bushy,

dark eyebrows came by my carrier and said, "I'm a Catholic priest, son. Pray with me . . . ," and began moving alongside. As I recall, the priest went a few steps into the operating room with me. Before he left he said something like, "Bless you, son. You'll be well."

A squad of masked people with caps and gowns was waiting. One man expectantly spread the fingers of both hands and carefully placed the webbed parts against each other. Someone touched the IV device over my head. Then the lights went out.

I suppose it was the next day when I awoke to see a large, kindly presence looming before me. "I'm from the Old Corps, Lieutenant. But we from the Old Corps want to thank you for what you in the New Corps have done. I'm pinning this on . . . now . . . because you've earned it."

"Could this be Heaven?" I wondered. Then the burly figure stepped back and I faintly discerned that the man was wearing green utilities with the sleeves rolled up. It was General Walt. I tried to say thank you but lapsed into unconsciousness once more.

Later that day I awoke to find several of my men, who had been slightly wounded earlier, standing around my rack in pajamas and dressings. They seemed to be looking at me disbelievingly. I tried to say something upbeat and cheerful, but found I could not talk. Before I went off to sleep again, all three said, "Good luck, Sir."

The next thing I recall, I was on an airplane and someone there told me I was "going home."

SIX

★

Clark Air Force Base

Whoever it was who told me that I was homeward bound was wrong, and this subsequently caused me no small amount of distress. Thinking that I was being shipped home to the States, when I awoke to find I was at Clark Air Force Base Hospital, in Manila, I was disappointed and disoriented.

The first few weeks at Clark were in many ways a continual nightmare. I was unconscious much of the time. And when I was awake, often I was not fully aware of what was going on around me. Thus the chapters that follow are somewhat more fragmentary and disordered than the previous ones.

For much of what was perhaps the first ten days I had great difficulty focusing my eyes and speaking. On one of these first nights at Clark, I dreamed I was still commanding 3d Platoon; I woke up yelling orders and feeling "rammy." I had to be almost physically restrained by a nurse and an Air Force hospitalman. The latter said something like, "Lieutenant! *Settle down!* You've been very seriously wounded. You're not a platoon commander anymore. You're not in Vietnam. You're in Clark Air Force Base Hospital in the Philippines. Do you understand that?" I had already lost a great deal of blood—my medical records indicate that I received seventy-nine pints in transfusion—had numerous injuries, and virtually every wound was badly infected. Also, I was not immediately aware that I had developed a serious case of double pneumonia. For the first ten days or so after I was wounded my mother received a number of cryptic telegrams from the commandant of the Marine Corps. On the sixteenth she received a message that included the following:

> . . . your son First Lieutenant James J. Kirschke U.S.M.C. became ill in the Republic of Vietnam. His illness has been diagnosed as severe pneumonia. He was treated at the First Medical Battalion and was evacuated to the U.S. Air Force Hospital, Clark Air Base, Philippine Islands for further treatment. He was placed on the very seriously ill list. His prognosis was guarded. His recovery is not assured. Your anxiety is realized and you can be assured that he is receiving the best of care and you will be kept informed of all significant changes in his condition . . .
>
> Additional information received this headquarters subsequent to our initial report . . . your son First Lieutenant James J. Kirschke U.S.M.C. was injured 9 January 1967 in the vicinity of Quang Duy Xuyen, Republic of Vietnam. He sustained multiple fragmentation wounds from a hostile explosive device while on patrol.
>
> Wallace M. Greene, Jr.
> U.S.M.C.
> Commandant of the Marine Corps

Had my condition allowed, the doctor would probably have amputated soon after I arrived at Clark. As my condition was, the doctors hoped I would be able to aerate my lungs sufficiently to clear the pneumonia and grow stronger quickly enough so that I would be able to withstand major surgery.

In order to effect the first of these, I had often to work with the medical staff in doing a series of deep-breathing exercises supplemented by the use of a "bird machine," primarily a breathing mask appended to a tank containing pure oxygen. At least four periods a day I did inhalation therapy with the plastic mask held up to my face. In my condition, those exercises were among the last things in the world I wanted to do. It is primarily a tribute to the staff at Clark that I performed the exercises on schedule. I may also have been helped somewhat by the fundamental orneriness of my nature. I was not willing to surrender to death, however painful life was at that time.

During the first two weeks I underwent surgery several times—mostly for wound debridements—but there were also attempts to repair my numerous fractures. In my condition, those operations were indeed risky.

After each operation I had intense pain, but almost from the time I was wounded, I tried as best I could to fight the pain and to master it.

The hospital regimen combined with my rapidly debilitating physical condition when I was at Clark and afterward made maintaining a sense of dignity difficult. The contrast between my situation in the hospital and the one I had so recently experienced as a platoon commander could hardly have been greater. Yet I believe now that whatever small successes I had in mastering the pain, in fighting and resisting it with whatever determination I was able to muster, not only helped me maintain a sense of self-worth but also helped to provide me with strength that would sustain me after I was discharged from the hospital and retired from the Corps.

I would not wish to go through the same degree and kind of suffering again yet I feel that the experience has not been without value. The small, private, "midnight standoffs," and "3 A.M. victories," as I thought of them, are my permanent possessions, possessions in many ways more valuable and durable than some material honors and awards.

One morning early in my stay at Clark an enlisted medic working in the intensive care ward woke me to change my bed. When he pulled back the stained covering sheet, I began to take stock of my condition for the first time. From mid-chest downward my body was swathed in heavy dressings, soaked in colors from bright crimson to deep rust. Some of the stain was from my leg wounds.

A 3.5-inch rocket round is intended to knock out a tank. And an antipersonnel fragmentation grenade will almost always kill a man if it explodes beneath him, as the one that hit me did. And a homemade box mine, "An Hoa model," often killed most people within fifteen meters. Few people survive being hit by all those devices at the same time. I was fortunate to be alive. Nevertheless, I had dozens of wounds.

Among them were multiple fractures of both legs as well as numerous fragmentation wounds from my jaw downward.

Holes had been cut in the dressings on both sides where machines were either sucking fluids out of my hips or pumping others into them. Around my privates another hole had been cut from which a yellow catheter ran out of my penis and disappeared over the side of the bed. I smelled horrible, but just then that was the least of my concerns.

My left hand was wrapped in a large, white dressing that also covered half my forearm. Into one arm was inserted a needle that supplied whole blood, suspended in a transparent sack affixed to a stand on one side of the bed. Into the other arm another needle was taped that dripped a flow of clear liquid (presumably nutrients) from a bottle suspended from a stand on the other side of my rack. Still another needle entered my chest around the pectorals. And that one connected to a tube of some kind of liquid that seemed to be running from overhead into my chest.

Because of the jaw wound, for the time being I had a bandage around my chin as though I had the mumps. It made speaking difficult. Which may have been just as well. A tracheotomy had been done, presumably to help me breathe: a three-inch tube inserted in my throat approximately two inches below the Adam's apple. A noise that sounded to me as though someone were shoveling snow on the sidewalk outside issued from the "trach" every time I breathed. And when I spoke, a strange whistling noise trailed after every word.

While my bed was being changed, one Air Force medic held me, effortlessly, above the bed as another one changed it. Less than a month before I had been strong enough myself to carry wounded men to safety, and now I was so weak and debilitated that a not overlarge medic was holding me as if I were a child.

"Could this be Hell?" I wondered. "Please, God, help me to be a man," I prayed to myself then as on occasion since. Soon after the rack change the medic moved away, and I enjoyed again the supreme liberty bestowed by sleep.

One day I had not yet recovered from the painful turning and lifting involved in the rack changes when a pink-faced, overweight Air Force doctor entered the room followed by several nurses. Without a word of greeting he grasped the transparent, plastic face piece for the "bird machine," told the nurses what it was, and placed it firmly against my face for what seemed an overlong session. As he did this, he explained in a hearty, southern drawl the way the machine worked. He paused for several minutes more to lecture the nurses, and turned again to tell me in the most impersonal manner to take "ten more deep ones." After that, without once having acknowledged my presence as a human being, he led the nurses out behind him.

On the basis of my own admittedly limited firsthand experience of patient care such as that, I am led to speculate that impersonal medical treatment probably accounts for far more complications and deaths than the medical profession realizes. I recall remarkably few such incidents in my own medical history; but I wish I could say there had been fewer.

For most of the first six weeks after I was wounded I was too weak to write, too weak to feed myself, on all but one memorable occasion, too weak to sit upright without support or even to raise an arm unassisted. For most of my time at Clark, when I had the strength, I dictated letters home that were written by a Red Cross volunteer. The first such letter I have a record of was to my mother, on January 21, and reads as follows:

Dear Mom:

I was wounded in action and sent here to Clark Air Base Hospital, Philippine Islands.

They tell me I have multiple fractures in the lower extremities and many other injuries. Don't know for sure how long I'll be here, but hope to be home by Spring; perhaps before.

The hospital is modern and well staffed, and I am getting excellent care.

Will try to keep you posted on my developments.

Write.

Love,
Jim

One Red Cross hospital volunteer who was especially nice to me at Clark was Kitsy Westmoreland, wife of Army General William Westmoreland. As I remember her, Mrs. Westmoreland was a petite, middle-aged woman with thick, dark eyebrows. She was always neat and emanated a kindness and warmth that were almost physical in their intensity. She seemed to me to be very concerned about myself and the other badly wounded men in the intensive care unit at Clark. My impressions are that she came to visit with us at least every third day. Virtually all of the nurses and Red Cross Gray Ladies I met while in hospital I liked very much, and Mrs. Westmoreland was one of the nicest of that fine group.

I account it a blessing that for my entire stay in the Clark ICU I was the senior military patient there. I often did not have very much strength to speak, but when I did I tried in whatever small ways I could to cheer up the other fast-fading men in the beds around me. If a word of encouragement from myself appeared to cheer any of those troops, I usually felt immediately better off myself. Like them, I was struggling, but whatever I could say to help them in my strange-sounding, whistle-voiced ways afforded me a boost in the fight I was going through. It may be that love helps heal both the giver and the receiver.

One of those I was unable to reach was a badly wounded South Korean Marine whose heart, I had been told, had stopped beating for about as long as possible without inducing death. The absence of oxygen to the brain, the nurse told me, brought on the man's violent hysteria. For a longer time than I should like to recall, he racked next to me. I do not believe he slept at all during that time but screamed nearly continually, at full volume, hour after hour. As he did, he banged his head, arms, and legs repeatedly against the restraining bars surrounding his bed and vehemently struggled to get out. In an unsuccessful attempt to restrain him, the staff had not only tied him down but covered his rack with two layers of heavy netting. That required the full muscle of four large members of the staff and took nearly an hour. Soon thereafter he not only broke the restraining straps but penetrated the netting as well, clambered promptly over the metal restrainers, rose up briefly over me, and fell with a heavy slap onto the deck between our beds. Needless to say, his activities did not do much to help the rest of us recover.

I never actually spoke to the doctor who worked on my hand, and only recall seeing him on two occasions. I was told he was a hand specialist who traveled to hospitals throughout the Far East working on servicemen whose hands had been injured in Vietnam. He did fine work. Just after I was wounded, my left hand looked gruesome. In fact, I feared I would lose it. Yet it healed more readily than most of my other wounds, and within several months of my injuries I was able to use my hand nearly as well as I could before I was wounded. I am missing now perhaps an inch and a half of one metacarpal. My left hand, therefore, has a shortened middle finger and looks odd. But the injury has caused me little inconvenience over the years, and I am able to use my left hand almost as easily as my right.

The injuries to my lower extremities were to prove more serious, but that was not the fault of the doctors. A wise and skillful surgeon friend has intimated that, had I suffered the same injuries in an accident outside most hospital emergency rooms in the United States at that time, I wouldn't have received such good treatment or, more than likely, even survived.

The doctor whose patient I mainly seemed to have been at Clark was a young orthopedic surgeon whose name I believe was Sweterlitsch. He was tall, thin, and had as kindly a manner as possible that was still in keeping with medical effectiveness.

Doctor Sweterlitsch, of course, did not work on me alone but rather seemed to me to coordinate the work of a team of medical personnel including the hand doctor, respiratory therapists, internists, ear-nose-and-throat doctors, urologists, general surgeons, anesthesiologists, physical therapists, and so forth.

However good they are, though, surgeons and other medical support people are not masters but servants.

They can do a great deal to assist the natural powers inherent in living flesh but cannot replace them.

During the weeks that I was in the intensive care unit at Clark, several men died there, and from my limited observations not all of those who did seemed the worst off physically. In almost every case I recall, before a seriously wounded man "went," he more or less announced that he had given up, that "this was all too much to take," or words to that effect. Soon thereafter, the next of kin—usually a mother or wife of the injured serviceman—arrived. The announcement was, in all cases I recall, the sign that the end was near. Within a day of the first visit by the next of kin, the chaplain would be at the foot of the wounded man's bed for a time. Usually within another day the doctor would be summoned by a nurse or hospital attendant, the man examined, and the body soon covered and then wheeled quietly away.

"If the spirit is willing, then the flesh often is also" was a motto I silently formulated and repeated to myself many times on those dark days and mostly lonely nights. Not until many months afterward did I learn that the Marine Corps, believing I would not long survive, had offered to fly my mother to Clark but that, for complicated reasons, she had had to decline. As I look back today I am sure it was best for both of us that she did not make the trip.

On January 25 something occurred that I believe now was almost as important in keeping me alive as all the expert medical treatment I had thus far received. I had my first mail call in the hospital since I had been wounded.

In this first batch of letters at Clark were nearly three dozen letters, including twenty-four from my former troops. A Gray Lady whose name I do not recall sat down beside me that morning to read each letter aloud to me. Several were from close friends, teammates, and athletic coaches who had heard at first merely that I was ill. A letter dated January 15, for example, had been sent me by my former high school end coach, John Lavin. At the time, John was still unaware that I had been wounded and thought that I had just contracted pneumonia. His letter reads in part as follows:

Dear Jim,

My brother Joe just informed me that one of my boys had to be flown from Vietnam to Clark Air Force Base Hospital for medical care. At first, I was really concerned; I couldn't understand how Jim Kirschke with all my Inside-Outside drills could be hit. Joe related your entire medical report; I was quite relieved to find out that you were attacked by an army of bugs, that required only you and your system to combat. As I recall my young friend and end Jim Kirschke, his most serious problem in football was thinking, working and fighting too hard. I spent most of my coaching time trying to relax this intense competitor; so I feel extremely optimistic about your speedy recuperation.

When you receive this letter I am sure your main concern will be for your mother. My brother Joe is a Captain in the U.S.M.C.; he had the responsibility of notifying your mother and family. I can assure you that this unpleasant duty was handled properly.

I called your family today. I'm afraid they concur with me that you're too damn stubborn to let germs keep you down even for a short period. . . .

Jim, I hope I've taught you something about the best utilization of "time-outs." Take your recuperation as serious as you have always undertaken work, play and duty.

In church today, with my wife Lill, Kimberly Anne (6), and John Jr. (3), in between John Jr's. high dives, flips, spins, kicks, punches, hugs and kisses, the John Lavin family said a few for you.

Best wishes and regards.
John Lavin

Another packet of letters had been written by members of my 81 Platoon in 3/5 and forwarded to me from 2/5. At the time, none of those men had as yet learned that I had been wounded. Among this batch were letters from each of my section leaders in 81s as well as from many of their troops. The two I received from Staff Sergeant Thomas were typical in spirit of this group of letters:

January 5, 1967

Hello Lt. Kirschke,

The Section and I thought you may like to know how we are doing. You know how the bum scoop goes around and you were supposed to be wounded. I'm glad to hear [lately that] that was a farce. . . .

They're starting to replace the Section Leaders. But you know Gy. Sergeant Rockdale. He just isn't going to take anyone for a replacement for one of his Section Leaders. . . .

We've told the new troops about you, Sir. And how outstanding your Platoon was. . . . We have the best. And I'm trying to leave with the best remaining here and carry on the original 3/5 tradition of the *best 81 Platoon in the Marine Corps.*

I'm sure you'll do a great job as a teacher and coach if you so choose civilian life. But I'm hoping we in the Marine Corps will be the lucky ones to reap the harvest of your leadership. For many years to come.

I'm privileged and honored to have served with you. I know many more men would have liked to say these same words before you left but couldn't. I think I can say it for the whole platoon.

Captain Vorreyer, the old S-4, is L Company C.O. now. He keeps saying, "if the bubbles don't level, kick the base plate."

That should be a good closing statement to the 81 M.M. MORTAR PLATOON Commander.

Respectfully,
Wesley L. Thomas
S.Sgt. U.S.M.C.

Of the other letters in that batch from the troops in 81s, Corporal Williams's was especially moving. Big Mike thanked me sincerely for helping the men in training and in combat. His robust letter said more about him than it did me, and closed with the words, *"I SALUTE YOU, SIR,"* in large capitals.

The letters I received from the men of 3d Platoon I asked the Gray Lady to save to read last. By the time she got this far she was crying so hard she had to excuse herself to try to regain her composure. She was unable to, however, and had to find another Red Cross volunteer to finish this duty. I was glad for the break, since I also needed the time to "get myself together." A few minutes later she came back to resume the reading.

From my former rifle platoon the letters I received that day from Lance Corporals Jiminez and O'Connor were typical of the ones I received from the troops. Jiminez's letter ends, "I'll never forget you and your undying courage, and I'll always be proud to say that I served under Captain James J. Kirschke. Respectfully yours, Thomas W. Jiminez L/Cpl., U.S.M.C."

Lance Corporal O'Connor's letter was dated January 16, 1967, and reads exactly as follows:

Dear Mr. Kirschke,

We heard that you were going to pull threw alright. That was sure some good news. The Chaplain said mass that night for your speedy recovery. We know that it took a lot of strength to pull threw, but we all figured that you could make it all right. I know all the guys in the plt. miss you because you were the best plt. commander we ever had. An you came to us when we needed someone an did such a good job.

We have a new Lt. in who is going to take over the thrid plt. [Author's note: 2d Lt. Earl F. Smith. He was killed in action on Operation Tuscaloosa, January 26, 1967.] An Gunny Burns is going to be are plt. Sgt. Sgt. Hoole and Sgt. Honeycutt don't go out in the field anymore [Author's note: because they had less than a month on their tour]. I never did thank you but I think that was a fine thing you did having all thows people from Pa. send Xmas cards. An you could see how it brought the moral of the men up. I guess you will be going back to the states pretty soon. Well thats about all I can think of. I'll keep praying for you an may God bless you.

> Your
> Friend,
> L/Cpl.
> James (Terry) O'Connor

At the time of their writing, I do not believe that either O'Connor or Hoole knew that, for me, the issue was still in doubt. Sergeant Hoole's letter I believe was read to me last. His letter was dated 1/17/67 and reads in part as follows:

Dear Sir,

Just a few lines wondering how you are feeling and to let you know that I am thinking of you. I hope you are making it alright. I'm sure you will, your very strong sir.

It really hurt when you got it. The hole platoon felt so bad when we got back in. This platoon will always be the best. You made this plt., and I'm only proud to say I was among the men of 3rd PLT. H-2/5. *YOUR PLT, SIR!* It will always be your's.

Gunny Burns came out after he heard about you getting hurt. Gunny told me that I won't be going back out in the field anymore. . . .

Sir, if you are going to be shipped to one of the hospitals in the states, wherever you are I'll go and see you. I never meet an officer like you before. You would talk about your future to me just like I was one of you's, an officer. You would listen when I wanted to say something, You never mind, because I was only an E-5 plt. Sgt.. You were happy just the same. Even though you had to help me do my job sometimes. You were always there when I had any problems that I should of handle myself, but you would help me.

You were just great Sir.. I hope we can get together someday and just bring up old times we had together. Sir, please get well soon and I promise if I can find out where you are in the states, if you are transferred to the states I'll look you up. Take care and God be with you. I'll say the Rosary for you.

Your friend,
Ron

By the time the second Red Cross woman had finished reading this mail, the morning was nearly over and we had cried so much we had no tears left. I did not know it at the time, but the next day would be the day of the big battle during Tuscaloosa. Lieutenant Smith was killed that day and Gunny Burns moved up under heavy fire to take command of 3d Platoon. As Jerry Doherty related to me months later at the Philadelphia Naval Base O Club, Mike Litwin's platoon that day overran a Main Force regimental CP. While doing this, our company was receiving heavy fire from the left flank, which 3d Platoon was then defending. Had our platoon not held their ground when Mike's men were doing such a good job, it would have cost Hotel Company dearly.

I was sitting at a table in the O Club when Jerry told me how my men had performed that day. He also told me he had asked Gunny Burns if he would be able to hold his ground. When Jerry related the Gunny's response to that question, it was not just because I had had too much to drink that I was unable to choke back the tears.

The Gray Lady had not been gone long at all when Dr. Sweterlitsch and the day shift charge nurse moved into the room. The doctor stood at the foot of my bed and passed his hand back and forth over the bulking bed frame; the nurse stood stiffly, a pace or two behind him, with her arms folded. Doctor Sweterlitsch had his head down as he began to speak. I do not recall the precise words, but he said in essence that my pneumonia was now pretty much cleared but that I had a bad case of gangrene in my lower extremities. If he did not operate right away I would die from the gangrene. I would die, in other words, if he did not amputate . . . tomorrow.

"Amputate tomorrow!"—the words flew at me across the space that separated us and brought me back to the present like a slap. If ever in my life till that time I felt prepared to face such an operation, it was then. With the first words from my friends and former troops still ringing inside my chest, I felt I could face anything. I wanted to live.

A permission form I was to sign was shown and read to me by the chief nurse. She had to sign it for me as I recall because I was not yet strong enough to grasp the pen. Doctor Sweterlitsch stayed where he was as that formality was completed. I looked up at him again, and he looked back for a second that seemed pregnant with empathy. Then his professional side took over and both doctor and nurse walked out.

The operation took place the next morning. I waited on a carrier in the hallway outside the OR for what seemed a very long time. The hallway was long and dark and well waxed. I do not recall feeling any special sense of panic, but I remember having prayed quite a bit while I was waiting. There seemed to be no one else in the corridor around me. Anyway, I was too groggy and tired to have strength for conversation.

When my carrier moved into the OR, I sensed an almost palpable emotional chill. I heard the sound of loudly running water as I entered. Everybody inside was masked, but I could tell by the way they carried themselves that it was not their average operation.

The anesthesiologist leaned over my face and addressed me in tones that one would use in addressing a child or an octogenarian.

The next thing I recall I was in the recovery room. I was very sore and very cold—so cold my teeth were chattering; I was shaking as though I were having a severe malaria attack. Somehow I managed to get the nurse's attention and she brought at least two more blankets to cover me with. She also brought some water.

Before long, people came to move my carrier onto an elevator and back to ICU. The next time I woke up, Doc Sweterlitsch was standing next to me. "Sorry we couldn't save the left one at all," he said. Instinctively I looked down to my thigh. Nothing there but the sheet. "You have a pretty good B.K., now, though," the doctor continued, not looking at me any longer but turning the pages on the chart.

"What's a B.K., doctor?"

"Below the knee amputation," he said. I looked down and saw no lump in the sheet where my right foot should have been, and felt a hollow-sick feeling roll over me like a wave. The first few days after the amputations I felt physical pain exceeded previously only by the explosion itself and the impact I felt when I landed. My family, too, must have felt no small amount of sorrow and pain at the same time. On the twenty-sixth my mother received the following telegram, done at 11:33 A.M.

. . . your son underwent surgery on 26 January 1967 at the U.S. Air Force Hospital, Clark Air Base . . . for amputation of the right leg below the knee and he had disarticulation of the left leg. His present condition and prognosis are critical and he is still being carried on the very seriously ill list. Your son tolerated well during surgery. . . . Your concern is realized and you are assured that James continues to receive the best of care. You will be kept informed of all significant changes in his condition.

> Wallace M. Greene, Jr.
> Commanding General
> U.S.M.C.
> Commandant of the
> Marine Corps

After that operation, as before it, the mail I received did more than I can say to aid me in recovering. Each one helped bolster my morale inestimably. Some of the mail came from friends and former teammates in Philadelphia, some from former coaches, and even more from my troops, NCOs, and fellow officers. PFC Zlatunich had been my radio operator and messenger virtually the entire time I was platoon commander of the 81s. I am not sure if he had yet learned I had been wounded. His letter was typical of those I received from the troops in 81s:

Dear Sir:

Hope this letter finds you well. I wish I had the chance to see you off when you left. I saw you getting on the truck but I didn't know you were being transferred. I'm sure sorry I missed you. . . .

I really learned a lot from you—the only thing I wish is that the Platoon, you and I could have stayed together. I think all the men resented you for all the P.T. you made them go through, but after you were gone there wasn't one who said a bad thing—they all respected you and thanked you for what you had done. They were proud and they had a lot to be proud of. . . . I hope we can get together some day. It would be nice to have a reunion or get-together with all the men.

If I can ever be of any help to you. . . . I would feel insulted if you didn't ask.

Take care and write soon—

Jim

I do not believe Staff Sergeant Thomas knew, as yet, that I had been wounded when he wrote the following letter, which I received shortly after my first amputative surgery. In this letter Sergeant Thomas said a number of nice things, then closed with these words:

> If I ever have the respect of eighty-seven men like you had from this Platoon, I'll consider that I'll have done something. If there is ever anything we can do for you, your wish is our command.
>
> > Respectfully yours,
> > Wesley L. Thomas

During these days also I received at least two letters apiece from Staff Sergeant Oliver and Gunnery Sergeant Killinger. Both section leaders were already aware that I had been seriously wounded; I am almost sure that both also knew I had lost my legs. Sergeant Oliver's letters were written with a kindness and consideration typical of him. In a P.S. to one letter, he remarked that all of the men asked for me and said they wished I was still with them. Corporal Harrison, especially, said I should "keep my chin up."

In Killinger's letters there was much information about how well his section continued to do in combat in the final weeks of their tour, and how they had continued to perform after I had left. Although I am almost sure he was aware of my injuries by this time, Sergeant Killinger refrained from mentioning them even once. These letters I found briskly cheering in much the same way I had always found Killinger himself to be in person.

Gunnery Sergeant Rockdale never wrote—that was not his way—but he told Gunny Killinger to send me his best.

A major I had served with earlier in my tour wrote a long, businesslike letter not unlike the pair I had received from Killinger at this time. Major Shearer, however, concluded as follows:

> I guess you can tell by now I've been avoiding the big subject, buddy. What the hell do you say to a guy like you who has lost both legs, Jim? I couldn't feel any worse about it

if they were my own. 'I'm sorry' seems so damn inadequate, but I guess that covers it as well as anything I can muster. . . . I know you have the guts to bounce back and make it anyplace. I couldn't have misjudged you that badly. The Corps is going to miss guys like you though, and I think that is going to be the hardest part to accept, but accept it you must and make the best of it. . . .

Got to get back into the program—there's still a war on here you know, and sometimes I'm not sure who the hell is winning! Till next time—keep your chin up tiger.

> Best personal regards,
> Your buddy,
> Bill Shearer

From lieutenants Larry Cullen, Roger Pullis, and J. D. Murray I received several long and typically morale-boosting letters that could only be appreciated in their entirety. All of the letters said, in essence, "the old Gang's pulling for you," and they meant more to me than much medicine.

Among the letters I received from my 3d Platoon troops after I lost my legs, the one from PFC Marvin Redeye, with its bittersweet news, I am sad to say is typical:

March 8, 1967

Dear Lt.

Just a few lines to say hello an let you know how things are over here.

First off, on behalf of the 3rd PLT. and myself, we want to thank you for everything that you did for us. We all appreciate it very much. And I'm sure if there's anything we can ever do for you, we'd be more than willing to do so. We want you to know you'll always be remembered among us. You were a good friend, as well as a good leader. It was our pleasure to serve with you.

There aren't many of the people left here that you would remember. Most of them are new people from the States or other units. These last few Operations have taken quite a few people. But we still have the same spirit the PLT. has always had. . . .

That's it for now. I'll write from time to time to let you know how we're doing.

Sincerely,
Marvin

Of the many letters from South Philadelphia I received when I was at Clark, the one from John Verica, Jr., was among the most inspiring. John, a former football and basketball coach of mine at St. Monica's C.Y.O., said he knew I would overcome my injuries. He concluded his letter by saying: "I know you will rise above the average man in this grown up jungle we live in because you have the inner serene justified confidence in your own abilities."

Also at Clark I received several batches of letters, apparently from youngsters, all of which were enjoyable, and some poignantly so. Unfortunately, none of the youngsters put a return address on their envelope or dated their letter, so I had no idea where to respond when I got well.

Dear Lt. Kirschke,
I am sorry to hear about your accident, but those things just happen.
I hope the weather is nice where you are at.

From,
Marsha

Dear Lt. Kirschke,
It is not the end of the world for you. You will still have fun when you get home to your family.

Yours truly,
Jean

Dear James:
I think you are one of the best men in the world because you risked your life for millions of others. I hope your legs are feeling better and you will rise from your bed. I love you.

Truly yours,
Mark

When I was in hospital—both at Clark and in the States—many people sent money to me in envelopes. Most of those likewise had no return address, and many notes bore no signatures whatsoever. The following, which came to me with a postmark from Levittown, Pennsylvania, was typical:

February 9, 1967

Dear Captain Kirschke:

This isn't much for what you have done, but, *"Thank you."*

Sincerely,
Mrs. I. Fredman

How can one estimate the value of such support? I do not think it is possible. Even such fragments as I have quoted, from many hundreds of letters, telegrams, and anonymous gifts, I believe provide some indication, though, of the generosity that helped make possible my recovery. Yet I was not the only person who benefited from the warm support. Before she died, in 1979, my mother told me she had received many telephone calls and letters that made life much easier for her in those weeks of waiting. The following letter, dated January 23, 1967, from a former college English teacher and World War II Marine infantry veteran, is in many ways typical of the kinds of assistance extended to her:

January 23, 1967

Dear Mrs. Kirschke:

. . . I have sons of my own. If they emerge into manhood with the qualities that I recognized in Jim, I will be most thankful.

Sincerely yours,
Claude Koch

Between the twenty-sixth and the thirtieth I had surgery several more times. At least one of these was a stump "revision," a surgical euphemism meaning several more inches were removed. On the thirty-first, in the handwriting of a Red Cross volunteer, I sent the following to my Aunt Nancy:

January 31, 1967

Dear Nancy,

Since I last wrote to you I've been on the operating table several more times. They removed a further portion of my right leg but only shortened it a bit.

The shrapnel wounds in my left hand have just been temporarily splinted and hand feels real good. My other minor wounds are healing well.

I am getting a little scrawny. This is mainly due to a lack of exercise. When I get back to Philadelphia, however, I plan to go back to a physical therapy program like a maniac.

Philadelphia has the best physical therapy facilities so this will be good. . . .

I still have no release date as yet, however, I figure within 2 weeks. I am receiving a great volume of mail and it is very encouraging.

J.J.K.

I am almost certain, nevertheless, that at this time I did not yet know for sure where I would be sent in the States. In January, in fact, my family received word that, if I pulled through, I would be sent to California. In my references about going to Philadelphia, I may have been wishing out loud.

As to my "scrawniness," I spoke the truth. Before the month was over I had received an additional fifty-five pints of blood in transfusion, had dropped in weight to just over eighty-five pounds, and had already had at least six more trips to the operating room. By early February, I resembled General "Skinny" Wainwright after he had been liberated from a Japanese POW camp, except that I had two fewer limbs and numerous suppurating wounds whose odors proved so strong I could barely stand myself. Except for a certain light that some said they saw in my eyes, I evidenced no trace of the robust good health I had generally enjoyed before I was wounded.

From a medical standpoint I was in poor condition, yet I do not think I was altogether lacking in vitality. Incredible as this may seem, one of the best-looking nurses at Clark developed a serious crush on me. This astonished me no less than the healthy members of the staff, some of whom seemed jealous.

On February 1st I dictated a short note to my mother:

Dear Mom:

I am resting and eating much better now. Today I take my first whirlpool and the way my body responds to these whirlpools will mean whether I come home in a week or a month. I am resting much better, thinking of you.

Love,
Jim

As I reperuse this note, I notice that on the envelope I had dictated my return address as H-2/5 [2d Bn., 5th Marines] rather than Clark Hospital. As I look back on that day from the perspective allowed by time, I believe that in dictating my former unit's return address I may on some level have been denying that I really was in the hospital. Analogously, I believe I may also have been attempting to summon right away whatever physical courage I had been able to show as a platoon commander. I was aware that I would need all the fortitude in my possession to handle the ordeal I faced for the first time that morning. At Clark and at the naval hospital I had basically two kinds of wound debridements: surgical and nonsurgical. Of the latter I must have had perhaps fifty in all during my first three months in the hospital. All of those were painful.

At Clark the debridements were done in a small whirlpool machine. Before each session I was wheeled on a carrier into the PT room, where I was lifted, dressings and all, off the horizontal carrier and into an already filled whirlpool tub. The lifting and placing for over two months I found incredibly painful, as in my weakened condition almost every major movement was. After I settled into the tub the therapist turned on the machine, and two water guns began shooting jets of water into my hips. When the dressings on my wounds became thoroughly soaked, both the therapist and a heroic black hospitalman removed the many dressings and sponges that had adhered to my numerous wounds. Most of the smaller wounds had begun to scab over, but the skin had shrunken over the bones. It proved impossible to perform this duty without pulling away both scabs and flesh in the process. Needless to say, these debridements were torture sessions from beginning to end.

In the few minutes after the whirlpool had stopped running, I looked down to assess "the damage." I was not a pretty sight: my left hip was fully open and suppurating profusely, a slab of discolored flesh where the entire left leg as well as the hip joint had been removed. On the right side the bone of my iliac crest was visible, protruding from a large, infected wound over my right hip. From my stump, several inches of bone appeared beneath a tissue of sagging flesh which surrounded it. A large chunk of shrapnel had sliced my lower abdomen straight across, from left to right, and that wound also drained steadily for months afterward. A piece of shrapnel had struck my right hip bone and ricocheted inward, leaving a hole in my right hip larger at the time than an open hand (eventually the iliac crest would have to be "revised" several times, by more than three inches, and further surgery done to close the wound). Although I could not see it at the time, I had another wound just above my buttocks. By the time of my first whirlpool treatment at Clark, that wound was already as large as a fist, and gaining size steadily since my frontal wounds were so serious and painful that I would not be able to be turned onto my stomach for more than two months.

In addition, the numerous scars on my arms, hands, and shoulders were then various shades of crimson, purple, yellow, and pink—far more gruesome-looking than they are today. I had also suffered severe spinal injuries during the blast; those bothered me more then than they do now.

As early as February, moreover, the kidney problems had begun, and these continued until mid-1967, at which time I had to have surgery to clear the problem. Among the shrapnel wounds in my stump, the one that had severed my right femoral artery caused extensive nerve damage, but at the time that problem was one of my least concerns.

In the whirlpool sessions, the therapist's unpleasant task was to reach into the tub as the water flowed over my wounds and snatch the wet dressings. As he did this, I was almost always supported by an assistant who ran his forearms under my armpits. Until April, except for the day of my first mail call, I did not have the strength to support myself upright.

It happened that nearly every one of these nonsurgical debridements at Clark took place at the same time that a thirtyish Army or Air Force pilot, a major, had his PT sessions in the workout room. The major had been wounded in the leg while flying a light jet plane mission over South Vietnam. Almost always when I came in, he was either mounted on an exercycle or about to. He was a distinguished-looking gentleman with graying hair and distinctive features. When I was wheeled in we always exchanged polite greetings. As the pain of the debridements became more intense, my cries and screams grew louder every minute, and the major pedaled his bike faster and faster so that by the end of every session he had had a very fine workout indeed.

That gentleman often stopped in to see me on the ward and asked if there was anything he could do to help me. Before he returned to duty—in another flying billet—he came to say good-bye and wish me luck. What courage it must have taken for him to return to combat, knowing as he did that he might end up in the same circumstances as me.

The therapist at Clark was a pleasant, athletic-looking fellow almost exactly the same age as me. At every phase of the debridements I feel that he suffered at least as much as the major and myself. As with Doc Sweterlitsch, I don't think the therapist could have been nicer or more considerate and still performed his duties. Although I do not recall his name, he wrote to me when I was back in the States and came to visit me as soon as he returned. When he came to see me, I am embarrassed to say, I was cool and short with him almost to the point of being rude.

Behavior such as this characterized my conduct with far too many people who came to visit me after I was wounded. As I reflect upon those months, I wonder, Why did anyone ever come to see me more than once? That many came again and again says far more about their goodness than it does about the patient they came to visit.

Even at Clark, of course, there were light moments. Often, for instance, I cracked small jokes with the troops about some of the more eccentric hospital personnel who worked with us. And the following incident, which took place in early February, is worth relating.

At one morning's linen change, the two Air Force medics working with me were laughing as I woke up. One held me easily above the bed as the other pulled off the stained sheets from the night before.

"How do you feel this morning, Sir? A little dizzy?"

"Why, yes, I think so," I responded woozily. As I looked down at the bed, it seemed to be spinning slowly beneath me. Both men laughed as I asked why they had inquired.

"You'll find out soon enough," they responded as they moved to their next chore, laughing mischievously as they departed.

Some time later an Air Force enlisted man (Airman Gonzalez?) with an El Paso Spanish accent appeared in the doorway.

"Good morning, Sir! How do you feel this morning? Dizzy?"

"Yes, quite a bit," I said, my trach trailing the words with an eerie whistle.

"I just figured I'd stop by this morning and see the person who has all my drunken blood in his veins!"

The story I pieced together from several sources was this: I have A-negative blood, one of the hardest types to match. After one of my operations I lost so much blood that I exhausted the supply of A-negative in the blood bank at Clark, and the Air Force medic was the only person at Clark at the time who had A-negative blood, but he was in Manila on liberty that night. The commander reportedly authorized the military police to track the man down. After checking several bars he was most often said to frequent, the MPs at last found him, drinking and carousing for all he was worth!

The MPs reportedly parked their wagons outside the place on a busy strip in Manila and left their emergency lights flashing when they went in. They found our partying medic, approached him, asked for his ID, then escorted him briskly away.

"Hey, now, come on. I haven't done anything wrong!"

he told me he had protested; the MPs said only, "Never mind, we'll explain as soon as we get you going."

He said they had someone from the blood bank already aboard the van and ready to draw blood as soon as the man entered. As my Chicano brother explained it, they had almost begun to draw his drunken blood before they explained to him why he had been so abruptly seized.

I believe Army General William Westmoreland commanded the American forces in Vietnam for the entire time I was there. I had the impression that many people thought he was an unfeeling martinet. During my stay at Clark both he and his wife came to visit our ward many times. I do not think anyone who saw the look on his face when he came to visit us in the hospital at Clark could ever say he was coldhearted and selfish. If I were a commanding general I could have found more desirable ways to pass my leave time in Manila than in spending whole days visiting horrible-smelling, half-dead skeletons like me.

While I was at Clark I also received several visits from Lt. J. D. Murray, Lt. Jeff Ketterson, and a lieutenant named (Ken?) Davis. Murray I had served with in 3/5. He was not at Clark then because he had been wounded, but because of some temporary duty. I believe he stopped in to see me every day he was in Manila. When he returned to Vietnam he extended his tour for six months and soon thereafter earned the Navy Cross for his heroism. The last I heard he was a major.

The two lieutenants, however, were seriously wounded. Both had gone through Basic School with me. Ketterson and I had served together for a time in the 2d Division. His hometown was Millburn, New Jersey. He had sustained at least one nasty .50-caliber wound through the chest.

Lieutenant Davis was a modest officer from Virginia. He had run cross-country in college and was one of the few lieutenants at Basic School able to beat my time in the three-mile run with full equipment. Both Davis and Ketterson, it seemed to me, took considerable risks in visiting me as often as they did, and they must have known so at the time since their wounds were open also, and they must have known that mine were extremely infected. Moreover, I smelled so horrible at the time that I could barely stand myself. I know I was not good company, and was probably depressing to visit, yet those officers' steady and courageous visits gave my sagging spirits a big lift.

One day at Clark, Dr. Sweterlitsch came to see me at the PT room just before a whirlpool session. He could hardly have picked a better time to broach this subject: "Well, we've looked everything over, and we feel now you're probably able to go home."

"What's that?"

"We think you're ready to go back to the States, Jim."

"What hospital will I be going to, Doc?"

"We'll be sending you to the East Coast center for orthopedics."

"Where's that?"

"The naval hospital in Philadelphia."

"The Philadelphia Naval Hospital"—the words were as magic to me. The hospital was only a few blocks from the neighborhood where I grew up and where I had lived for most of my first twenty-two years.

The doctor hurried on to say that I should not worry about "making the trip" since a good friend of his, another doctor his age, would be returning on the flight with me. I would not therefore be alone on the flight, since the other doctor would be nearby all the time to render any assistance I needed.

I was not worried in the least; I was buoyed by the prospect of returning to Philadelphia soon. Our flight departed the day after I received "the word." I flew out of Manila on February 11, 1967.

SEVEN

Going Home

The flight home was in many ways an extended nightmare. I was sustained throughout, however, by my knowledge that at the end of it I would be in a hospital very near home. Moreover, the doctor, who was from New York City, could hardly have been more supportive.

The day of our flight was hot and moist with a brutal sun, the first sunshine I had felt in well over a month. I was laden with blankets and placed on the deck at the rear of the military bus that would take us to the runway. The doctor who was to accompany me had not yet arrived, and my stretcher was just inside the rear hatchway, which was open. Since my head was aft, the sun beamed steadily onto my face for what seemed an eternity. By the time the rest of the passengers had come aboard I was already drenched with perspiration. My mouth felt as though it were full of cotton.

Before we started to move we were given an extended ditching-procedures lecture. I could not tell what kind of condition the other men aboard were in, but I thought to myself, if our plane goes down in mid-ocean, what a disappointing morsel I would make for some hungry shark. I doubt if I weighed eighty pounds at the time.

For a long time after I left Clark, my hip and abdominal wounds were so severe I was unable to lie on my stomach. Since I had to be always on my back, had lost so much weight, and had the large back wound to begin with, my lower spine and tailbone had pierced through the skin and caused no small amount of misery, especially during the long flight home.

The flight itself did not begin well. Just after takeoff I had a strong urge to urinate. An Air Force medic stumbled valiantly up the aisle with a duct. After I used it and handed it back to him, the plane lurched into a sharp climb and shuddered as it did, causing the attendant to fall over my body, which hurt, and splash the contents of the duct all over the dressings freshly changed that morning. I had no dressing changes on the lengthy return trip despite that early dousing.

The flight across the ocean was rougher than I would have hoped. Many of the men aboard moaned intermittently throughout. From the man on the rack above me, fluid of some kind dripped fairly steadily throughout the first leg of our flight.

On the East Coast there was a bad storm in mid-February 1967. Mostly, I trust, because the Philadelphia Airport was socked in, we made a number of stops before we got to Philadelphia. En route we stayed in *at least* five different hospitals. The places I recall for sure we stopped were: Japan, Alaska, California, Ohio (at Wright-Patterson Air Force Base we stayed at least one night, but I think three), a hospital near Washington, D.C., and one in Dover, Delaware. As I recollect, before we arrived in Philadelphia we even went up and down the East Coast a bit.

In the D.C. area hospital, Bethesda, I think, I was placed in isolation in a semiprivate room with a Marine corporal from Arkansas named Jim Hardin. Hardin had one above-knee amputation. Both of us must have had serious infections and were thus placed in isolation. I remarked to Corporal Hardin, however, that they had put us together because we were the worst-smelling patients they had ever encountered—a comment he loved. Shortly after I said this, as if on cue, an attendant came with something—I believe it was a small packet of mail that had caught up with us from overseas. Rather than bringing the items to us (Hardin and I were both on IVs and confined to bed), this person hastily opened the door and flung the mail onto our beds from a good six feet away. Coming when it did, this gesture elicited several minutes of laughter from the two of us. We were both so loud that all the attendants at the hospital stayed away from the two crazy Marines as much as possible for as long as we were there.

Like a pair of characters out of Samuel Beckett, the two of

us passed the better part of the twenty-four hours we were together in isolation by making up jokes and humorous songs. Hardin got a special kick out of a poem I made up that had the words, "half a leg, half a leg, half a leg onwards." With my tracheotomy whistle as accompaniment, it sounded fine.

Our plane set down at the Philadelphia Airport around 2 A.M. on a cold, windy Saturday. The doctor who had accompanied me was a tall, calm, bespectacled fellow with dark blond hair. Like a number of successful New Yorkers I have met, he might just as well have stepped off a farm down South as come from the concrete-and-steel caverns of Manhattan. Proust was probably right when he remarked that "exceptions to the rule are the magic of existence."

As our plane taxied in I had another strong urge to urinate. This time I told the doctor.

The other patients were off-loaded ahead of me and taken away on a bus. I was placed on a stretcher just off the runway, about thirty meters away from the plane.

"Jim, my plane may be leaving in five minutes," the doctor said. "I'll go ask a corpsman to bring you a duct right away."

He leaned over my stretcher and said in a considerate manner, "I wish you the best of luck, Jim. You deserve it."

The wind poked its fingers at different places along my shivering frame as I lay on the stretcher waiting for the duct. Over one more year in the hospital was ahead for me—thirteen months that would include a half-dozen more operations and no negligible amount of suffering. The other patients who had been aboard with me had been taken away, and the runway was deserted. I did not know yet that I would be going to emergency surgery again in less than four hours. I did know that the hospital I was going to was less than a mile from the South Philadelphia neighborhood where I was raised, and my heart sang with the prospect of returning.

No single, dramatic homecoming awaited me. No one big blast—no confetti, brass bands, and large, cheering crowds—then all forgotten. Only the steady, kindly, tactful, enduring support of many, many family members, neighbors, and friends. Friends who visited me continually for the next thirteen months. Friends who came with presents, tactful advice, homecooked meals of all kinds, homebaked cakes and pies, bottles of booze, cases of beer, T-shirts that had "fallen off the truck," good memories, warm understanding, unfailing encouragement, and no small amount of love. Friends who stayed with me for long stretches of time, sometimes just to listen to my plans and dreams, and help me to ride over the waves of pain in whatever ways they could. Friends who did more than I can say to help me straighten out my thoughts about my injuries and the part I would allow them to play in my life. Friends almost all of whom I never bothered to thank in the ways I should have for kindnesses beyond praise. And whatever was true of my friends was doubly so for the members of my family; those, too, I never thanked adequately for helping me as they did.

The portholes of the evacuation aircraft spangled the runway nearby with ovals of light on the snowdrifts beside me. As I waited, I prayed the pain that throbbed through my lower body would ease somewhat, and that the corpsman would come quickly with the duct so I would not have an accident worse than the one our flight had started with.

Several minutes more and I stopped listening to the roaring jet engines and observing its frame and looked up at the iron-dark sky. Gradually, I was able to see that many stars shone. About the time I began to feel that I could hold out no longer, I heard a rapid footfall beating along the runway toward me. When the medic was still some distance away, I threw back the blankets and got ready. He pulled up just short of me and presented a cold metal duct.

"There," he said, gasping for air. "I see I just made it," he said, his voice exhaling large puffs that blew quickly away with every word.

"Mmhmm."

"As soon as you're finished, Sir, we'll get the Lieutenant aboard this ambulance that's coming along now."

As I returned the duct, he asked, "Where are you from, Sir?"

"Philadelphia," I said. . . . "South Philadelphia," I added as he grasped the urinal with both hands in front of him.

He took a half step backward and I could see him straighten just a bit: "Welcome home, Lieutenant."

GLOSSARY

AFB Air Force base.

air burst Explosive device that detonates aboveground.

air strike Surface attack by fixed-wing fighter-bomber aircraft.

AK A Soviet bloc assault rifle, 7.62mm, also known as the Kalashnikov AK-47.

AO Area of operations, specified location established for planned military operations.

Arty Artillery.

ARVN Army of the Republic of (South) Vietnam.

beaucoup or **boo koo** French for "many."

Bird Dog A small, fixed-wing observation plane.

blood trail Spoor sign left by the passage or removal of enemy wounded or dead.

bush The jungle.

C-4 A very stable, pliable plastique explosive.

C rations or C rats Combat field rations for American troops.

C&C Command & control.

cammo stick Two-colored camouflage applicator.

Capt. Abbreviation for the rank of captain.

Chicom Chinese Communist.

Chinook CH-47 helicopter used for transporting equipment and troops.

chopper GI slang for helicopter.

chopper pad Helicopter landing pad.

CO Commanding officer.

Col. Abbreviation for the rank of colonel.

contact Engaged by the enemy.

CP Command post.

DMZ Demilitarized Zone.

Doc A medic or doctor.

double-canopy Jungle or forest with two layers of overhead vegetation.

FAC Forward air controller. Air Force spotter plane that coordinated air strikes and artillery for ground units.

finger A secondary ridge running out from a primary ridgeline, hill, or mountain.

firebase Forward artillery position, usually located on a prominent terrain feature, used to support ground units during operations.

firefight A battle with an enemy force.

fire mission A request for artillery support.

fix The specific coordinates pertaining to a unit's position or to a target.

FO Forward observer. A specially trained soldier, usually an officer, attached to an infantry unit for the purpose of coordinating close artillery support.

G-2 Division or larger intelligence section.

G-3 Division or larger operations section.

grazing fire Keeping the trajectory of bullets between normal knee-to-waist height.

gunship An armed attack helicopter.

H&I Harassment and interdiction. Artillery fire upon certain areas of suspected enemy travel or rally points, designed to prevent uncontested use.

HE High explosive.

helipad A hardened helicopter landing pad.

Ho Chi Minh Trail An extensive road and trail network running from North Vietnam, down through Laos and Cambodia into South Vietnam, which enabled the North Vietnamese to supply equipment and personnel to their units in South Vietnam.

hootch Slang for barracks or living quarters.

hot A landing zone or drop zone under enemy fire.

HQ Headquarters.

hug To close with the enemy in order to prevent his use of supporting fire.

hump Patrolling or moving during a combat operation.

IAD Immediate Action Drills; they teach immediate response to certain situations.

I Corps The northernmost of the four separate military zones in South Vietnam. The other divisions were II, III, and IV Corps.

immersion foot A skin condition of the feet caused by prolonged exposure to moisture that results in cracking, bleeding, and sloughing of skin.

incoming Receiving enemy indirect fire.

intel Information on the enemy gathered by human, electronic, or other means.

KIA Killed in action.

LAW Light antitank weapon.

LMG Light machine gun.

LP Listening post. An outpost established beyond the

perimeter wire, manned by one or more personnel with the mission of detecting approaching enemy forces before they can launch an assault.

LPH Landing port helicopter. A converted fixed-wing aircraft carrier used as a helicopter launching port.

Lt. Lieutenant.

Lt. Col. Lieutenant colonel.

LZ Landing zone. A cleared area large enough to accommodate the landing of one or more helicopters.

M-14 The standard issue 7.62 millimeter semiautomatic/ automatic rifle used by U.S. military personnel prior to the M-16.

M-60 A light 7.62mm machine gun that has been the primary infantry automatic weapon of U.S. forces since the Korean War.

M-79 An individually operated, single-shot, 40mm grenade launcher.

MACV Military Assistance Command Vietnam. The senior U.S. military headquarters after full American involvement in the war.

Main Force Full-time Viet Cong military units, as opposed to local, part-time guerrilla units.

Maj. Major.

Marine Force Recon U.S. Marine Corps divisional long range reconnaissance units similar in formation and function to U.S. Army LRP/Ranger companies.

Medevac (or dustoff) Medical evacuation by helicopter.

MG Machine gun.

MIA Missing in action.

MOS Military occupation specialty.

MP Military police.

NCO Noncommissioned officer.

NDP Night defensive position.

net Radio network.

number one The best or highest possible.

number ten The worst or lowest possible.

nuoc mam Strong, evil-smelling fish sauce used to add flavor to the standard Vietnamese food staple—rice.

NVA North Vietnamese Army.

O–1 Bird Dog Light, single-engine, fixed-wing aircraft used for forward air control.

OP Observation post. An outpost established on a prominent terrain feature for the purpose of visually observing enemy activity.

op Operation.

op order Operation order. A plan for a mission or operation to be conducted against enemy forces, covering all facets of such a mission or operation.

overflight An aerial reconnaissance of an intended recon zone or area of operation prior to the mission or operation, for the purpose of selecting access and egress points, routes of travel, likely enemy concentrations, water, and prominent terrain features.

P–38 Standard manual can opener that comes with government-issued C rations.

pen flare A small, spring-loaded, cartridge-fed signal flare device that fired a variety of small colored flares used to signal one's position.

PFC Private first class.

pith helmet A light tropical helmet worn by some NVA units.

point The point man or lead soldier in a patrol.

POW Prisoner of war.

PRC-10 or **Prick Ten** Standard-issue platoon/company radio used early in the Vietnam War.

PRC-25 or **Prick Twenty-five** Standard-issue platoon/company radio that replaced the PRC-10.

PRU Provincial reconnaissance units. Mercenary soldiers who performed special military tasks throughout South Vietnam. Known for their effective participation in the Phoenix Program, where they used prisoner snatches and assassinations to destroy the VC infrastructure.

pulled Extracted or exfilled.

punji stakes Sharpened bamboo stakes imbedded in the ground at an angle designed to penetrate into the foot or leg of anyone walking into one. Often poisoned with human excrement to cause infection.

Purple Heart A U.S. medal awarded for receiving a wound in combat.

PX Post exchange.

radio relay A communications team located in a position to relay radio traffic between two points.

R&R Rest and recreation. A short furlough given U.S. forces while serving in a combat zone.

rappel Descend from a stationary platform or a hovering helicopter by sliding down a harness-secured rope.

reaction force Special units designated to relieve a small unit in heavy contact.

rear security The last man on a long-range reconnaissance patrol.

RPD/RPK Soviet bloc light machine gun.

RPG Soviet bloc front-loaded antitank rocket launcher used effectively against U.S. bunkers, armor, and infantry during the Vietnam War.

RTO Radio/telephone operator.

saddle up Preparing to move out on patrol.

sappers VC/NVA soldiers trained to penetrate enemy

defense perimeters and destroy fighting positions, fuel and ammo dumps, and command and communication centers with demolition charges, usually prior to a ground assault by infantry.

satchel charge Explosive charge usually carried in a canvas bag across the chest and activated by a pull cord. The weapon of the sapper.

search and destroy Offensive military operation designed to seek out and eradicate the enemy.

Sgt. Sergeant.

short rounds Artillery rounds that impact short of their target.

short-timer Anyone with less than thirty days left in his combat tour.

single-canopy Jungle or forest with a single layer of overhead tree foliage.

sitrep Situation report. A radio or telephone transmission, usually to a unit's tactical operations center, to provide information on that unit's current status.

Six Designated call sign for a commander, such as Alpha-Six.

SKS Communist bloc semiautomatic rifle.

smoke A canister-shaped grenade that dispenses smoke used to conceal a unit from the enemy or to mark a unit's location for aircraft. The smoke comes in a variety of colors.

snatch To capture a prisoner.

snoop and poop A slang term meaning to gather intelligence in enemy territory and get out again without being detected.

socked in Unable to be resupplied or extracted due to inclement weather.

SOI Signal Operations Instructions. The classified codebook that contains radio frequencies and call signs.

spider hole A camouflaged one-man fighting position frequently used by the VC/NVA.

Spooky AC-47 or AC-119 aircraft armed with Gatling
   guns and capable of flying support over friendly
   positions for extended periods. Besides serving as an
   aerial weapons platform, Spooky was capable of
   dropping illumination flares.

spotter round An artillery smoke or white-phosphorous
   round that was fired to mark a position.

S.Sgt. Staff sergeant (E-6).

staging area An area in the rear where final last-minute
   preparations for an impending operation or mission
   are conducted.

stand-down A period of rest after completion of a
   mission or operation in the field.

star cluster An aerial signal device that produces three
   individual flares. Comes in red, green, or white.

stay-behind A technique involving a small unit dropping
   out or remaining behind when its larger parent unit
   moves out on an operation. A method of inserting a
   recon team.

TAC Air Tactical air support.

tacnet The frequency network for the appropriate
   battalion-level communications.

TAOR Tactical area of responsibility. Another designation
   for a unit's area of operations.

TDY Temporary duty.

Top Slang term for a first sergeant meaning "top"
   NCO.

triple-canopy Jungle or forest that has three distinct
   layers of overhead tree foliage.

VC Viet Cong. South Vietnamese Communist
   guerrillas.

warning order The notification, prior to an op order, given to a Marine combat unit to begin preparation for a mission.

WIA Wounded in action.

WP or **willy pete** White-phosphorous grenade or mortar round.

INDEX

DIARY OF AN AIRBORNE RANGER
A LRRP's Year in the Combat Zone

by Frank Johnson

When Frank Johnson arrived in Vietnam in 1969, he was nineteen, a young soldier untested in combat like thousands of others—but with two important differences: Johnson volunteered for the elite L Company Rangers of the 101st Airborne Division, a long range reconnaissance patrol (LRRP) unit, and he kept a secret diary, a practice forbidden by the military to protect the security of LRRP operations. Now, more than three decades later, those hastily written pages offer a rare look at the daily operations of one of the most courageous units that waged war in Vietnam.

Undimmed and unmuddied by the passing of years, Johnson's account is unique in the annals of Vietnam literature. Moreover, it is a timeless testimony to the sacrifice and heroism of the LRRPs who dared to risk it all.

Published by Ballantine Books
Available in your local bookstore

PAPA BRAVO ROMEO
U.S. Navy Patrol Boats at War in Vietnam

by Wynn Goldsmith

Here is a river rat's graphic, harrowing account of fighting in Cong-infested Mekong Delta. In Vietnam, river warfare was often conducted in the dark. It was always dangerous, sometimes fatal—especially in the eastern end of the Cong-plagued Mekong Delta. In 1967, U.S. Navy Lt. Wynn Goldsmith was the "river rat" who led the first MK II PBR patrol boats in brutal combat.

This gripping account is a tribute to these brave men and their agony, sacrifice, and heroism.

Published by Ballantine Books
Available in your local bookstore

PHANTOM WARRIORS
Book II

by Gary A. Linderer

During the Vietnam War, few combat operations were more dangerous than LRRP/Ranger missions. PHANTOM WARRIORS II presents heart-pounding, edge-of-your-seat stories from individuals and teams. These elite warriors relive sudden deadly firefights, prolonged gun battles with large enemy forces, desperate attempts to help fallen comrades, and the sheer hell of bloody, no-quarter combat. The LRRP accounts here are a testament to the courage, guts, daring, and sacrifice of the men who willingly faced death every day of their lives in Vietnam.

Published by Ballantine Books
Available in your local bookstore

UTTER'S BATTALION
2/7 Marines in Vietnam, 1965–66

by Lt. Col. Alex Lee, USMC (Ret.)

In May 1965, the entire 2nd Battalion, 7th Marine Regiment embarked for Vietnam. Captain Alex Lee was there—and here he brings to gritty life the full tour of 2/7. From the search-and-destroy missions to the sudden violent ambushes in the hills and valleys west of Qui Nhon, Lee describes how Marines battled monsoons, malaria, and the enemy as they crept through terrain infested with Viet Cong caves and hideouts. Although they faced a life of constant danger and occasional mindless confusion, in their seemingly endless marathon of effort, agony, and sacrifice, the Marines of 2/7 never faltered, never stopped giving their best.

Published by Ballantine Books
Available in your local bookstore